# Who Let the Dogs In ?

# Who Let the Dogs In ?

## Molly Ivins

*Incredible*

*Political Animals*

*I Have Known*

First published in Great Britain in 2005 by
Allison & Busby Limited
Bon Marche Centre
241-251 Ferndale Road
London SW9 8BJ
*http://www.allisonandbusby.com*

This edition published in arrangement with Random House USA,
a division of Random House, Inc.

A catalogue record for this book is available from
the British Library.

10 9 8 7 6 5 4 3 2 1

ISBN 0 7490 8332 8

Printed and bound in Great Britain by
Bookmarque Ltd, Croydon, Surrey

To my brother, Andy,
who makes me laugh more than
anyone I know. *Viva* Chateau Bubba.

# Contents

# *Introduction*

The editor of this book is Jonathan Karp, an alarmingly bright young man who appears to be about fourteen years old. He says he considers this my "career retrospective."

"Jonathan," I explained, "that makes me feel slightly dead."

So here I sit with a smart kid's selection of "my best work," trying to figure out if it means anything. Do we have a Theme here? Are there Underlying Meanings? Refrains? Have I done anything for forty years except laugh at the perfectly improbable nincompoops who get themselves elected to public office?

I guess the most amazing refrain is that I still love politics, and I think it matters to every American in more ways than most of them ever guess. Also, I still think it's funny. I consider that especially moving testimony, given that American politics is in a state of open corruption and intellectual rot.

I have been optimistic to the point of idiocy my whole life, a congenital defect. I assumed that as I grew older I would become an unnaturally cheerful old fart. Instead, I find both journalism and politics, the two fields I have cared about most, in a parlous state, and rather than coasting out on a long, merry burst of laughter, I am buckling up for what looks like a last hard stand against Mordor. Natch, I'm sure we'll win. But we need a trumpet call in here—for attention, for help, to battle. Now *is* the time for all good men (and women) to come to the aid of their country. Attention must be paid. Work needs to be done.

I may be an optimist, but I am also as frightened as I have been for this country since the Saturday Night Massacre under Richard Nixon, when I really thought he might call out the troops. In a different way, almost with our permission, I think we're that close to losing all of it – the Constitution, freedom, rule of law, even the dream of social and economic justice.

Did you know that in nineteenth-century America, politics was the entertainment that more than filled in for both television and movies? It was the equivalent of all the college and professional sports teams added together—people listened to politicians giving loooong speeches as though . . . as though their lives depended on it. It was considered better than the zoo, better than the circus, better than the Friday Night Lights. And it wasn't about who won or lost, it was about how your life would turn out. Americans understood that; they knew their decisions mattered.

Where did it go, that understanding? When did politics become about *them*—*those people* in Washington or *those people* in Austin—instead of about *us*? We own it, we run it; we tell them what to do; it's our country, not theirs. They're just the people we hired to drive the bus for a while. I hear people say, "I'm just not interested in politics." "Oh, they're all crooks anyway." Or *"There's nothing I can do."*

Because I have been writing about politics for forty years, I know where the cynicism comes from, and I would not presume to tell you it is misplaced. The system is so screwed up, if you think it's not worth participating in, then give yourself credit for being alert. But not for being smart. How smart is it to throw away power? How smart is it to throw away the most magnificent political legacy any people has ever received? This is our birthright; we are the heirs; we get it just for being born here. "We hold these truths to be self-evident, that all men [and women!] are created equal, that they are endowed by their Creator with certain unalienable Rights, that among these are Life, Liberty and the pursuit of Happiness. —That to secure these rights, Governments are instituted among Men, deriving their just powers from the consent of the governed, —That whenever any Form of Government becomes destructive of these ends, it is the Right of the People to alter or to abolish it." More than two hundred years later, people all over the world are willing to die for a chance to live by those ideals. They died in South Africa, they died at Tiananmen Square, they're dying today in Myanmar.

Don't throw that legacy away out of cynicism or boredom or inanition: "I'm just not interested in *politics*." "There's nothing I can do."

You have more political power than 99 percent of all the people who have ever lived on this planet. You can not only vote, you can register other people to vote, round up your friends, get out and do political education, talk to people, laugh with people, call the radio, write the paper, write your elected representative, use your e-mail list, put up signs, march, volunteer, and raise hell. All your life, no matter what else you do—butcher, baker, beggarman, thief/doctor, lawyer, Indian chief—you have another job, another responsibility: You are a citizen. It is an obligation that requires attention and effort. And on top of that, you should make it into a hell of a lot of fun.

Having fun while fighting for freedom is, as you will see from this book, my major life cause. I see no reason why we should not laugh, and in fact I think we should insist on it.

So if all this is so gloriously funny, what went wrong? We won the cold war after fifty years, and suddenly our politics is sour, angry, ugly, full of people who can't discuss public affairs without getting all red in the face. The tendons stand out in their necks and their wattles start to shake like a turkey gobbler's. Good grief.

Plenty of blame to go around for this revolting development, but those who deliberately corrupt our language for political advantage deserve some special ring in hell. One is Rush Limbaugh, a silly man. Another is Newt Gingrich, who has done much to poison the well of public debate: "sick," "twisted," "pathetic," "bizarre," "traitor."

But I think far more damaging is the planned, corporately funded, interlocking web of propaganda—the think tanks underwritten by corporate funders, the "academic journals" underwritten by corporate funders, and right-wing newspapers, radio, and television, not to mention low-life, bottom-feeding scandal-mongers, all funded by huge right-wing money. Hillary Clinton once called this "a vast right-wing conspiracy," but it is not. It is all right there, out in the open; it has been growing before our eyes for more than thirty years for anyone to see.

Coming up in East Texas, I knew many racists and batshit John Birchers, as well as a few splendid Goldwater libertarians. For a long time, "conservative" was just another word for "racist" in Texas: some were more polite than others. I first ran across another form of conservatism in the Rocky Mountains in the late 1970s as the "Sagebrush Rebellion" or "Wise Use" movement, corporate-funded anti-environmentalism.

From the beginning, it was all about right-wing money—H. L. Hunt, Coors, Mellon-Scaife—that old batty anti–New Deal money that was always behind the Republican right. They were against taxes on rich people and against taxes on business, didn't want limits on pollution, didn't want limits on exploiting natural resources. Greed is good, the market is God—same old sorry claptrap we have heard since the era of the robber barons. Unleash capitalism and everything will be dandy, as though Ayn Rand and Milton Friedman were actually saying anything new. Sheesh.

Having been born and raised amongst foot-washing Baptists, I've never considered them strange or Other. They are my friends, my neighbors, and my kinfolk. Good people—they care for the sick and visit shut-ins, and they have the best hymns. They didn't used to be political. I suspect that changed for three reasons: *Roe v. Wade; soi-disant* (as we often say in Lubbock) sophisticates who created resentment by dissing and dismissing believers; and manipulation by political professionals. Abortion is an issue over which one of the sides is unable to agree to disagree. The obvious and perhaps flip answer on abortion is that if you believe abortion is murder you shouldn't have one. If you believe that every fertilized human egg is in fact the precise equivalent of a full human being, no one, including the government, should be able to force you to have an abortion.

People (especially men) tend to be uncomfortable with discussions of female plumbing, so I apologize for bringing up what an old friend calls "dank, womblike subjects." Still, approximately one fourth of all fertilized eggs are swept out on the menstrual tide before they even get near to implanting themselves in the uterine wall, and we do not hold funerals over Kotex or Tampax. I suggest to you this means that the beginning of life is not a single specific event, but rather a process that deserves increasing respect as it continues toward birth—precisely the tripartite system set up under *Roe v. Wade* (and if you hear *Roe v. Wade* described as "abortion on demand," you are listening to a liar).

I respect those who oppose abortion, but I do not think they have a right to use the law as an instrument of coercion against people who do not believe (and it is a matter of faith) as they do. They have no right to make this decision for someone else, nor does the government. Some women do not have the physical, psychological, or economic resources to bear a child. There were an estimated one million abortions a year in this country before *Roe*. Abortion can be safe and legal, or dirty and illegal. It cannot be stopped.

The anti-choice crowd have every right to make their arguments, but I think they are being used. Ditto the people who think gays are an abomination. I do not think the Christian right is driving what is happening in this country politically, nor is it even an equal partner with economic fundamentalism. There's a large extent to which the Christian right is being played for a bunch of suckers by country club conservatives who are interested in nothing more than their own pocketbooks.

Everybody knows God is nonpartisan, but I swear Jesus was a liberal—the best, the biggest, the original bleeding heart—the one who embraced the outcasts, the model for us all. Just read the stuff in the New Testament written in red. Don't ever try to convince me that Christianity is right-wing. As for the economic conservatives, who are driving this entire insane detour away from liberty and justice for all, well, as Wright Patman once observed, "The rich and powerful in our country are very greedy. This has many times been demonstrated. It is natural that they should seek ever more power and wealth, but where there is greed there is no vision. And as the Good Book says, where there is no vision, the people perish."

We are witnessing such an astonishing demonstration of greed, such a ridiculous maldistribution of wealth. The average CEO makes three hundred times as much as the average worker. (In 1982, it was just forty-two times.) The richest 1 percent of Americans have 33.4 percent of the total wealth of the country, while the bottom 80 percent have 15.6 percent. According to government data, in 2000, the richest 1 percent had more money to spend after taxes than the bottom 40 percent. Between 1990 and 2003, CEO pay rose 313 percent. The S&P 500 rose 242 percent. Corporate profits rose 128 percent. Average worker pay rose 49 percent. Inflation rose 41 percent. This is not capitalism, this is some sick, extreme deformation of a system that always needs regulation.

How many ways can you measure what's wrong? According to the Census Bureau, poverty is getting worse and household income is falling: The poverty rate is 12.1 percent, or about 35 million people, including 12 million children. Median household income dropped 3.3 percent between 2001 and 2003. Between 2002 and 2004, the richest 1 percent of Americans got $197 billion in tax cuts under the Bush plan. *The Wall Street Journal*'s editorial page, a fountain of misinformation, moans about liberals who want "class warfare" and "income redistribution." Since 1962, there has been a 17 percent decline in federal revenue from progressive taxes and a 135 percent increase in the share of revenue from regressive taxes. There has been a 67 percent drop in the share contributed by corporations and a 17 percent increase in individuals' share. The disparities are becoming worse, not as a consequence of some inexorable economic law, but as a direct result of unfair taxation and unfair legislation.

So, what? We're supposed to think a mere vote outweighs a $2,000 campaign contribution? Not to mention the $2,000 from everyone on the entire corporate masthead—a little campaign-money trick called "bundling." Beloved fellow citizens, it stinks, it rots, it is disgusting and full of worms—it is not just not working for us—this system is screwing us. Oldest saying in politics: "You got to dance with them what brung you." Not that hard to figure out how to fix it. Public campaign financing—kick in a couple of tax dollars to pay for campaigns, so when pols get elected, they got nobody to dance with but us, the people.

Public schools and health care are falling apart while the right sits around griping about high taxes. What is this, France under Louis XIV, with aristos and peasants? Working-class people are getting screwed, and Lord knows it's not because they're not working hard. We finally get a so-called recovery, and none of the profits go to the workers.

Come on, Americans: This sucks. Democracy and capitalism are separate systems: one political, one economic. Capitalism is the best system yet invented for the creation of wealth, but it does dog on its own for social justice; it must be mitigated; it needs to be refereed by government intervention (and the refs damn well better not be on the take). Otherwise, we're going to end up like the banana republics in Latin America—rich people shut up behind high walls and the rest of us in slums. This is not rocket science. We've had decades and even centuries of experience with capitalism: We know how to harness it so it works for most of the people most of the time.

As I look at the "career," it's hard for me to remember what it was like to be naïve, but I have never been able to move beyond the experience of being shocked by people who think it's OK to lie, cheat, and steal in politics. My old friend Linda Lewis and I once came to agreement on what we consider the irreducible minimum of decency in politics, based on our experience with a sorry class of pseudoliberals called "poverty pimps": Don't Steal the People's Money.

Here are a few other things I have learned or come across that might be useful to you as citizens.

- "When Dr. Johnson declared patriotism to be the last refuge of a
  scoundrel, he underestimated the potential of reform." —Roscoe
  Conklin, U.S. Senator from New York, 1890 (I used to think
  "reformer" was a noble word, until I met the Medicare Prescription
  Reform Bill, otherwise known as "How to Brown-nose Big
  Pharmaceutical Campaign Contributors While Literally Screwing
  the Life Out of Old Folks.")
- "Being a man is not letting anybody be humiliated, not letting

the people around you feel degraded." —from *Kiss of the Spider Woman*

• One of the wisest editors I ever had was Dick Cunningham, who observed, "American journalists inherit the freest press in the world, but they enslave themselves to two masters: the conventions of their craft and the limits their society puts on what is acceptable thought." How many times have I been clocked by various kinds of thought police? One of my faves is the condescending "You do realize, Miss Ivins, that the polls show the great majority of Americans do not agree with you." No shit? The struggle to escape conventional wisdom is, in my opinion, made much easier by avoiding Washington, D.C. I like to pretend it's easy for me to say, "Aw, kiss my ass." What is in fact terrifying to me is how often I accept "what everybody else says."

• Huey Long observed: "If totalitarianism comes to this country, it will surely do so in the guise of 100 percent Americanism."

• I've had encounters with sexism that range from infuriating to depressing to hilarious, but my favorite is still the Texas lawmaker who said in all sincere admiration, "Young lady, you got huevos."

• There are 148,000 people in prison in Texas; 72,000 of them are there for nonviolent crimes.

• "News is something someone wants to suppress. Everything else is advertising." —Lord Northcote

• "The character issue is driving all the characters out of politics." —Jan Reid

• "Racism is not the KKK; it's when there's serious inequity and not a passion to do something about it." —Pat Hayes, president, St. Edward's University

• "Many conservatives despise government and perhaps for that reason disregard civilities suited to its functioning. People who despise government should not be entrusted with it. Important kinds of public spiritedness are foreign to them." —George Will

• "I wouldn't ask a plumber how he treated his wife and children before letting him loose on the leaking toilet." —P. D. James

So here we are in the glorious election year of 2004, with a boring stiff in one corner and stupefying incompetence in the other. *Now* they all ask: "Who knew Dubya Bush would be this bad? I realize there is nothing more annoying than someone who says, "I told you so." But dammit, the next time I tell you someone from Texas should not be in the White House, would you *please* pay attention? I knew him, but even I hadn't counted on what fear would do to him. Fear makes people do terrible things. I also think Bush is badly advised, chiefly by Dick Cheney and also by that whole nest of neo-cons in the Defense Department. One of the most elementary mistakes you can make in politics is to listen only to people who agree with you. How could they be so stupid? Karl?

Reading Douglas Brinkley's book *Tour of Duty* is enough to give one hope for John Kerry, but it also leaves one wondering, "So what the hell happened to the guy?" His career since then is not a profile in courage. The record isn't bad, but he seems to suffer from extreme political caution. Of course, every criticism of Kerry can be countered with the unanswerable argument "Compared to Bush?"

Not an inspiring speaker? Compared to Bush? (My favorite is still the time the president informed us we had enjoyed an enduring 150-year alliance with Japan.)

Flip-flops? Compared to the man who opposed the 9/11 Commission, the Intelligence Review Board, the Department of Homeland Security, nation-building, McCain-Feingold, the Middle East peace process, summits, free trade, the corporate reform law, consulting the UN about Iraq, consulting Congress about Iraq, letting Condi Rice testify, etc.? Hell-o-o?

What more can be said about the mess in Iraq? The consequences of ignorance in power are disastrous. We knew Bush didn't know anything about foreign affairs, and the great tragedy of his presidency is that the mother of all foreign policy crises occurred on his watch. But he was supposed to be surrounded by people who knew more. Paul Wolfowitz, architect of the Iraq invasion, assured Congress before the war, "There is no history of ethnic strife in Iraq."

While Iraq is clearly hubris carried to the point of insanity—it's damn hard to convince people you're killing them for their own good—there is a quieter and creepier agenda as well: the steady erosion of freedom, the contempt for legal process, the secrecy, and the unleashing of corporate greed on the environment. Through good times and bad, through terror attacks and wars, Bush has remained consistent about one thing: cutting taxes for the rich. They said it would be "the CEO administration," and so it is. What is astonishing to me is the irresponsibility.

Fiscal irresponsibility, leaving staggering debts to be paid for by future generations. Economic irresponsibility: As Paul Krugman observed, if you eat ten chocolate bars in a row, you will get a burst of energy, but it's not good for your health in the long run. Environmental irresponsibility: To simply ignore global warming, to pretend it's not happening, is so stupid. Mercury, carbon dioxide, mad cow disease, arsenic—they behave as though corporate profits were more important than people's lives. Irresponsible about terrorism, we have thrown away the goodwill of the rest of the world, ruptured alliances, threatened friends, and publicly dismissed and condescended to the United Nations. We have done nothing but create more terrorists and cost ourselves the most valuable tool that exists in hunting them down: international cooperation.

Benito Mussolini, who knew whereof he spoke, said "Fascism should more properly be called corporation, since it is the merger of state and corporate power."

"So, Stanley, a fine mess you've gotten us into this time." And what's to laugh about in this sorry pass? There's always that reliable cheerer-upper: Things could be worse. For example, the current governor of Texas is a lot dumber than the last one, and he could run for president. And things could get better. I think we have taken a wrong turn, but that doesn't mean we can't get back on the high road. It's already been a great political year, in that the Internet has finally arrived as a major political player, and all to the good. Interactive politics, people participation, and, best of all, money—real, serious political money, being raised in small amounts from regular folks. Wow, that's new, and that's important.

Rejoice, beloveds, we'll weather this brush with fascism and come out as noisy and as badly behaved as ever, our politics back to the usual national Roller Derby. As Marianne Moore said, "It is an honor to witness so much confusion."

Who Let the Dogs In ?

# The Reign of
# Ronald Reagan
# and
# Big George

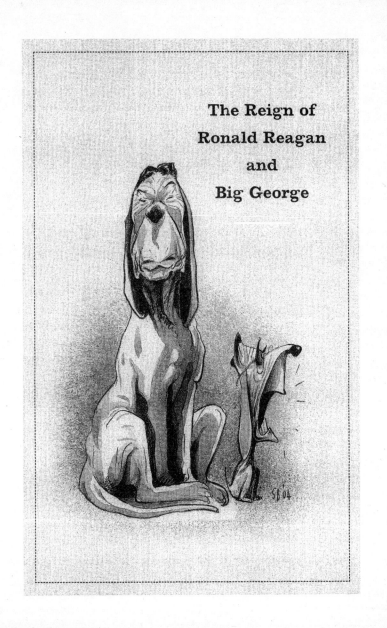

# How to Survive Reagan

◾

MANY CITIZENS of progressive political persuasion are finding that, soulwise, these are trying times. To be a liberal in the Reagan Era—not to mention being a lefty, pinko, comsymp—strikes most of us as damned hard cheese. Duty requires the earnest liberal to spend most of his time on the qui vive for jackbooted fascism, in a state of profound depression over the advance of the military-industrial complex, and down in the dumps over the incurable nincompoopery of a people addicted to *The Newlywed Game.*

Beloveds, fear not, neither let yourselves despair. Rejoice. I bring you good news. As a lifelong Texas liberal, I have spent the whole of my existence in a political climate well to the right of that being created by Ronald Reagan and his merry zealots. Brethren and sistren, this can not only be endured, it can be laughed at. Actually, you have two other choices. You could cry or you could throw up. But crying and throwing up are bad for you, so you might as well laugh. All you need in order to laugh about Reagan is a strong stomach. A tungsten tummy.

Mike Zunk is a fellow we used to know who tried to get into the *Guinness Book of World Records* by eating a car—ground up, you understand, a small bit at a time. He just took it in as a little roughage every day. We always thought of Zunk as a Texas-liberal-in-training. The rest of us toughen our stomachs by taking in the Legislature a day at a time. And now, lo, after all these years of nobody even knowing we were down here, it turns out Texas liberals are among the few folks who know how to survive Reagan. We feel just like Rudolph the Red-Nosed Reindeer.

It may be true, as Tom Lehrer believes, that satire died the day they gave Henry Kissinger the Nobel Peace Prize. But then, as Gore Vidal recently observed in another context, one must never underestimate the Scandinavian sense of humor. You have to ignore a lot of stuff in order to laugh about

Reagan—dead babies and such—but years of practice with the Texas Lege is just what a body needs to get in shape for the concept of Edwin Meese as attorney general. Beer also helps.

Here are six perfectly good reasons to keep laughing during the Reagan administration:

- Things are not getting worse: Things have always been this bad. Nothing is more consoling than the long perspective of history. It will perk you up no end to go back and read the works of progressives past. You will learn therein that things back then were also terrible, and what's more, they were always getting worse. This is most inspiriting.
- Things could get worse. The fact that they probably will should not be used as an excuse for tossing away this golden opportunity to rejoice in the relative delightfulness of our current situation. Is there anything to cheer us in the realization that Ed Meese is attorney general? Yes. It could have been Jesse Helms. And may yet be. Let us give thanks for Ed Meese while we yet have time.
- There is always the off chance that adversity will improve our character. Since we are all the spiritual children of the Puritans, we secretly believe suffering is good for us. I am putting this spell in the wilderness to good use myself: That awful tendency we liberals have to bleed from the heart over victims of cruelty and injustice is so offputting. One of my New Year's resolutions is to not feel sorry for Texaco, Inc., victim of manifest injustice though it is. I hardly ever heard of anything so awfully unfair as Texaco having an $11 billion judgment put against them when it wasn't even Texaco that screwed over Pennzoil in the first place. And then they have to pay a $13 billion bond to appeal the case. Gosh, it's a good thing I have a will of iron or I'd be hard put to suppress those little twinges of sympathy.
- We're not responsible for any of this stuff. No matter how bad it gets, no matter how much they foul things up, it's not our fault. We've got a guilt-free eight years here, team, and given the amount of guilt we have to carry around with us when we have any say in how things get done, this should be our shining hour.
- A redundant reason to keep right on chortling through the Ronaldan Age is on account of lefties are more fun than righties by definition. Ever been to a YAF convention? By comparison, SDS was

a Marx Brothers movie. What's the point of doing good if you can't have fun doing it? You want to wind up looking like Jeane Kirkpatrick? So smile.

• The Reagan administration is genuinely funny, honest it is. From the time we whipped Grenada in a fair fight to the day the old boy dropped off the wreath at Bitburg, this administration has been nothing but laughs. James Watt! Killer trees! Ketchup as a vegetable! Reagan cures the deficit! This is great stuff. You can't make up stuff this good.

In fact, there's another perfectly good reason to be grateful to Ronald Reagan: He's so amazing that zillions of future writers are daily being discouraged from ever trying their hands at fiction.

**March 1986**

# The Fudge Factory

A FEW YEARS AGO, Jules Feiffer drew an Everyman who offered, in serial panels, these observations about the state of the nation:

1. Truth hurts.
2. Before truth, this was a happy country.
3. But look what truth did to us in Vietnam.
4. Look how the truth fouled us up in the 1960s and the 1970s.
5. Truth has changed us from a nation of optimists to a nation of pessimists.
6. So when the president makes it a crime for government workers to go public with the truth, I say, "Hoorah!"
7. And when he bars the press from reporting our wars, I say, "About time!"
8. America doesn't need any more truth.
9. It needs to feel better.

Ronald Reagan, Feiffer observed elsewhere, represented "a return to innocence; a new moral, ethical, and political Victorianism. Reagan's Victorianism transcends truth. It circumvents politics. It gives America what it demands in a time of insoluble crisis: fairy tales."

Lately, through no initiative of its own, the American press has been debunking fairy tales and once more telling depressing, pessimistic, hurtful, unhappy truth. With predictable results. "The nation's news organizations have lost substantial public esteem and credibility as a result of the Iran-Nicaraguan affair . . . according to a new Gallup Poll for the Times Mirror Company," said a front-page story in *The New York Times* on January 4.

What we have really lost is popularity. People don't like being roused from the rosy Reagan dream that it's morning in America, so they turn on the messenger who brings the bad news.

Here is a sample—a letter to the editor of my local paper, the *Austin American-Statesman:* "Like sharks circling, the news media are in a feeding frenzy. They would love to bring down a very popular president. From the beginning, President Reagan's foreign policy has been under attack. First it was Grenada, but that turned out to be a triumph; next it was the bombing of Libya. During that attack, we were deluged with quotes from *Pravda* and *Tass,* but, alas, that too was triumphant for Reagan."

The letter writer, Jean Whitman, continued: "The media are delighted that irresponsible and traitorous congressmen are leaking top-secret information to them.... Consider the media score: They love Castro, hated the shah; they champion the leaders in Zimbabwe and Angola, where tribal murder is now common; they champion the African National Congress, a communistic party, in South Africa. They ignore the plight of Afghanistan. They so divided the country, making heroes out of the SDS and Jane Fonda, that the real heroes came home to hostility after fighting a horrible war in Vietnam."

Whitman is as serious as a stroke, and while there may not be many citizens who hold her detailed agenda of grudges, the 17 percent drop in confidence in the television news and the 23 percent drop in confidence in the credibility of newspapers uncovered by the Times Mirror poll do represent a kill-the-messenger response.

The reaction is predictable, of course, but that isn't helping the press deal with it. Like the Supreme Court, the press follows the election returns. And the press, like politicians, wants to be popular. The trouble with waking up America so rudely, after six years of letting it slumber happily in dreamland, is that we're now being greeted with all the enthusiasm reserved for a loud alarm clock that goes off much too soon. "Ah, shaddap!" "Turn it off!" "Throw it at the cat!"

And when the going gets tough for the press in America, the press fudges, the press jellies. That's what we're doing now. We are retreating to a fine old American press cop-out we like to call objectivity. Russell Baker once described it: "In the classic example, a refugee from Nazi Germany who appears on television saying monstrous things are happening in his homeland must be followed by a Nazi spokesman saying Adolf Hitler is the greatest boon to humanity since pasteurized milk. Real objectivity would require not only hard work by news people to determine which report was accurate, but also a willingness to put up with the abuse certain to follow publication of an objectively formed judgment. To escape the hard work or the abuse, if one man says Hitler is an ogre, we instantly give you another to say Hitler is a prince. A man says the rockets won't work? We give you another who says they will.

"The public may not learn much about these fairly sensitive matters, but neither does it get another excuse to denounce the media for unfairness and lack of objectivity. In brief, society is teeming with people who become furious if told what the score is."

The American press has always had a tendency to assume that the truth must lie exactly halfway between any two opposing points of view. Thus, if the press presents the man who says Hitler is an ogre and the man who says Hitler is a prince, it believes it has done the full measure of its journalistic duty.

This tendency has been aggravated in recent years by a noticeable trend to substitute people who speak from a right-wing ideological perspective for those who know something about a given subject. Thus we see, night after night, on *MacNeil/Lehrer* or *Nightline*, people who don't know jack about Iran or Nicaragua or arms control, but who are ready to tear up the pea patch in defense of the proposition that Ronald Reagan is a Great Leader beset by comsymps. They have nothing to offer in the way of facts or insight; they are presented as a way of keeping the networks from being charged with bias by people who are replete with bias and resistant to fact. The justification for putting them on the air is that "they represent a point of view."

The odd thing about these television discussions designed to "get all sides of the issue" is that they do not feature a spectrum of people with different views on reality: Rather, they frequently give us a face-off between those who see reality and those who have missed it entirely. In the name of objectivity, we are getting fantasyland.

**March 1987**

# Killing the Messenger

∎

RON AND NANCY. Let's face it, they were the eighties. OK, so his mind is mired somewhere in the dawn of social Darwinism, and she's a brittle, shallow woman obsessed with appearances, but then, it was that kind of decade, wasn't it? No fair blaming it on them—they were what the country wanted. They never made you think, never had any doubts, never met a problem that couldn't be solved by public relations, and they didn't raise your taxes. It was Don't Worry, Be Happy City—all done on borrowed money, with glitz and mirrors, while the social fabric rotted, the infrastructure crumbled, the environment slowly became nightmarish, and the deficit grew and grew. The least we can do is thank them for the wonderful memories.

The charm of Ronald Reagan is not just that he kept telling us screwy things, it was that he believed them all. No wonder we trusted him, he never lied to us. That patented Reagan ability to believe what he wants to—damn the facts, full speed ahead—gave the entire decade its *Alice in Wonderland* quality. You just never knew what the president would take into his head next—or what odd things were already lurking there. His stubbornness, even defiance, in the face of facts ("stupid things," he once called them in a memorable slip) was nothing short of splendid. It made no difference how often you told him something he didn't want to believe. The man *still* thought you could buy vodka with food stamps, that he never traded arms for hostages, and that the Soviet Union has sent billions of dollars of weapons to the Sandinistas. This is the man who proved that ignorance is no handicap to the presidency.

One of my favorite episodes came early in the administration, in 1981, when then secretary of state Alexander Haig announced to an appalled world (we hadn't twigged yet) that the Soviet Union was using chemical warfare in Southeast Asia, spraying a lethal "yellow rain" on remote tribes that led to a terrible sickness and then death. The godless commies were apparently practicing on remote tribal people to see if the poison worked. Oh, the horror.

Later, scientists around the world identified the "yellow rain" as bee doody. It seems that Asian bees occasionally leave their hives, fly up to a considerable altitude, and dump en masse. The resulting clouds frightened the tribes but never, it turned out, killed anyone. The Reagan administration never withdrew the charge and never apologized for it.

In 1986, when Reagan was told the Congressional Budget Office had statistics showing a dramatic redistribution of wealth from the poor to the rich, he twinkled endearingly and said, "Oh, I don't think that's true." That's a classic example of the simplicity, the straightforwardness of his approach to unwelcome news. It was one of his favorite phrases.

By December 1987, the deficit had become so staggering that a "budget summit" was called between the White House and Congress. The deal was that Congress had to come up with half of an agreed-upon sum by making cuts in social spending and that Reagan would come up with the other half by cutting military spending. The congressional delegation arrived at the White House and laid out its cuts. Reagan then laid out his new military budget, but it had no cuts in it—it had increases. "Mr. President," said Speaker Jim Wright gently, "you were supposed to *cut* the military budget."

"Oh, spending on the military doesn't increase the deficit," replied Reagan cheerfully. "Cap," he gestured to the end of the table, "explain it to them." Looking slightly sheepish, since he was talking to the members of Congress who know most about financing government, Caspar Weinberger rose to his feet and launched into a spiel he had obviously given often before. He said money spent on the military goes out into the economy, you see, and is spread around and then it trickles down, you see, and then it has a multiplier effect, and because of the multiplier effect, the Treasury gets back more money than it spends on the military, you see, so it doesn't increase the deficit at all. And then he sat down. Reagan turned confidently to the congressmen and said, "You see?" He had then been president for seven years.

He was the candidate of the Moral Majority and the Religious Right: Unfortunately, his entire administration was so riddled with corruption that much of it is still being uncovered. The man brought James Watt, Ed Meese, Ray Donovan, and Silent Sam Pierce into the cabinet. He brought Michael Deaver, Lyn Nofziger, Donald Regan, John Poindexter, and Oliver North into the White House. In 1985, the last year for which we have the full numbers, 563 federal officials were indicted and 470 convicted, a tenfold increase over the high-water mark that was reached with Watergate. It's gotten worse every year since and may go even higher this year, if only because of the HUD scandal.

As for Nancy, my own feeling is that it's unfair to pick on her—irresistible but unfair, in that the only reason she ever entered the public eye was as Reagan's consort. Whatever vanities, follies, selfishness, or even excesses of loyalty that may distinguish her, none of them would have ever come in for public lampooning had the woman married a rich dentist. Many, including Donald Regan, saw her as the power-behind-the-throne, as the stronger, more manipulative partner, as the one who supposedly made Reagan into a right-winger to begin with. Oh, Poop. That's just the same old sorry sexist stereotype about the scheming woman that's been used against every wife-of-a-powerful-man from Napoleon to Lincoln to Roosevelt. There's no evidence that Nancy Reagan's occasional interference in her husband's schedule, staff, or public presentation was ever anything more than protectiveness or perhaps overprotectiveness. That he was slightly dotty by the end of his second term was clear to everyone, and her fierce desire to protect him from demands beyond his fading abilities can only be considered commendable in human terms.

Of more legitimate public concern, although probably of marginal impact, is her effect as a role model. Mrs. Reagan chose to be—first, last, and always—a wife. By the testimony of her own children, it was a role she put well ahead that of mother. That she has no independent life is apparent. He *is* her career and she is unquestionably an enormous political asset to him. I never met an honest man yet, no matter what his politics, who wouldn't confess that he would adore to have a woman look at him the way Nancy *always* looks at Ronnie. "The Gaze" was famous among journalists and political insiders. Through every single speech of his, Mrs. Reagan looked at him with total attention, as if she were witnessing one of the wonders of the world. It was a fantastic performance when you consider how many times she had to sit through that drivel.

So here's to Nancy, the Gaze, and eight years of not much else. When not calling her "friend," the astrologer, to see if it was a good day for the president to travel, she followed the advice of her image maker and sought to shed her reputation as a vain, vapid clotheshorse by valiantly combatting the drug epidemic with the most ringingly inane and inappropriate slogan in the history of folly: "Just Say No." All who have been saved from drugs by Nancy Reagan, please raise your hands. Thank you.

# Bush Leaguer

■

I WAS JUST ABOUT to celebrate George Bush's long and distinguished career as a raving twit when he up and jumps all over Dan Rather, thus transforming his image from Tweety Bird to Chuck Bronson. "If I hear Iran-contra, he's gonna hear Miami" (a reference to Rather's famous walkout), Bush is said to have snarled before the big broadcast bout began. A clash of titans. Cover of *Time*. The whole schmear. And I thought it was just another politician refusing to answer questions.

My favorite moment in the whole flap came the morning after, when Rather, carried away by the thrill of it all, said he had intended no disrespect, was merely intending to do his job. "I have the greatest respect for the office of the vice presidency," said he. Is that right? Next month, Dan Rather's career as a raving twit.

Before the Great Confrontation, Bush had been having some bad days. While campaigning in Iowa, he was confronted by a woman who demanded to know why he is in favor of abortion. Absolutely untrue, said the veep, I am not in favor of abortion, I am totally opposed to abortion. After the meeting broke up, Bush approached the woman, who had a Jack Kemp flier in her hand. Bush took the flier away from her, tore it into pieces, looked at her, and said, "Fini." Fini? *Fini?* He used French in Iowa? *Quel fromage!* I'm getting worried about the veeper.

When he lost a straw poll in Iowa a few months ago, he blamed it on supporters who were off "at their daughters' coming-out party or teeing up at the golf course for that crucial last round." This comment did not burnish the man's image as a son of the soil.

Then *The Wall Street Journal* asked him what went through his mind when his plane was shot down in World War II. "Well," replied Bush, "you go back to your fundamental values. I thought about Mother and Dad and the strength I got from them. And God and faith, and the separation of church and state."

The thought of George Bush, his plane blown apart by Japanese gunfire, hurtling toward the Pacific while he meditates serenely on the separation of church and state—well, come on, admit it, *you* wouldn't have thought about the separation of church and state.

And then there was the most memorable day of the 1984 campaign. Now, you have to understand that all politicians have days when nothing will go right. This one started in Minnesota, where the veep had to get up at 6 A.M. to milk a cow in order to demonstrate his concern for the plight of the American farmer. He showed up wearing a properly plaid wool shirt—but he had it on under a State Department suit. Either he had forgotten how to milk or the cow was a Democrat. He had also forgotten that cows are retromingent, a word one doesn't often get to use.

It went on like that all day. Every time they handed him a baby, it would start screaming as though it had just been stuck with a safety pin. He got to Green Bay, Wisconsin, and told the crowd how much he liked the Minnesota Vikings.

This was just a few days after the debate in which Bush accused Walter Mondale of having said that our marines in Lebanon "died in shame." Mondale had said no such thing; he said the marines had died in vain. Bush then held a ridiculous press conference trying to prove with a dictionary that "in shame" and "in vain" mean the same thing. Mondale was furious, and when asked to comment said, "George Bush doesn't have the manhood to apologize."

Bush was in Wisconsin by the time this comment was relayed to him and he was asked to respond. "On the manhood thing," said the veep, "I'll put mine up against his any time." Reporters stood there, pencils frozen. "Did he say that? Did you hear him say that?"

*The Washington Post* was driven to describe him as "the Cliff Barnes of American politics—blustering, opportunistic, craven and hopelessly ineffective all at once." Which was as nothing, of course, compared to the fact that Bush voluntarily renounced his Texas citizenship in 1984, taking a $123,000 tax deduction by claiming his real residence is in Kennebunkport, Maine. It came as quite a relief for those of us who had been trying to explain how a Texan could behave so much like a Yankee.

---

THERE IS ALWAYS a curious duality in reactions to George Bush. Some people listen to him and immediately say, "Preppy dweeb." Others hear him on a good day and come away impressed, saying, "This guy has a lot of knowledge and a lot of experience. He is not a lightweight." I have never forgotten his courageous defense of his vote in favor of the 1968 Civil Rights Act. There was hell to pay in his district back in Houston when he came home—screaming, abuse, threats—but he wouldn't apologize, wouldn't back down. He just said, "All in all, it's a good law."

As it happens, that's the last time I can recall Bush doing anything that required courage. He is one of those people neither time nor circumstance has treated kindly. God knows, he started with enough gifts and talents and advantages, but somehow he seems to become less as he gets older.

Trouble with Bush is, he's a lickspittle even when he has a choice. Go back to Watergate and look at his record.

Bush was named ambassador to the United Nations by Nixon and then Republican Party chairman in the midst of the Watergate scandal. The stink of corruption from that administration was the least of it—the arrogance, the contempt for the law, the killing, the despotism—Nixon was probably certifiable by the end. Through it all, George Bush burbled inanely, chirruped cheerfully, and ignored all sins large and small.

He was a toady, a bootlicker, and a sycophant. He didn't have to do that. He didn't need a job.

**March 1988**

# The Word's the Thing

■

TOLD YOU SO. I *told* you George Bush was going to turn out to be more fun than a church-singin'-with-supper-on-the-ground. How can you not love his thing thing? They asked him why he thought he was trailing Michael Dukakis, and the veeper said it's the problem he has with "the vision thing."

He's also having a little difficulty with the minority thing. A few weeks ago, Bush was commiserating with a black ghetto kid who said he hated homework. "Ah," said Bush, "*comme ci, comme ça.*" Yo, mo'-fo'. Reporters traveling with Bush have taken to keeping track of his French. "He's back on '*C'est la vie.*' Three times today."

Next, Bush was interviewed by Ted Koppel, whom he kept calling "Dan." Koppel was finally reduced to pleading, "Please, Mr. Vice President, don't call me Dan. It's so Freudian. Call me Peter, call me Tom, anything but Dan."

I think this is not a Dan thing but a word thing with Bush. While trying to express how close he is to President Reagan, Bush said, "For seven and a half years I've worked alongside him, and I'm proud to be his partner. We've had triumphs, we've made mistakes, we've had sex." He didn't mean that: "Setbacks, we've had setbacks," he quickly amended. There's just slippage from time to time in the links between his mouth and his mind.

The continuing debate over whether Bush is a Texan surfaced again during the state Democratic convention, when some fun-lovers rented Bush's "home"—his address of convenience, a suite at the Houstonian Hotel—and held a Bologna Bash and Boogie here. The bookcases in Bush's "house" feature *Reader's Digest* Condensed Editions. Also, it should be noted for the record, real Texans do not use the word *summer* as a verb.

Texas Agriculture Commissioner Jim Hightower, reflecting on Bush's "stay-the-course" strategy, said, "If ignorance ever goes to $40 a barrel, I want the drillin' rights on that man's head."

**August 1988**

# Brave New Age

I HAVE JUST RETURNED from a New Age spa. I am in harmony and in balance, I am integrated, in touch with Father Sky and Mother Earth, living in the now and open to the universe.

I went to get in touch with my body. High damn time, too. My body and I have not been on speaking terms for years. "Listen to your body," they kept telling us, "listen to your body." My body just rolled along like Old Man River, he don't say nothin'.

Finally, on the fourth day, I said to it, "Body," I said, "how'd you like to go to the Vigorous Toning with Resistance Class at 9 A.M.?"

Clear as a bell, my body answered, "Listen, bitch, do it and you die." Great, I'm finally in touch with my body and it turns out to have the personality of an unpleasant Mafioso.

I heard from it several more times that week. It stopped a mountain hike one morning by announcing, "You have a stone in your left shoe, stupid. Stop and take it out." That kind of thing. Never got any friendlier.

I hardly ever get to be on the cutting edge of a trend, but here I am, fair chockablock with mind-body awareness. This is the latest development in the fitness craze. The people who brought you jogging are now out to aerobicize your spiritual life. Meditation has married the long-distance hike and the push-up can be improved by crystals.

The spa, Rancho La Puerta in Baja, California, is a lot like camp for grown-ups, just with different b.s. Instead of singing "Kumbaya," we went to T'ai Chi and learned the Dance of the Five Elements. I tried meditation and seriously considered spending half an hour a day for the rest of my life concentrating on the sensation of air going in and out of my nostrils. I decided against it.

Spend a week eating nothing but baby vegetables in strange colors (the tomatoes are yellow, the lettuce is red, the bell peppers are purple) and it will make you feel better.

I just get tired of all the concentration on self. My body, my spirit, my right brain, my center, my chi, my chakras. Don't any New Age people ever feed the hungry, clothe the naked, or shelter the homeless? They do spend a lot of time Visualizing Peace.

TWO YEARS AGO, I went to an Old Age spa near Dallas, also known as a fat farm, where the ladies all wore their daytime diamonds to exercise class in the swimming pool. Even at Old Age spas, they try to improve your self-esteem. My friend Marlyn went to a walking clinic and the instructor told her she had perfect stride. I went to makeup class and the makeup lady assured me I have a *fabulous* space between my eyes. But Marlyn topped even that: Her masseuse told her she has *great* elasticity.

I knew we were in trouble one night at the Old Age spa when a lady proposed we go around the dinner table and each say who we were going to vote for in November. Instead of saying, "Bush," as I had hoped, all the ladies in their daytime diamonds said, "George, of course." Marlyn had to confess to being a Democrat. There was a horrified silence and the lady who had proposed the game asked, with perceptible disgust on her face, "Do you . . . *work*?"

I like the New Age much better, but I got in trouble there, too. I was stuck one afternoon when we were instructed, "Think of something about yourself you really like and then hold it close to your center: because before we can have peace in the world, all of us must each learn to love ourselves." Oh hell, where's my center? What do I like about myself? World peace depends on it. Then it came to me: I have a *fabulous* space between my eyes. I tucked that right into my center.

In keeping with the New Age spirit of detachment, I refused to become upset upon returning to Texas and finding that some tanker called the *Mega Borg* was leaking oil all over our beaches. (Sounds like something from a space-invaders movie, no? "We're at Warp Six now, sir, and the *Mega Borg* is still gaining on us!")

What is is meant to be, quoth I serenely. And you see how well it works? The *Mega Borg* stopped leaking, Congress refused to amend the Bill of Rights in order to deter flag burners, and George Bush came out for new taxes. Ommmmmmmmm.

# Confusion, Uproar, and Upset

YOICKS! THE PEROT-NISTAS are upon us. Here in Texas, where the vertically impaired billionaire who sounds like a Chihuahua is running ahead of both President George Bush and Bill Clinton in the polls, the Perot-nistas are everywhere. It makes my populist heart beat faster, it does, it does, to watch all those ladies in polyester pantsuits and guys in lime-green leisure suits scouring the countryside for signatures on their petitions, not a natural-fiber snob in the whole herd.

They're organizing themselves, you know. Choosing their own state chairs, setting up their own committees and work shifts. It's almost like ... well, it's sort of ... what I mean is, it looks a lot like democracy in action, friends. So naturally the entire Establishment is shitting bricks. Isn't it lovely?

What a splendid year this has been: confusion, uproar, and upset. The three candidates who have enjoyed surges, much to the horror of the Insiders (I'm never exactly sure who I mean by that, but George Will looking as though his hemorrhoids were paining him always comes to mind), are Patrick Buchanan, Jerry Brown, and Ross Perot. What all three have done is crystallize and articulate our discontents and anger. Alas, none of them has put forth much of a program to fix things. Still, it's been great fun to watch the Beltway Boys squirm.

Even My Man George is distressed. He sent for his son George the Younger, called Shrub, to fix his campaign. Shrub Bush told friends his daddy thinks "the speeches are not too good and no one is bringing him any initiatives." One is left with an image of the president sitting in the Oval Office, pounding both fists on his desk like a hungry camper, crying, "Bring me initiatives, bring me initiatives." Twenty-six years in government, and he hasn't a single thought of his own about what might usefully be done to fix things.

Having tried to preempt Bill Clinton's initiative on the Soviet Union and having gotten caught at it, having swiped Clinton's initiative on education and having gotten caught at it, Bush is now reduced to repackaging his own non-initiatives. Thus, we hear from various underlings who solemnly assure us the president is prepared to put $50 million into saving the cities. Same inadequate $50 million already on the books. He named health insurance as top priority in his State of the Union address, but we now hear he will not send any health-insurance legislation to Congress.

CONGRESS ITSELF finally got off its collective duff and is about to pass the critically needed Spending Limit and Election Reform Act. No fooling this time. No Lucy and the football, where the House passes it but the Senate doesn't or vice versa. But as of this writing, Bush says he will veto it. Jeez, this is depressing.

One seldom sees Bush being an actively bad president—inadequate, hesitant, silly, wrongheaded, short on the vision thing, yes, but not often just dumb and mean like this.

Bush is barely bearable anymore except in his silly mode. In one of his silly moments, he introduced a speech to a Republican fund-raiser in Florida by meditating first on how to win. "Let's ask Steinbrenner how the Yanks win. My friend George. By one run." And then on how pleasant it was to go to a strawberry festival and eat shortcake without having to get permission from Congress.

His goofy-guy mode is getting weirder. In addition to tangling himself up in hopeless half-sentences, he now gets his gestures backward. He'll say, "And the deficit is growing bigger and bigger," while gesturing lower and lower toward the floor. Or, "I want to bring people *together*," while gesturing as though breaking something apart. Dave Barry thinks he's gotten better since he stopped taking Halcion, but I think he's had a relapse. During his press conference on his new proposal to provide aid to the former Soviet Union, Bush said, "I will say that I think it is enough and that it's what we ought to do right now and fight like heck for what we believe in here. And I think it is."

Any meditation on My Man George's health brings us ineluctably to the veep, who is quietly doing a great deal of damage these days. While Johnny

Carson and Jay Leno continue to immortalize his deer-frozen-in-the-headlights reaction to any question more complicated than, "How ya doin'?" the veeper and his Council on Competitiveness are quietly giving special privileges to corporate buddies. This is the real stuff.

**June 1992**

# The Chihuahua

A COLLEAGUE FROM OUT OF state called to inquire, "What is it about these Texas runts?" He meant the political runts with attitude.

"I'm talking about Ross Perot, Claytie Williams, John Tower, Bill Clements. What is it with these people?"

I explained that it is not easy to be a short, male Texan. If you can't be a long, tall Texan, our tradition calls for you to weigh in with at least 130 pounds of bad attitude to make up for it. Nor is the phenomenon limited to Republicans and right-wingers. For example, both Jim Hightower and Sam Rayburn could be listed as runts with attitude, except that, since they're Democrats and thus politically correct, we would have to call them vertically impaired, or possibly differently abled, heightwise.

Several readers have written to object to my having referred to Ross Perot as a Chihuahua. Actually, this was not intended as a reference to his size, or even to the size of his ears: It was his voice I had in mind—he yaps. Now, my readers have pointed out that Perot's physical characteristics, including his stature or lack of it, have nothing to do with his qualifications for the presidency, with which I heartily concur. I was merely attempting a descriptive analogy. He does sound like a Chihuahua. Under no circumstances would I suggest that this bars him from the presidency. Harry Truman also sounded like a yapping dog, but it had no effect on his presidency.

Well, much as I have enjoyed playing with Perot, whom I actually rather like, I'm afraid it's time to point out a few of his failings beyond Bad Haircut.

Ross Perot is a liar. It's really quite striking and leaves me with a certain respect for professional politicians, who lie with such artistry, such deniability, such masterful phraseology that they can always deny their denials later on. Perot lies the way Henry Kissinger used to lie, but without Kissinger's air of grave, weighty authority. Perot just flat-out lies. What's more, when he lies, he accuses everyone else of lying. He never said this, he never said that, he never said the other. They're making it all up. They're all liars. They're all out to get him. You should check on their reputations (hint, hint).

Some bidness expert explained the other day that Perot lies like that because he's an entrepreneur, and those guys are always out on such limbs that they have to lie. It was a new theory to me.

Perot is seriously into paranoid, right-wing conspiracy theories. Actually, this is not news; we've known this about him for years. But now we have to do some serious thinking about what it means to have a president whose grip on reality is both infirm and elastic. By now your humble servants in the ink trade have documented Perot's connections to Lyndon LaRouche–ites, Christic Institute fantasists, Ollie North at his wiggiest (Perot says Ollie is lying, Ollie made it all up, no such thing ever happened), and various oddball spin-offs of the there-are-still-POWs-in-Asia theory.

Ross Perot spies on people. Perot keeps saying he didn't know anything about instances of Electronic Data Systems employees being spied on—maybe so. But he hired a private investigator to snoop on Senator Warren Rudman of New Hampshire, hired a PI to snoop on some of the contra stuff, sent his own company lawyer and two pilots to check into part of the October Surprise scenario, offered to show "secret," supposedly incriminating photos to the *Fort Worth Star-Telegram* publisher and to a *Washington Post* reporter.

I don't like the way the guy plays. If he can't have it all his way, he takes his ball and goes home. Whether it's the promise of a big donation to a Dallas charity or General Motors, Perot's been a bully and a quitter. And no matter whom he crosses or who crosses him, his story is always the same—he's completely in the right and the other guy's completely in the wrong.

I think it's a damned lousy idea to vote for anyone who's paying for his own campaign. You've all heard me complain for however long you might have been reading this column about the way we finance elections in this country. It's sorry, it's sleazy, and it's got to stop. But the biggest loophole in the campaign law right now is that it puts a $1,000 limit on contributions to campaigns for federal office unless it's your own campaign. Well, dammit, we already know this system is giving us a government of the special interests, by the special interests, and for the special interests. The players in politics all have big money or access to it—that's what's wrong with the government of this country. That's why the average citizen is getting screwed.

OK, so maybe we figured that at least Perot wouldn't owe anything to the usual chorus of special interests—I mean, if it was all his money, maybe he'd actually work for us.

But look, in the first place, it's bad enough the extent to which rich people and their bought lackeys already run this country—why make it worse?

In the second place, look at Perot's proposals. He, like Bush, favors a cut in the capital gains tax: That's the move that helps rich people. He also wants to take away Congress' power to levy taxes. In a speech to the National Press Club, he proposed this startling notion and said, "You say, 'Well, that means a constitutional amendment.' Fine." I don't like people who think it's fine, chop-chop, no big deal, to change the Constitution of this country. I think Madison and Jefferson and Adams and all those guys were wiser than Ross Perot. I think they put the right to tax in the branch of government closest to the people for good reasons.

Perot says he wants to throw out the current tax system and start with a blank piece of paper. But he hasn't said what he wants to write on it, because people think issues aren't important.

Ronnie Dugger has pointed out that since presidents have already ripped up one of the major constitutional powers of Congress—to declare war—and Perot wants to remove another, that would leave Congress with just one important power—to spend. Except that Perot wants the right to veto any appropriation passed by Congress. Let's see, that would give him war, peace, taxes, spending—can anyone think of anything else he'd need to be our first dictator?

**July 1992**

# Bush's One Conviction

■

BREWSTER COUNTY— Sheesh, *everybody* is pickin' on our man George. I am fixin' to get vexed about it. That tacky George Will even wants Bush to drop out of the race and let some other Republican carry the GOP banner.

The R's are actin' like a bunch of spooked wildebeests, stampedin' in panic. "Eeek! Eeek! Bush is gonna lose! Let's all run around in circles!"

The current conventional wisdom consists of the same bright lads who were putting out magazine covers a few months ago like "Why Clinton Can't Win" (*New Republic*, May 4). And to mention their performance a year ago recalls these same shrewdies yammering about how the Democrats shouldn't bother to nominate anybody on account of George was such a five-inch putt for reelection.

These ninnies have gone and forgotten everything they ever told us about why George Bush is a great president. For example, he writes lovely thank-you notes. Always has. For years and years now, Bush has been writing thank-you notes whenever anyone does something nice for him. Personally handwritten. Also, he has very nice manners and is a credit to his momma.

I grant you "Shut up and sit down" is not perfect manners—when stressed, George does get testy—but I'm talking normal situations here.

And now the whiners have started in on Bush's inability to express himself. Otherwise known as George in his doofus mode. Mr. Will wrote, "The Bush campaign, like Bush himself, uses words not to convey meaning but as audible confetti."

For example, when Ross Perot was a threat, Bush's people eviscerated him as emotionally unstable, anti-constitutional, a potential tyrant, and an actual ignoramus. When Perot withdrew, Bush's people promptly praised him as "wise" and "courageous."

To them, words mean nothing because nothing means anything—nothing, that is, except power or, more precisely, office. They do not even have the gravity that comes from craving power to effect change.

Oh, poot. I have spent a considerable chunk of my life since 1966 studying the bizarre form of verbal dyslexia that afflicts George Bush. Year after year, I was there, taking verbatim notes and then anxiously studying the resulting jumble of words in my notebooks. Like an anthropologist carefully, delicately investigating an ancient site, I have sifted through those strange middens of verb-less, pronoun-less sentence fragments in search of meaning.

George Will wrote: "Such corruption of language indicates political nihilism. Bush's meandering rhetoric stopped being amusing long ago, when it became recognizably symptomatic of two things. One is the incoherence that afflicts a public person operating without a public philosophy. The other is Bush's belief that he need not bother to discipline his speech when talking to Americans because the business of seeking their consent is beneath him."

We always knew those right-wingers were short on compassion, but that is downright merciless. Again and again, George Bush has cried out for help, has tried to explain to us what the problem is: "Not good on the vision thing. Can't talk the fancy talk."

Being hopelessly inarticulate didn't hurt Gary Cooper in *High Noon*. Why does Will think a leader needs to be able to communicate? Or, for that matter, need to have something to communicate? Is this not just a bit hypocritical coming from the man who kept telling us Ronald Reagan was a great leader? Do we honestly think the Great Communicator's mental life was lightning swift and crystal clear?

Do you remember Reagan's testimony when they called him as a witness in the Iran-contra trial?

The pathos of George Bush, born into an English-speaking country of English-speaking parents, would touch any heart of more permeable stone than the basilisk that occupies George Will's chest.

I'm not saying I ever thought that writing lovely thank-you notes was sufficient qualification for being president. I am just recalling what the Republicans of the world told me four years ago when they got to enumerating Mr. Bush's excellencies.

For those of you interested in the results of my years of study in Bushology, yes, it is my conclusion, after lo these many years, that George Bush truly does believe in something. The current joke is wrong: "Bush, like John Gotti, does have one conviction. He believes in a capital gains tax cut!"

**August 1992**

# Bit in the Balls

■

N OW, LOOK, SOMEONE has got to write about George Bush telling the story about the gladiator who bit the lion in the balls. You cannot count on the David Broders of the world to keep you posted on the bizarre excesses of campaign dementia—people like that are paid to take the whole schmear seriously. This column feels it has some responsibility to keep track of political ludicrousness on grounds that the republic is sorely in need of all the laughs it can get.

This column is in no way qualified to comment on the psychological implications of the gladiator-lion story, but we are prepared to parse the sucker for political meaning, because we believe there is a high probability future historians will cite the gladiator-bites-lion's-balls story as the turning point of the entire 1992 campaign. For those of you who missed this whole deal, here is the story told by the president of the United States—as Lyndon Johnson used to remind us, the only president we've got—on Thursday at the annual convention of the American Legislative Exchange Council, a group of conservative state lawmakers, in Colorado Springs, Colorado. This is not quite a verbatim rendition—I was too stunned to take notes fast enough—but any possible alterations will be noted:

"This all reminds me of the old story of the fierce gladiator who killed every lion they could throw at him. Finally, the other gladiators went to and they got the worst, meanest lion there ever was. Then they buried the great gladiator in the center of the arena in sand up to his neck, and they unleashed the terrible lion. The lion charged the great gladiator, and it made its first pass, jumping over the gladiator's head. As he did, the gladiator reached up and took a very ferocious bite in a very sensitive place in the lion's anatomy. And the lion howled in pain, ran for the exit, and fled from the arena, and the lead centurion ran out and attacked the gladiator, saying, 'Fight fair, dammit, fight fair.' "

At this point, there was confusion in the audience: Who was the lion? Who was the gladiator? Was this a history lesson in the first sound bite? But the prez went on to explain: "Every time I tiptoe into the water with this guy, they start yelling, 'Negative campaigning, negative campaigning.' " Get it? Bush is the gladiator buried in sand up to his neck; Clinton is the most ferocious lion, and the other centurions are maybe the press or the Democrats. Or maybe the Democrats are other lions. Or what.

Now, Bush has lately been in his tweeter-and-woofer mode, which has nothing to do with sound systems but is a semidescription of his habit of alternately making tweeting and woofing sounds while campaigning. (What happens, folks, to those of us who listen to the president a lot is that we, too, start treating words like confetti: We just throw a lot of them up in the air and they come down in random patterns, and we assume you'll know what we mean—it's catching.) You could tell when he announced to an astonished nation earlier in the week that he was our "moral compass." Those who tend to think of him as a moral weather vane were left whomper-jawed, as one so often is by our only president. I mean, just try saying that aloud: "George Bush is my moral compass."

Quite naturally, when I saw a headline on the day after the gladiator-bites-lion story saying, "Bush's Campaign Dismisses Four Speech Writers," I assumed those responsible for the gladiator-lion story had been given the ax. But no, according to *The New York Times*, the triumphant victor in the speechwriter infighting is the very fellow who put the gladiator story in the speech. According to the *Times*, "Mr. Bush told a long anecdote provided by his new speechwriter, Steven Provost, who has been supplying him with increasingly folksy flourishes intended to help him connect with the common man."

OK, commoners, are we feeling connected? Here's the conventional wisdom on the gladiator situation: Bush is unfairly buried in sand—the economy is unfair to him, Japan was unfair to him, the tear gas during his triumphant tour of Panama was unfair to him—he's up to his neck. Clinton is this ferocious lion and his most sensitive point is bimbos, so Bush will go for the bimbo bite and then claim to be the victim. All clear?

I realize that while I have been engaged in this exhausting explication of text, all of political Texas is in a state of chaos and confusion because state Senate redistricting is once more in the twilight zone. As things now stand, thirteen Senate nominees of assorted parties are no longer living in the districts they are running in, a slight electoral impediment. This ungainly mess will probably go all the way to the Supreme Court, proving once again that when the Texas Legislature sets out to mess something up, nobody does it better.

But it's easy to handicap the whole deal: Pay no attention to the sniveling, hypocritical Republicans. Had the sniveling, hypocritical Republicans now crying, "Foul!" not hijacked the Senate redistricting plan in a secret midnight judicial coup (which we must all admit was a terrifically shrewd political move) in the first place, we wouldn't be in the present pickle. The R's may jerk this thing around in the courts long enough to force a special election for the Senate seats, but on the whole, both legality and minority representation are on the side of the D's.

**August 1992**

# Character Issue

Alice laughed. "There's no use trying," she said.
"One *can't* believe impossible things."
"I daresay you haven't had much practice,"
said the Queen. "When I was your age, I always
did it for half-an-hour a day. Why, sometimes
I've believed as many as six
impossible things before breakfast."

THROUGH THE LOOKING-GLASS

CHARACTER, SAYS GEORGE BUSH, is the issue. George Bush. Says character is the issue.

Character, one supposes, comprises both principles and integrity. What are George Bush's principles, this man who accuses Bill Clinton of waffling? George Bush has been on both sides of the abortion question. He has been on both sides of civil rights. More recently, he has been on both sides of new taxes. He has been on both sides of Saddam Hussein. He says he is for a balanced budget amendment while the deficit has increased to $288 billion and he has asked for more money than Congress has actually appropriated. He has been on both sides of "voodoo economics."

In 1964, George Bush campaigned against Ralph Yarborough as a staunch opponent of the 1964 Civil Rights Act, the first great piece of civil rights legislation that gave blacks the right to eat in the same restaurants and drink out of the same water fountains as whites. He was wrong, he was mistaken, and he has never admitted it. Why doesn't he admit it? George Wallace has.

As a Republican, despite his heritage from both his mother and his father as a moderate Republican, he first became active in the Goldwater wing of the party. Later, he became a moderate. Then he became a Reaganite. Then he became whatever he has been for the past four years.

Those who were around during Watergate may recall Bush's inane, burbling denial of the entire stinking mess. Those who recall his vice presidential years may recall why George Will described him then as "the tinny, yapping lap dog of the Reagan administration."

George Bush and principle. There is one single issue on which George Bush has been resolute through the years, despite its unpopularity and defeat—a capital gains tax cut that would disproportionately benefit the wealthy.

George Bush and integrity. You may recall when he said on national television that Walter Mondale had said our marines in Lebanon "died in shame." Mondale had said they died "in vain." Bush tried to prove with a dictionary that Mondale *meant* "in shame."

You may recall his 1988 campaign—a vapid, racist exercise featuring the flag and Willie Horton, conducted while he carefully concealed the extent of the savings and loan fiasco and lied about his involvement in the Iran-contra scandal. In this campaign, he has descended into rank McCarthyism with his unfounded charge that there was some impropriety about Clinton's having visited Moscow during a tour of European capitals and with his demagoguery implying that it was unpatriotic to oppose the war in Vietnam.

One reason Bush won in 1988 was his famous interview with Dan Rather about Iran-contra—Bush blustered, he fulminated, he attacked Rather—but he never answered the questions. And the reason becomes more apparent every day. He was not "out of the loop." From the George Shultz memo to Tuesday's revelation of the John Poindexter cable that lists Bush among those supporting secrecy and concealment of the entire operation. A month after that cable was written, Bush made a speech saying, "Let the chips fall where they may. We want the truth. The president wants it. I want it. And the American people have a right to it. If the truth hurts, so be it. We've got to take our lumps and move ahead." But he went right on with the cover-up and is still lying about it today.

His entire administration is embroiled in a massive cover-up of Iraq-gate, the illegal use of American grain credits by Saddam Hussein to buy weapons. To cover up this piece of folly, the administration had to interfere in and then botch the prosecution for the largest bank fraud in the history of this country. The CIA, the FBI, and the Justice Department are now engaged in investigating one another in the farcical fallout. It would be more farcical if Americans hadn't died fighting Iraq.

In every campaign speech he gives, George Bush is guilty of massive hypocrisy. In every campaign speech he gives, he twists his opponent's words (as he does on Clinton's stand on the Persian Gulf War), he twists his opponent's stands, and he twists his opponent's record. He is guilty of hypocrisy about the Clean Air Act, the civil rights legislation he was finally forced to sign, the tax bill he agreed to ("Congress twisted my arm," he whines).

Sure George Bush is a decent individual—he's polite, he's loyal, he's kind to his children, and he has that endearingly goofy streak (did you catch his reference to "90/90 hindsight" the other night?), but in his public life, George Bush has been anything but an exemplar of principle and integrity. When has George Bush stood for anything in his public life except the protection and advance of George Bush? To suggest otherwise is a sick, sad joke.

**October 1992**

# The 1992 Vote

■

LITTLE ROCK— I can think of one and a half reasons to vote for George Bush. The first is entirely selfish. But then, they tell us this is the year of the "What's in it for me?" voter.

What's in it for me as a political humorist is that George Bush is just fabulous material. Bush-speak, the thing thing, that gloriously daffy streak he has—"Read my lips," 90/90 hindsight, "the manhood thing."

Lord, but I would miss that goofy, preppy, golden retriever–like part of his personality, those moments of transcendent dorkiness when we all stand there trying to believe he's just said what he did.

If you have any mercy in your hearts for those who make a living being funny about politics, take pity on us. Mark Russell is going to commit suicide if we elect Bill Clinton. *Saturday Night Live* will fall on its collective sword. Russell Baker will molt and decline. Mike Royko will be stuck with Chicago, and I'll be stuck with Texas.

Not that Texas isn't more than enough, but Bush has been *such* a boon.

The half-reason is foreign policy, and for none of the usual reasons cited by either Bush or the conventional wisdom.

I don't think Bush had do-squat to do with ending the cold war. Forty-four years of bipartisan American foreign policy and its own internal weakness killed off the Soviet Union. If any one person deserves a lot more credit than anyone else, well, they gave the Nobel Peace Prize to Mikhail Gorbachev for a reason. He was the one who put his life on the line.

Likewise, it seems to me that Bush's leadership during the Persian Gulf War is canceled out by his stupidity in having armed Saddam Hussein in the first place. However, I do think Bush deserves credit in an area in which he hardly ever gets it, and that's south of our border.

I grant you that saying his policies in Central America are better than those of Reagan is damning with the faintest praise in all of human history. And I'm willing to grant that the North American Free Trade Agreement, as now negotiated, may well result in the faint sucking sound of jobs going south. But I still say that Bush—with his "Hello, Jorge, this is George" style of telephone diplomacy—has done better than any president since Kennedy (who mostly had plans rather than accomplishments) in improving our relations with both Mexico and Latin America.

Except, of course, for Bush's ongoing drug-war follies. There is immensely more the United States could do to help both our neighbors and ourselves south of the border, but the beginning, the minimum, has to be what Bush has accomplished.

He has recognized the importance of the region and given Latinos the respect they deserve and accorded them the dignity they must have.

And for the rest? Even if Bush has finally, belatedly developed some ideas, some weak domestic agenda, what makes anyone think he would have any better luck putting it into place next term than he has in this one?

Gridlock government will not only continue, it can only get worse with a bunch of sore-loser Democrats dominating Congress.

As a lame duck, Bush will have even less clout. His judicial appointments won't get any better. The rot of cynicism and corruption that infected the second Reagan term will be back in spades.

And frankly, this Iraq-gate mess is so rank, I'm afraid Bush will be impeached over it. Not the failed policy with Saddam Hussein—that was just a dumb mistake—but the cover-up.

Like Watergate, the initial mistake was not as poisonous as the lies that followed. The Bush administration has clearly jacked around with the prosecution of a criminal case, this immense BNL scandal out of Atlanta, and they're going to get nailed for it. The taxpayers have been nailed for a billion bucks. Just what we need, a second-term administration totally absorbed in an impeachment fight while the economy continues to unravel.

And if you really want to depress yourself, there's always the possibility that Bush will croak and leave us stuck with Quayle. Although personally, I have always thought God would never be that unkind.

As for the Perot option, damn, damn! I wish with all my soul that had worked out. I would have loved that more than anything in the world. An anti-establishment populist with no strings on him, owing no one, not having to dance with a single special interest, just going up there to do the will of the people.

That is the dream of my life. We may never get this close again, and it is breaking my heart. I would have given my left arm for Ross Perot, and my right as well—except for one thing.

The guy's a wrong 'un. He is just not a democrat. The other night on television with David Frost, he kept saying, "I'm the only one who listens to the people." Bull. Perot listens to no one. Or more precisely, what he means when he says "the people" is the people who tell him, "Ross, we love you." Everyone else, he's x-ed out.

It's his way or nothing. That's why he quit the first time. He gutted his own corps of volunteers except for the ones who would tell him exactly what he wants to hear. That squirrelly little part of his brain that will never allow him to admit he's wrong about anything comes up with these fantastic rationales for his own flaky behavior. A Perot presidency would be like the time of the papist plots in England. Conspirators sighted everywhere, evidence no object.

Look, I'm not a shrink, I can't tell you why he's like this. I just know from studying his record that Perot is not temperamentally suited to lead this country. He does not have the patience. He does not have the knowledge, and despite his seeming common sense (when he's not sitting there with springs coming out of his head), I don't think the man has the first idea how to go about getting anything done in D.C. Worse, he couldn't and wouldn't stand having anyone around him who did know.

George Bush once said the key thing we should watch, the one thing that would tell us more than anything else, was who he chose for vice president. Bush chose Dan Quayle. Perot chose Admiral Stockdale. Stockdale is admirable in many ways, but he is not a democrat, and he could no more function as president than he could put on a pink tutu and dance *Swan Lake*.

So that leaves Clinton. I reserve the right to make fun of Bill Clinton from now to infinity, but he is bright (actually, amazingly bright), and he has a sense of humor about the world and about himself. He genuinely likes people, even the ones who don't grovel at his feet, and he listens, which is an unusual trait in a politician.

He is a serious student of how you get government to work. In fact, that is the great passion of his life. More than that, I don't guarantee. Clinton is gonna have to dance with the people what brung him, and I do not know if he has the political courage to change that system. So maybe the best solution is to go out and vote for him and make sure he knows we *all* brung him.

Finally, to all my old friends and to all my old enemies concerning what I fear will always be the Defining Moment for our generation, I think the question now is not whether you went to Vietnam or whether you didn't, whether you fought in the war or whether you fought against the war. I think the only question is whether we can find a president smart enough never to make a mistake like that again.

**November 1992**

# Dan Quayle I

■

**M**ADISON, WIS.— How nice. Vice President Dan Quayle has joined the Lost Values Task Force, also known as Doing Nothing.

In a speech Monday that may yet prove to be the high-water mark for disconnection-from-reality for the entire four years of the Bush-Quayle administration, the veeper gamely blamed the Los Angeles riots and all other manifestations of urban unrest and social decay on—declining values.

Not the sky-high unemployment rates, not the rotten schools, not the lack of housing, or the lack of opportunity, or redlining, or the health-care double-bind that keeps mothers on welfare. In sum, not on poverty at all, but, as he put it, the poverty of values.

He also managed to blame Murphy Brown, but, in a memorably charitable moment, he allowed, "It would be overly simplistic to blame the social breakdown on the programs of the Great Society alone." Have to agree with that, don't you? But said the veep, "It would be absolutely wrong to blame it on the growth and success most Americans enjoyed during the 1980s."

Unfortunately, Quayle is wrong. Most Americans did not enjoy growth and success during the eighties, and those who enjoyed it least were the urban poor, who just rioted. Perhaps this is even more relevant than Murphy Brown; what do you think?

During the past two years, we have gotten several studies of the economic impact of the eighties, all of them grim. The latest studies show that 60 percent of the wealth created in that decade went to the richest 1 percent of Americans. An additional 14 percent of the wealth went to the richest 2 percent. And yet another 20 percent of the new wealth went to those in the richest 20 percent, leaving 6 percent of the new wealth to be spread among the remaining 80 percent of Americans.

The vice president says the answer is two-parent families, but according to a study done by the Congressional Joint Economic Committee, based on Census Bureau data through 1989, two-parent families are having to run harder than ever just to stay in place. Their income in inflation-adjusted dollars rose 8 percent between 1979 and 1989. That includes all income levels. It was a rate of growth one half of that in seventies, one fourth of that in sixties, and one fifth of that in the fifties. The study did not show the effects of the current recession, which obviously worsened the trend. Every study of the poorest people in America shows them losing ground sharply, in both income and job opportunities. Watts today is worse off than Watts in 1964. If any of this is Murphy Brown's fault, Quayle should inform Miles Silverberg soonest.

I certainly agree with the vice president that some people in this country have lost their sense of values. On the other hand, that's not all that happened to them. For example, homeless people didn't lose their sense of values until we stopped building low-income housing. Kids didn't start hanging out on street corners in the ghetto all day until manufacturing jobs started to disappear. (It is a little-known fact that America's school dropout rate, always high, was disguised for years by the fact that school dropouts could get manufacturing jobs, which years of struggle by the unions had made into high-pay employment.)

Now we hear much sober analysis and hand-wringing over the fact that inner-city residents just don't want to work. Really? What were those three thousand people in a Chicago ghetto doing last winter, lined up in the freezing cold hours before dawn to apply for a couple of hundred good jobs at a new hotel? Why is it that every year in Harlem, when the applications open to get summer jobs provided by the Business Alliance, hundreds of teenagers line up on the sidewalk twenty-four and even forty-eight hours in advance to make sure their applications get considered?

It is one of those odd little facts of life that poor people work harder than rich people. People who dig ditches and scrub floors and pick crops put in longer hours at backbreaking labor than dentists and stockbrokers, that's all— as any college kid who's ever worked summer labor will tell you.

I like getting lectures on values and hard work from Dan Quayle, who recently charged the taxpayers $27,000 for a golfing weekend (took the company plane). I think Dan Quayle knows a lot about values. For example, frat-boy Quayle made lousy grades in college, but he got into law school anyway by using family pull to take a slot reserved for a minority student on scholarship.

He supported the war in Vietnam, thought it was a fine war; he just thought somebody else should fight it, and that's why he used family pull to get into the Indiana National Guard, so he wouldn't have to go. As Dan Quayle told us during his 1988 debate with Lloyd Bentsen, his grandma used to tell him, "Dan, you can grow up to be anything you want to be." His grandmother was Mrs. Martha Pulliam, one of the richest women in the country, owner of several newspapers, part of a very powerful and influential family. So you see, Dan Quayle is in a position to tell us all about what's wrong with moral values in the ghettos and the barrios; and all about how any kid in this country can grow up to be anything he wants to be, as long as he works hard and gets good grades in college and serves his country and joins the same fraternity as George Bush and keeps up his golf game at the taxpayers' expense.

Dan, shut up.

**May 1992**

# Dan Quayle II

∎

T HERE IS NO shortage of symptoms that Things Are Going to Hell, so it's a bit like bringing heat to Houston to point out one more. Still, this is such a vacuous little quirk, I'm distressed by it. Two political books have come out this spring, and the mediocre one is doing quite well while the superb one is getting little attention. Not an unusual tale in publishing, but still worth decrying, methinks.

On display everywhere, with a first printing of 750,000, on the bestseller lists, is Dan Quayle's woodenly written, self-justifying compendium of twaddle called *Standing Firm*. Even the little touches of malice aren't what they're cracked up to be. Everyone's to blame but Quayle for all his problems.

While Quayle was veep, I was often asked if the press wasn't treating him unfairly. I said I'd be inclined to agree, except that I'd covered him during the '88 campaign and found him dumber than advertised. I privately thought he was dumb to a point that was alarming. Now Quayle informs us that wasn't him in '88—he knows he was awful, but his handlers made him do it. I'm sorry, but there was no way to know that at the time. And that first impression did stick.

On the strength of this book, I'd say Quayle isn't as dumb as advertised, and he has a legitimate grievance, having been publicly ridiculed as a border-line moron for years. What doesn't change is one's sense of his limitations. As Peter De Vries once observed of a character, "Deep down, he's shallow." Quayle is the quintessential suburbanite whose world is divided into "us"—who play golf at the country club, vote Republican, love our families, go to church, and are mighty white—and "them"—who by implication not only don't believe in God or love their families but who he actually claims "treat people worse" than conservatives.

Quayle quotes as unfair what seems to me a genuinely perceptive descrip-tion of him by George Will: "that the conservatism I'd demonstrated was less a creed than 'an absorbed climate of opinion, absorbed in a golf cart.' " I suspect you'll wind up agreeing with Will if you read this book. The most amazing part is Quayle's heated defense of his service in the National Guard on the grounds that he wasn't given any special treatment to get in; he shows not the faintest awareness that the entire war was fought on a class basis. The book does contain a few giggles; my favorite is the description of "Lee Kuan Yew, an impressive public figure, a true geopolitical thinker." That's Lee Kuan Yew, the dictator of Singapore.

Quayle's book is in astonishing contrast to Madeleine Kunin's memoir, *Living a Political Life*. Kunin served in the Legislature and then as lieutenant governor and then governor of Vermont for six years before bowing out. Her book is infinitely more reflective than Quayle's, about both government and political life, and also stands in striking contrast to Quayle's placid, imper-turbable good opinion of himself. If you want to study how much difference being an economically comfortable white male makes in the American psyche, compare these two books. Kunin suffered agonies of self-doubt, constantly questioned herself as to whether she was doing the right thing, and dealt con-stantly with the challenge of being female in a male world.

"It was shocking to me to see how susceptible I continued to be to that most chronic symptom of female insecurity: feeling like a fraud," writes the woman who was three times elected to the highest office in her state. She writes beautifully about the seductive nature of power, the struggle to keep her sense of self and of others free from the effects of power.

Compared with Kunin, Quayle still looks like a shallow frat boy. This is the first book written by an American woman who has succeeded in politics, and its searing honesty sets an extraordinarily high standard for the new genre. I'd also recommend it to anyone who has ever considered running for office at any level. It's as realistic an account of the troubles and rewards as I've ever come across.

May 1994

# The Baptist Boys

∎

ON THE CLINTON BUS, CORSICANA, TEX. — It is a show, and a good one at that. I'd recommend it for everyone, regardless of political persuasion, who enjoys vintage American politics.

Our political life is now so dominated by television that it's wonderfully pleasant to be able to wander down to the courthouse—or the mall—in your own hometown and listen to the guy who wants to be president while he's out there sweating in the sun with everyone else.

That the entire show is carefully orchestrated for television is just one of the facts of contemporary life.

Clinton is an exceptionally good campaigner. I make this observation in the same spirit in which one would note that Joe Montana is an artist on the football field, even if one were a Cowboys fan. What is, is. The "liberal media" is not inventing Bill Clinton.

A couple of notable things about Clinton as a campaigner: His stamina is incredible, and he tends to get stronger as the day goes on. He blends gentle ridicule of the whole Bush era with a "We can do it" pitch that is actually classic Reagan—we're the optimists; they're the pessimists.

He has a standard litany of what he plans to do if elected. To my surprise, the one that crowds like most is the national service idea. Clinton wants to set up a national college trust fund, so any American can get a loan to go to college. Then, he emphasizes, the student will have to pay back the loan, either with a small percentage of his or her earnings after graduation or by giving two years to public service—as a teacher, as a cop, working with inner-city kids, helping old folks. As the list goes on, the applause swells. "We can rebuild this country, we can save our cities, we can do it, we can!"

Clinton and Al Gore have a lot of material to work with, given George Bush's record, his dingbat mode, and his latest goofy proposals. Both men needle the president constantly and are rapidly turning the "family values" convention to their own advantage. Meanwhile, the Bush team, now under Jim Baker, is already quicker at responding and has now dropped family values.

Bush probably made a mistake when he told the evangelical crowd in Dallas last weekend that the Democrats left G-O-D out of their platform (that was before Baker nixed "family values"). An Episcopalian really should know better than to try to out-Bible a couple of Baptist boys. Both Clinton and Gore can quote Scripture to a faretheewell, but the ever-magisterial Barbara Jordan, daughter of a Baptist preacher, used it most witheringly at the enormous rally in Austin. "Everyone who calleth to me, 'Lord, Lord,' will not get in. Who will get in? Those who do the Lord's work."

Much of the Texas tour, viewed as a whole, is an exercise in inoculation.

The Clinton campaign fully expects Bush to go on television with massive negative ad buys. In Texas, two obvious targets are guns and gays—if past Republican performance is a reliable indicator, the gay-bashing will be done below radar, on radio.

Clinton tried to defuse the gun issue (he supports the Brady bill, the seven-day hold on gun purchases) by citing Ronald Reagan's support for the Brady bill and touts it as a common-sense measure to help law enforcement.

The Republicans' Texas attack plan, entitled "September Storm," contains a memorable wincer. The R's refer to the political operatives with whom they plan to flood East Texas as "Stormtroopers": You don't have to be Jewish to flinch at that lack of historical sensitivity.

There are three qualities that make Clinton such an effective campaigner—energy, stamina, and joy. Of the politicians I have watched, he is most like Hubert Humphrey and Ralph Yarborough. He loves doing this—he gets energy from people.

A lot of politicians, Lloyd Bentsen, for example, move through crowds smiling and shaking, but the smile never reaches their eyes, and you can tell they'd much rather be back in Washington cutting deals with other powerful people. In his book *What It Takes: The Way to the White House*, writer Richard Ben Cramer suggests that Bush despises politics, considers it a dirty business, and consequently believes anything is permitted.

The different thing about Clinton is that he listens to people as he moves among them—Humphrey and Yarborough were always talking. Clinton listens and remembers and repeats the stories he hears.

I have read several of the poetic effusions produced by my journalistic colleagues about Clinton's bus tours and laughed. On Thursday evening, in the late dusk, moving among the thousands gathered on the old suspension bridge over the Brazos in Waco, I realized why so many of us wax poetic about these scenes.

It's not Clinton who's so wonderful—it's America.

**August 1992**

# Class War

■

LOS ANGELES, CALIF. — All right. Once more, Vietnam.

For those of you who are too young to remember; for those of you too old to have felt it intensely.

There were no good choices in those years. Early in the war, you might have believed in it. You might have been like John Paul Vann. Or even David Halberstam and Neil Sheehan, because the press believed in it, too, at the beginning.

But by 1969, no one believed in it. We had been told too many lies about why we were there. God knows the men running the war had long since stopped believing in our stated purposes there. David Beckwith, Dan Quayle's press secretary, said the other day that even Dan Quayle was opposed to war "as it was being fought" by 1969.

And what did he do to stop it? He voted for Richard Nixon, who had a "secret plan" to end it. More than twenty thousand Americans died in Vietnam after Nixon was elected, not to mention millions of Vietnamese.

There were no good choices. You could go to jail. You could go to Canada. Or you could go to Vietnam and kill or die for a cause you didn't believe in. You couldn't get conscientious objector status until later in the war. But you could get out of it if you were middle- or upper-class.

Because Vietnam was, from the American side, a class war from the beginning. It was planned that way.

General Lewis Hershey was in charge of the Selective Service System. His infamous pamphlet, "Channeling," made it all too clear that young American men had been divided into future members of the professional classes and cannon fodder. If Bill Clinton had stayed in Hope, Arkansas, and never gone to college, his butt would have been shipped to 'Nam. When Clinton says he got an induction notice while he was at Oxford but didn't pay much attention to it, of course he's telling the truth. No one was going to draft a Rhodes scholar, for God's sake, and everyone knew it.

As I recall, five men from Harvard were killed in Vietnam. There were a hell of a lot more from Odessa, Texas. For those of us who opposed the war, the rank unfairness of who had to go fight it was part of what we hated. When Dan Quayle joined the National Guard, 1.26 percent of Guardsmen were black.

Joining the Guard was a way to stay out of Vietnam, period. Yes, there were a few Guard units sent to 'Nam, and boy were they surprised. I had to laugh when I saw the quote from Retired Colonel Robert T. Fischer of the Indiana National Guard in last Sunday's *New York Times:* "Headquarters detachment just didn't take every turkey off the street. It was where the general was, and there were some of those guys they just didn't want. If they walk in the door and he looks like a dog and has hair down to here, you send them to another unit. When some trash bag came in the door, there were ways around these things without breaking any rules." They took only nice, clean-cut boys with connections, like Quayle.

When the long, miserable folly of Vietnam finally ended, I thought America would never do anything that wrong again. But we managed one more piece of cruelty and stupidity with regard to that war—we failed to honor and in some cases mistreated our own men who had fought it. Ten years later, Vietnam veterans gave themselves a homecoming parade. I don't know how many of you were there; the crowds were thin. There were no socko military bands because the government didn't spend a nickel on it. It was the weekend The Wall was dedicated that the vets held their own homecoming. The only member of the government who came was that fool John Warner from Virginia, may it not be forgotten. Do you remember how they looked, the Vietnam vets, rolling down the avenue in wheelchairs, straggling along in no formation? Almost all of them had hair down to here: Many wore bandanas around their foreheads. They must have looked like trash bags to Colonel Fischer. I don't think more than 1 percent of them could have gotten into the Indiana National Guard even at that late date.

After all that long history of unfairness and insanity, I did believe no more indignities could be heaped on that particular pile. Wrong again. Now, for political purposes, lies are being told once more. Quayle, who supported the war and took an easy out, now claims to be "proud" he "served," while Clinton was leading "anti-American" demonstrations in England. Not anti-American, Mr. Quayle, anti-war. Bush says Clinton called the entire American military "immoral." He didn't: He called the war immoral. It was.

No one who loved someone who was killed in Vietnam, and Bill Clinton did, ever confused being anti-war with being against those who served there. Many of us who love this country hated that war and still believe the highest patriotism was to oppose it. Mr. Bush now implies that someone who has not served in a war is unfit to be president, might be too easily inclined to risk American lives. I believe the opposite, although you could cite Ronald Reagan as evidence of Bush's thesis.

Clinton worked against the war in Vietnam; Al Gore served in it: I believe they each represent the best of our generation. One thing all of us of the Vietnam generation know for certain is that we cannot prop up a government that does not have the support of its own people. But the price of that lesson was too high.

**September 1992**

# The Year of the Woman

■

NEW YORK — The most conspicuous contradiction of the convention is the contrast between the Democrats' "Year of the Woman" emphasis and the punishment tour Hillary Clinton is on. Here are the Democrats featuring one woman candidate after another—bragging about their Senate candidates, massing their House candidates for photo ops, Ann Richards chairing the convention, Barbara Jordan keynoting, all hands being pro-choice out the wazoo—and poor Hillary is assigned to the Cookie Wars.

*Family Circle* magazine started the cookie fight by distributing the chocolate chip cookie recipes of both Barbara Bush and Hillary Clinton and asking people to vote on them. Sample batches of the cookies are being distributed, and partisan Democrats vote for Hillary's chocolate chips without even tasting Mrs. Bush's. Hillary Clinton, who is under orders from her husband's handlers not to say anything controversial or even substantive, has taken on the cookie project with characteristic zeal and intensity. This woman now knows enough about the making and distribution of chocolate chip cookies to become the next Famous Amos. If Clinton loses in November, she can make her cookie business into a Fortune 500 corporation.

But precisely because she has the smarts and the drive to do things like that—to become one of the best lawyers in the country or, if she chose, to be as formidable a political candidate as any of the women the Democrats have so proudly featured at the podium—she's considered a menace to her husband's campaign. His image guys (note: guys) want her to stay home and knit tea cozies lest the Great American Public take alarm.

Personally, I don't think any of this has anything to do with Hillary Clinton, who seems just as nice as she can be (I base this on all of two encounters with her) and has specialized in the area of law that helps children. It does, however, say a great deal about the ambivalence and confusion in this country over the changing roles of women. Wicked Women are a running theme in our culture, from the femme fatale of the nineteenth century to the castrating bitch favored in current films about career women who don't have enough sense to give it all up for a chance at marriage and motherhood. The Republican attack machine, a formidable instrument, stands ready to paint Hillary Clinton as someone akin to the Glenn Close character in *Fatal Attraction*, some ambition-crazed female without an ounce of natural warmth.

Women receive so many conflicting messages these days about how to behave and what is expected of us—sugar and spice, ruffles and lace, white gloves and gentility, stand by your man and good old mom (as long as she's not on welfare) get all mixed up with independence, holding a job, respect, achievement, and having a brain as well as a figure. Ellen Chesler's new biography of Margaret Sanger, the birth control advocate and early exemplar of emancipated womanhood, reminds us of how long we've all been struggling with these same contradictions. Frankly, if women didn't have a strong sense of humor, I think we'd all be nuts by now.

What interests me about the mass media's treatment of the recurrent conflicts caused by this mad mix of messages is their practically prurient interest in seeing women fight. "Catfight," "hair pulling," and "mud wrestling" are the beloved clichés of those who like to promote events where "the girls go at it." Setting women up to attack one another and then reporting on the ensuing festivities is a favorite media ploy and has been ever since the press tried to make nonexistent bra-burnings the equivalent of feminism in the 1960s.

Meanwhile, the convention's social scene is roaring along but may not again match the awesome display of New York power and glitter that turned out to meet Ann Richards at the Russian Tea Room Tuesday night. Richards, like most people in politics, is used to the politically prominent and long past being thrilled at meeting someone with a political title. But the crowd invited by gossip columnist and New York Texan Liz Smith (of Fort Worth, of course) was a mix of creative talent and media clout that left the press agape. Jane Pauley of television and her husband, Garry Trudeau, who does the "Doonesbury" strip, *Vanity Fair* editor Tina Brown and her husband, Harry Evans, of Random House, lyricist Adolph Greene, *New York Times* publisher Arthur Sulzberger, writers Peter Maas and Norman Mailer, Roone Arledge of ABC, on and on it went. Ann Richards may be governor of Texas, but she's still from Waco: She said later, "Can you believe they came to meet ME? I looked around that room and I felt like a stump."

Trudeau, by the way, is a fan of Texas comptroller John Sharp, who picked up on a Trudeau strip urging people who want to escape paying state income taxes to become titular Texans, à la George Bush. Sharp issued honorary Texan certificates to the thousands of "Doonesbury" fans and tax-dodgers who responded to the joke—and made money for the state doing it.

*July 1992*

# The Voters Speak

A LITTLE-KNOWN FACT about political writers, especially this one, is that if it weren't for the readers, we would go insane.

At this stage of a campaign, when we're wading around in b.s. up to our hips, trying desperately to cut through the bull so our readers can get some reasonably accurate picture of what's being proposed and what it will mean, it is, oddly enough, the readers who pull us through.

My election-year mail is a constant source of wonder and delight, not to mention an ongoing tribute to the common sense, variety, and creativity of the citizenry. Paul Tully, one of the great students and lovers of American politics, died last week, and I regret his death for many reasons, not least of which is that I never got a chance to show him the letter from the guy who figured out the thing about N.

It's about presidents whose last names end in N: Washington, Jefferson, Lincoln, Truman. It's staggering, the number of last-name-ending-in-N presidents we've elected. My correspondent not only noticed this, he went on to figure out the ratio of final N's compared to final anything-elses, and I'm here to tell you, the guy is onto something.

What, I have no idea. But his work confirms my long-held belief that we live in a great nation.

Three of my correspondents actually sat down and figured out their own plans for closing the budget deficit, which is three more than have done so in Washington, D.C. I shall forward their oeuvres to the next occupant of the White House. One bright fellow proposed a progressive income tax, table enclosed.

My least favorite writers are those who are on the government teat and also demanding that the government do less for everyone else and more for them. I regret to report that many on Social Security fall into this category. No, you did not pay in every nickel you are getting from Social Security. No, you did not earn the payments you are getting. You are, however, correct about the inadequacy of Medicare and the need for a long-term-care bill.

Instead of demanding more for yourselves, why not support national health insurance?

No sooner do I make a wish like that than, lo, I find the people are ahead of me again. The American Association of Retired People, a mighty lobby, is now concentrating some of its firepower not just on helping old folks, but on helping children as well, setting up programs for seniors to help kids and supporting the agenda of children's rights organizations. Bravo!

One modest suggestion I have to help people get a grip on how all this works is that the government begin printing Social Security checks in red after the brief period in which each recipient is in fact drawing out only what he or she has paid in, plus interest. Shouldn't be difficult to design a computer program for this purpose.

Now those moved to poetry by our electoral follies are a hardy breed. To make song out of madness requires much intestinal fortitude, but still the poets persist. I have received sonnets, lyrics, and limericks and heard from one poet "lariat," who writes in cowboy meter:

> Bush or Clinton, Clinton, Bush
> Now it's come from Shove to Push
> Mud is flying high and low
> How much lower can they go?

That's nothing: I once received a poem rhyming Attorney General John Mitchell with "Twitchell, Twitchell."

Parody is another favorite election-year form: "George Bush is my president; I shall know want. He maketh me to stand in unemployment lines; He leadeth me beside polluted waters. He restoreth my taxes, etc."

Several correspondents have reinforced another long-held conviction, which is that people who get their economic knowledge by reading the editorial page of *The Wall Street Journal* would be better off if they had remained in blissful ignorance, rather than coming to believe so much tripe and piffle.

Religion is a topic that touches off strong passions, pro and con. The wisdom of the founders ("Congress shall make no law respecting an establishment of religion, or prohibiting the free exercise thereof") is constantly demonstrated anew.

The family values correspondents fall into three categories, one of which I did not expect. Those who buy into the Republican presentation of family values are furiously angry. Those who think it's all a crock are given to giddy hilarity and rather rude suggestions about Dan Quayle and Murphy Brown. There are also a largish number of quite thoughtful letters on this topic, so thoughtful that I wish someone other than Quayle had introduced the subject for other than political reasons.

All in all, the mail reminds me of something that occurs to me quadrennially as we go through the electoral festivities: This is a pretty wonderful country, and there sure are a lot of people in it who care about what happens to it. That they seldom agree with one another, or me, is beside the larger point. Good on you all, and keep coming up with those amazing ideas and observations. Thank you.

**October 1992**

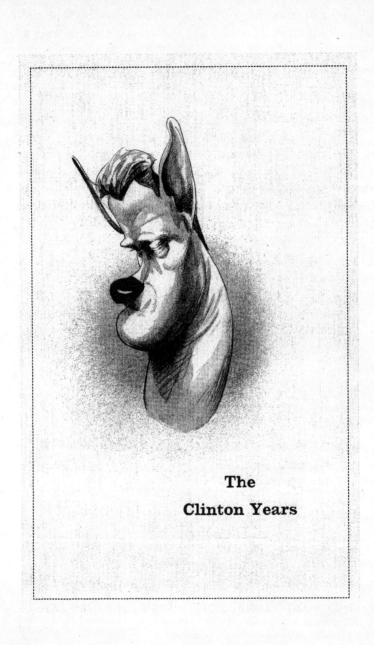

**The**

**Clinton Years**

# Hillary Clinton I

B OSTON, MASS. — Seems to be de rigueur to be in a tizz about Hillary Clinton these days. Everyone has an opinion about what she's doing, what she should be doing, and what she should not be doing.

Hillary Clinton has become the functional equivalent of a national Rorschach test of our attitudes toward the changing role of women. All the doubt, guilt, anxiety, and confusion we feel are being projected onto Mrs. Clinton, who is being made to stand for everything from a role model for working mothers to some fang-dripping militant feminist.

From my own brief acquaintance with Hillary Clinton, I'd say she's not only exceptionally bright, but also a kinder, funnier, and nicer person than is generally perceived. As we all get to know her, I suspect much of the controversy will die away.

For the nonce, however, she is in a bit of a pickle. She has heretofore been a person in her own right, not just a "wife of." But there is no practical way Hillary Clinton can continue to practice her profession in Washington—the potential for conflict of interest is just too great. Likewise, she cannot be appointed by her husband to any paying post in government—it's against the law. So Hillary Clinton, like Barbara Bush, Nancy Reagan, Rosalynn Carter, and Betty Ford before her, will become an unpaid, but clearly Very Important Counselor to the president.

Better Hillary Clinton than Joan Quigley. Joan Who? you say. Ah, how quickly they forget. Joan Quigley was Nancy Reagan's astrologer, the woman who cast the horoscopes that determined the precise minute at which President Reagan's plane would take off for summit meetings and other diplomatic trips. I'd rather have Hillary Clinton's brains and experience weighing in on the national fate than the alignment of Jupiter and Mars.

Hillary Clinton has two areas of special expertise—children's issues and the law. Seems to me Bill Clinton would be a fool not to listen to her on both. Hillary Clinton is an outstanding lawyer. If Bill Clinton were married to an outstanding physicist, I'd expect him to consult her about a good national science adviser and such topics as whether we'd be better off funding big science or a greater variety of research. Why ignore free expertise available right there in the home?

I also expect Mrs. Clinton to function as an extra pair of eyes and ears for her husband, as did Eleanor Roosevelt. Mrs. Roosevelt, who was better able to get out and around than her husband, brought matters to Roosevelt's attention he might otherwise have missed. Seems to me that's a good deal for Bill Clinton and the country.

As a long-standing Barbara Bush fan, I think Hillary Clinton should take a page out of her book. One reason Barbara Bush is such a comfortable first lady is because she's always just herself, not trying to be somebody else—she's not slim, she's not gorgeous, and she's not a great intellectual. So what? Likewise, I don't think Hillary Clinton needs to try to fit anyone else's idea of how a first lady should behave. She's a nice person, and we'll get used to the idea of a first lady who occasionally wears blue jeans and who can be mordantly funny.

As for the rest of us, perhaps we should stop with all the shoulds and shouldn'ts and let Hillary Clinton be herself. And we might also examine how our own prejudices and predilections are affecting our views of Mrs. Clinton.

I'm still startled when I think of the uproar during the campaign over the fact that Mrs. Clinton once put marriage in the same sentence with Indian reservations and slavery as an example of a legal dependency situation. Do you know anything about the legal history of marriage? Wives, until relatively recently, had no civil rights, no legal rights, and no property rights. Marriage in the nineteenth century was a classic example of a dependency relationship. And yet people carried on as though this simple statement of historical fact were some evil, anti-family view. And why beholdest thou the mote that is in thy brother's eye, but considerest not the beam that is in thine own eye?

November 1992

# Hillary Clinton II

**O**NCE UPON A midnight dreary, as I staggered weak and weary, out from under twenty-seven pounds of analysis of Bill Clinton's first one hundred days, it occurred to me that I actually had read something new in there.

I raced back to *Time* magazine's exegesis of Hillary Rodham Clinton's first one hundred days—when I get *The Weekly Reader* dissection of Chelsea's first one hundred days, I'll plow through that, too—Lord, why do I abuse myself like this?—and sure enough, there it was:

> A Republican consultant told a network newscaster that his job was
> to make sure Hillary Clinton is discredited before the 1996 campaign.
> Each day, anti-Hillary talking points go out to talk-show hosts. The
> rumor machine is cranking out bogus stories about her face (lifted),
> her sex life (either nonexistent or all too active) and her marriage (a
> sham). Many of the stories are attributed to the Secret Service in an
> attempt to give the tales credibility.

Excuse me, but when did this become common practice? I don't think I'm naïve—I've covered several Jim Mattox races—but this is a new one on me. Did the Democrats have someone assigned to discredit Barbara Bush? Did the seventies Republicans assign someone to go after Amy Carter?

Maybe it's because Hillary Clinton has an openly acknowledged policy-making role? Do the R's have someone assigned to discredit Robert Reich? Lloyd Bentsen?

I am especially interested because several journalistic colleagues passed along to me the phony "genuine, bona fide, straight from the Secret Service" tale about Hillary Clinton having heaved a lamp at her husband. Actually, that story was originally told about another political wife. When I inquired as to how they knew, I was assured "everybody in Washington is talking about it." Maybe they need to come to Texas to take a refresher course in political rumor-mongering.

The hundred-day thumb-suckers (as "think pieces" are known in our trade) fall roughly into four categories: (1) Clinton's full of energy and ideas and, despite some setbacks, has had a lot of success; (2) Clinton is a disaster; (3) In the long view of history, taking all this from the judicious, balanced point of view for which I-the-Writer am so noted, Clinton's glass is half-empty; and (4) One hundred days is a ridiculous standard on which to judge any president.

I especially like No. 4. When in doubt, wee-wee on the premise. That's my motto, too. All in all, the twenty-seven pounds of analysis is a study in the premise that there-is-no-such-thing-as-objectivity.

I am charmed by the extent to which we all seize upon those facts and events that conform to our point of view. *The Wall Street Journal*, which I for one consider a veritable Bible on the topic of political humor, chose to object to the president's sense of humor.

Specifically, its writers didn't care for his joshing at the White House Correspondents' annual dinner. (I believe it is a matter of historical fact that no one has actually been funny at the White House Correspondents' dinner since the Kennedy administration.)

It seems, among other errors noted by the *Journal*, the president hurt Rush Limbaugh's feelings with a remark that could be construed to imply that not only is Limbaugh a sexist, which he is, but also a racist, which he is not. This is the same Rush Limbaugh, a delicate flower of refined sensibilities, who refers to feminists as femi-Nazis, such a cute and appealing word play it could never offend anyone.

I'm awfully sorry Limbaugh's feelings were hurt. Especially since he would never take a cheap shot himself at either Bill or Hillary Clinton.

The blizzard of insider wisdom dumped on our heads by the hundred-day mark leaves me with an uneasy feeling. Clinton is either being faulted for being the opposite of George Bush (Clinton tries to do too much, whereas Bush never tried to do a damn thing about domestic problems) or for the same things for which Bush was faulted as though they were brand-new (Clinton still hasn't named all his appointees; it took Bush more than six months).

I am left with the impression the media are not being quite . . . fair.

I suppose I should be proud of my colleagues, in a way. Conservatives whined so long that the media were unfair to Reagan and Bush that at least now we can claim equal-opportunity, bipartisan unfairness.

But the media's collective treatment of Hillary Clinton still amazes me. There is, for example, nothing exceptional about the article inside *Time* about

Clinton, but the cover shows her with her head at what we assume is a combative tilt, and the headline is "Ascent of a Woman: Hillary Rodham Clinton is the most powerful first lady in history. Does anybody have a problem with that?"

It's certainly an in-your-face question. But nothing in the ensuing article indicates that she is aggressive or abrasive or shrill or any of those other words so beloved of journalists writing about strong women.

Let's see, when was the last time we saw a *Time* cover so at variance with the story it was supposed to illustrate?

Oh, yeah, I remember, that doozie of a photo of Gloria Steinem and Susan Faludi wearing black leather in what appeared to be a shabby men's room, with the headline, "Whither feminism?"

Oh, well, what's journalism without stereotypes?

**May 1993**

# Ol' One-Vote Bill

N EW YORK — Sometimes I feel like the last citizen left in America who thinks Bill Clinton is doing a fairly good job. Talk about being able to caucus in a phone booth. . . .

Clinton was at the National Governors Association meeting the other day, griping to his former fellows about how Washington works and "the air-filling bull that we hear so often in the nation's capital."

"People who try to work together and listen to one another instead of beating each other up are accused of being weak, not strong. The people that really score are the people that lay one good lick on you in the newspaper every day instead of the people that get up and go to work, never care if they're on the evening news, never care if they're in the paper, and just want to make a difference," Clinton said.

Well, Ol' One-Vote Bill has been through some rough fights recently, so I guess he's entitled to wax a little sentimental about his halcyon days in Little Rock, when it was all for one and one for all, or so it seems to him in retrospect.

But I spent some time in Little Rock last year talking to Arkansas legislators about Clinton's leadership style, and so far I've seen nothing that either surprises or disappoints me.

The best description I got of him came from a state senator who said, "He's like one of those broad-bottomed children's toys that when you tump it over, it pops back up. No matter how many times you push it down, it pops right back up again. That's Clinton. We reject one of his plans, and he comes right back at us saying, 'OK, then, why don't we try to do it another way?' "

I liked the sound of it then, and I still do. This is not the truly artful, Machiavellian arm-twisting and screw-tightening many of us were raised to admire in politics.

Let me tell you a possibly apocryphal Lyndon Johnson story. Supposedly it was late in Johnson's presidency, and the city of Wichita Falls had done dog-all about integrating its schools, not a move. So one day, Lyndon phones the mayor of the Falls and says, Tom, do y'all really want to keep Sheppard (the local air force base)?

Of course, Mr. President, we certainly do, said the mayor.

Schools. Integration. Tomorrow, said Lyndon, and hung up. And the next day, they integrated the schools.

Now I don't know if that's true, but it's told admiringly by people who like to see political power wielded with a heavy hand in a good cause. But those of you who recall the dark side of Lyndon's use of power (the reigning authority on the dark side is Robert Caro, two volumes so far) will also remember that we used to yearn for a better way to do things. For lack of a better description, we thought it would be nice if someone tried democracy for a change.

Lyndon, who liked to put people in a vise and twist till they screamed, used to say in public, "Let us reason together." In private, what he said was, "When you've got their peckers in your pocket, their hearts and minds will follow."

Bill Clinton actually believes in getting people to reason together, reach a consensus on a good plan, and then go forward.

Sometimes these different ways of using power are described in gender terms. Ann Richards says one of her frustrations with the Texas Legislature is that boys are taught from early on to win—and when someone wins, someone else loses. Richards thinks girls are socialized to find win/win solutions. My favorite example is what any smart mom does when there are two kids and one cookie. The first kid gets to divide the cookie, and the second kid gets first pick of the halves. You can generally count on the moms of the world to find solutions where nobody loses.

To my mind, while Clinton is not batting a thousand (he's barely batting .500), he deserves bonus points for taking on the toughest problems. We're looking at twelve years' worth of domestic problems that have been allowed to fester without action, and he's the spoon that's stirring the pot in Washington. He apparently just never counted on whatever is in that pot in Washington becoming more like cement than soup.

So Clinton's plans have been tumped over a couple of times now. The last thing we need is for him to start feeling sorry for himself. What we need and what he needs to do is pop back up again and try to find another way to get it done.

I'm sure Vince Foster's suicide made Washington look a lot darker to Clinton, but if I'm right that his greatest strength is persistence, he'll be back.

And those of us who always yearned to see power used in less coercive ways need to quit describing the president as "weak" because he doesn't club people over the head instead of getting them to reason together. The fight Clinton faces on health care is going to make the budget fight look like patty-cake. The amount of money being spent by the forces that find the status quo quite profitable, thank you, is staggering. My money's still on Clinton to find a way to at least start to fix this mess.

**August 1993**

# The First Year

■

ATLANTA — Having come to Atlanta for one of those "First Year of the Clinton Presidency" thumb-sucking sessions, I offered my own profession-centric view of the world by focusing on Clinton and the media. I felt obliged to review the record for this august occasion, and what's depressing is that there's so much evidence to support what I already thought: This president is getting trashed.

As an opinion writer who spent twelve years being generally unhappy with the presidencies of Ronald Reagan and George Bush, I consider myself an expert on trashing presidents. I once wrote an entire column on the subject of how to describe the Reagan quality that was then politely referred to as his being "disengaged."

"So dumb if you put his brains in a bumblebee, it would fly backwards" was one of my offerings. And Bush inspired several unkind reflections on my part; his inability to express himself clearly in the English language was fodder for many a column. How I miss him.

But I think you'll agree that there is a qualitative difference between wondering what Bush actually meant when he said something incomprehensible and a radio talk-show host telling jokes about Hillary Rodham Clinton performing oral sex. I think we have a problem here, folks.

The difference between the way Bill Clinton has been treated by the press in his first year and the way Reagan and Bush were treated is not a matter of one's political perspective. By now, there are several media studies comparing exactly the same story—"President makes major policy proposal" or "President signs bill"—and the wildly different treatment that Clinton has received.

On the theory that the press is always sycophantic toward someone who has come in with a big electoral majority—at least for a while—I went back to our last minority president, Richard Nixon. The exit polls in '92 showed that had Ross Perot not been in the race, his vote would have split evenly between Bush and Clinton, leaving Clinton with a clear majority. When Nixon was first elected in '68, the situation was far muddier: The George Wallace vote was also a Robert Kennedy vote, one of those populist phenomena that always confound pollsters. Of course, the country was in turmoil after '68, the Year Everything Happened. Opposition to the war actually escalated in '69, Nixon's first year in office, but it was not yet considered Nixon's war, so the vituperation was not aimed at him. Press and popular opinion were to give the guy a chance.

Somewhat closer to the mark is the first year of Jimmy Carter's presidency. Although Carter was cut far more slack than Clinton, who has been under steady and very heavy media fire since before his inauguration, there were undercurrents of the same vein of attack.

"This guy is from outside Washington; he doesn't understand how things work here; he's from a small, Southern, podunk state; he has white-trash relatives, etc." Perhaps the most significant difference between media attacks on Carter and Clinton is that Carter appeared to be more vulnerable to them than Clinton does. Carter always looked as though he were in pain, whereas Clinton appears to be actually enjoying himself, at least some of the time.

There are a number of psychobabble theories to account for the media's negativity toward Clinton. One is that Clinton is not a father figure; he's a brother figure and so much safer to attack. One is that the Washington press corps is trying to make up for its lamentable performance in the eighties (missed the savings and loan story, missed the Housing and Urban Development scandal, missed Iran-contra) by getting tough with Clinton. Another is that Clinton early on declared that he would not be a captive of the Washington press corps. He would go over its head directly to the people on talk shows and in town meetings. And so it decided to show him who needed whom in this town. And so on and so forth.

One of the alternative theories is that neither Clinton nor the media are at fault. They are both part of a political climate that has become so polarized and so paralyzed that no one talks about how to fix anything anymore.

As a recent minor example of what happens to Clinton with the media, the big Washington story a few weeks ago was that the administration had decided to concentrate on getting health-care reform passed this year. Except that instead of being about getting health-care reform passed, the story immediately became that Clinton was dropping the ball, breaking his promise and letting slide . . . welfare reform.

Now, Superman couldn't get two bills that size through Congress in one year, and it is clear to anyone who has looked at these problems that health-care reform is the key to welfare reform. What constantly happens to women on welfare is that they go out, get a job, and start making it on their own, and then one of the kids gets sick. And the only way they can afford a doctor is to go back on welfare. Ergo, you do health-care reform before you do welfare reform. This is not rocket science.

Exactly why the media have recently decided that a nonbreaking story (see *The New York Times,* August 1992) about an Arkansas S&L is now a story—the same media that ignored the S&L disaster during the eighties because Donald Trump was so much more interesting—is beyond me. I am a great believer in thorough research on politicians who make money while holding public office. Those who lose money and then fail to deduct it on their income taxes strike me as a bit less of a menace to the public at large than, say, Lyndon B. Johnson.

One of the many theories about all this is that Clinton is a victim of "changing standards." JFK could womanize; Clinton can't. Reagan could get away with having his California kitchen cabinet make him rich; Clinton can't have any questionable friends in Arkansas. And on the whole, aren't we a better nation for insisting that our public figures retroactively meet heretofore undreamed-of standards of purity? (While the media themselves, of course, are lowering their standards considerably about what's fit to print.)

I don't think so. Bobby Ray Inman might not have made a good secretary of defense because he's a classic military-industrial-complex graduate, not to mention his spook background, not to mention his less-than-impressive private-industry record. But he's right that making the housecleaner's Social Security payment a make-or-break issue is silly.

More than the petty list of specific transgressions (recall the tantrums when the Clinton people fired some folks in the White House travel office) is the cumulative level of cynicism and sourness that this kind of coverage has achieved. Beyond that lies a far more vicious climate of actual hate and contempt fostered by talk radio.

Clinton is a very intelligent man; he is extremely knowledgeable about both state and federal government and how they fit together. He has lots of ideas about how to fix things and is quite flexible about adapting his ideas to take account of other people's ideas and problems. He genuinely likes people. He's not mean, he's not autocratic, and he's not paranoid yet. The media have yet to give him the benefit of the doubt on anything.

**January 1994**

# Whitewater

■

I AM WORKING WOMANFULLY on the Whitewater scandal. I'm going to get a grip on it any day now. One of my secret vanities as a journalist is that I'm nonpartisan about ethical lapses, a veritable Ahab, I like to think, in relentless pursuit of do-badders of any persuasion.

I pride myself on the roster of Democrats and/or liberals I have roasted, toasted, and basted on matters both fiscal and moral: Lyndon Johnson, former House Speaker Jim Wright, Lieutenant Governor Bob Bullock, former attorney general Jim Mattox, former Texas House Speaker Gib Lewis, etc., etc.

It's just that every time I see Senator Al D'Amato waxing indignant about Whitewater, I start laughing. You have to cut me some slack on this: I used to work for *The New York Times*, where I covered D'Amato, who is one of the most awful weasels I ever ran across. Believe me, if you know Al D'Amato, watching him wax indignant about an ethical question is comic beyond all hope of redemption.

Nevertheless—operating on the theory that with all this horsepuckey around, there's bound to be a pony here somewhere—I have been studying Whitewater. Here's the deal:

Sixteen years ago—possibly on a cold, dark night—Bill and Hillary Clinton invested in a real estate deal that didn't pan out, lost about $60,000, and failed to take a deduction for the loss on their income taxes. So far, I fail to ignite. Like Queen Victoria, I am not amused by politicians who make money while holding public office, but I've never had to take a stand on a politician who lost money and failed to take a deduction before. Hillary Clinton later got shrewder about tax deductions, even taking off for donating Bill's old underwear to the Salvation Army, but that is apparently not part of the current complaint.

There follows the usual tangled tale of how the Clintons' partner in the real estate deal, James McDougal, owns this savings and loan called Madison Guaranty that gets into the usual S&L trouble. At which point there's the usual conflict of interest because Hillary Clinton has been hired to represent Madison Guaranty for the usual $2K-a-month retainer, and among other legal work, she represents McDougal before a state bank regulator appointed by her husband. Further conflict-of-interest charges loom on account of Hillary Clinton's being a partner in the Rose Law Firm in Little Rock, which represented several banks and S&Ls and then later, as per usual, also represented the government in the liquidation of banks and S&Ls.

At the Washington end, we get a big flap-de-do because some Treasury officials briefed some White House officials on how the Resolution Trust Corporation's examination of Madison Guaranty was coming along, and this is a big no-no because it might look like political pressure is being put on the RTC. Gawdawmighty, if there's a virgin left at RTC, I'd like to know who it is—gee, no one there ever would have guessed that the White House had any interest in Madison Guaranty; it's only been on the front pages for two years now.

The only truly distinguishing feature of the Madison Guaranty saga is how absolutely average it is. Notice that I am defending no one and nothing about it; I'm just telling you this story is as common as dirt. Talk about missing the forest for the tree. The Washington press corps has found itself a tree. Well, good on them. There just happens to be an entire darkling plain out there covered with the damn things.

Had the media bothered to cover the S&L scandal back when it was happening, this story would be considered a hopeless yawner. You think the Rose Law Firm looks funny on this? Try Akin, Gump in Dallas or any of dozens of other law firms in Texas alone. You think Texas looks strange on this? You should see some of the theft that was pulled off in California. You think the RTC might be questioned on its conduct of this case? The RTC should have been questioned, grilled, and bastinadoed years ago.

The Reagan administration set up the S&Ls to be looted in 1981. It was done, and then the very lawmakers who voted for the Garn–St. Germain bill, who took money from the S&L lobby, who pressured the regulators on behalf of their home-state contributors, had the nerve to set up an ethics investigation of five senators and call it quits. Except now, they want to make an example out of Madison Guaranty to get at the Clintons. Led by Al D'Amato.

Maybe it's pathetic of me, but I'm still not a cynic. I actually hope that Representative Jim Leach, who has a damn decent record on S&Ls, will use his hearing to get at what was wrong with the system, not just Madison Guaranty.

I think that if he and Representative Henry B. Gonzalez cooperated, the two of them could actually, finally, get after the whole forest and do a world of good in banking reform and regulation along the way.

I gave up on the tooth fairy and Al D'Amato a long time ago, but I still have faith in Leach and Henry B.

**March 1994**

# No Decency

■

EXCUSE ME, I must have a banana in my ear: I thought you said the Senate chaplain prayed for comfort for O. J. Simpson, including the line, "Whether he is innocent or guilty rests with our system of justice, but our hearts go out to him in his profound loss."

While your faithful media mavens were busy re-re-re-hashing the Simpson case last week, the dollar fell to a post–World War II low in the world currency markets, which means that the Federal Reserve will raise interest rates again, which means you're going to get shafted again. Whenever the economic recovery threatens to become serious, they call in Dr. Greenspan, who promptly puts a halt to it in the name of fighting inflation. Inflation, you understand, benefits debtors and harms lenders—i.e., the banks. Banks before people, that's Alan Greenspan's motto.

Oh, and nuclear war in Korea was averted.

Also, the president was accused of murder. Nah, not the old Vince Foster rumors; this is some guy in Arkansas who supposedly had the goods on Bill Clinton's sex life, and even though there is no evidence whatsoever, you can hear the president being accused of murder on a videotape being sold by the Reverend Jerry Falwell for forty bucks, plus $3 for shipping.

Even when he's not being accused of murder, the prez just cannot get a break. All the charmers who gritched about his speaking at the D-day ceremonies on account of he had enough principle to stay out of the Vietnam War would, of course, have been the very same people gritching if Clinton *hadn't* gone to Europe. I can hear Rush Limbaugh now: "How dare the president of the United States ignore this anniversary of our heroic landing in Normandy?"

Now Washington is all agog over Bob Woodward's book *The Agenda*, which (a) reveals that Clinton has a temper and (b) supposedly reveals that he's indecisive.

Now on the temper question, I have it on good authority that when he was informed that one of his aides had used a military chopper to get to a golf game, Clinton was so mad he nearly broke a chair by picking it up and slamming it on the floor. He further had several choice observations to make concerning the sea of problems he's facing and how, on top of all that, this dag-nabberty-blabbit, adjectival-deleted residue of bovine digestion (or words to that effect) had taken a chopper to go golfing.

Has no one in Washington any sense of history? For impressive presidential temper tantrums, you had to have heard Lyndon B. Johnson in full fury. Upon being informed that one of his aides had been arrested for indecent conduct in a men's room, LBJ turned the air so blue that Bird had to say, "Now, Lyndon." And she was used to him. (To the Johnsons' credit, they never abandoned the man or his family.)

As to Clinton's indecisiveness, wouldn't you think someone as smart as Woodward would realize that Clinton habitually agrees with whomever he's talking to? This is a good way to save yourself a lot of unnecessary arguments; it doesn't mean he can't make up his mind. I watched him once during the '92 campaign agreeing with a pod of advisers who told him not to mention race in Tyler, which was then in the throes of a nasty racial conflict. And then he agreed equally cordially with the advisers who told him that he had to address the question. He got off the bus still agreeing with everyone and proceeded to give, in its entirety, Martin Luther King Jr.'s "I Have a Dream" speech, which was the single best thing I've ever seen a politician do, except for the time Bobby Kennedy spoke to that crowd in Indianapolis the night King was killed.

I'm also sick of hearing that Clinton has no foreign policy or keeps changing it. Bosnia, Korea, Haiti—listen, I don't want us to go jumping into any of these places with both feet. If Clinton wants to push and test and probe and check around on what support he can get and then pull back and then start an escalating boycott, hell, I think that's just what he should do. You notice that none of these geniuses criticizing him has any good ideas on what to do in Haiti, because there are no good choices on Haiti. Einstein would be hard put to figure out which is the least horrible choice in Haiti.

After two years of listening to Limbaugh & Co. viciously attack his wife, insult his daughter, and constantly purvey lies, innuendo, invective, and propaganda, Clinton hit back last week, blasting these little creeps for their cynicism. So now his critics are criticizing him for that. Martha Gellhorn calls it "Trial by denunciation. Sentence by slander." At long last, have they no decency?

**June 1994**

# The Politician

■

Hartford, CONN. — It just never does come easy for Bill Clinton, does it? He lost money in a bad real estate deal in 1978, and they're going to hang that around his neck till kingdom come.

I have to add that Clinton has brought much of his trouble on himself, and the reason I have to add that is because a law was passed about four years ago; you may not know this, but the law forbids any journalist from ever saying anything either sympathetic to or admiring about Clinton without immediately adding, "But . . . " and then sticking in at least a little knife. We all obey this law religiously because anyone who breaks it will have his press pass removed or, worse, lose his cynicism stripes and stand convicted of being a sucker for spin.

It's especially important that no journalist ever give Clinton credit for an ounce of sincerity because, you see, we know him to be a Politician to the Bone. So is everybody else we cover, but we have to be especially cynical about the ones who are good at it.

It's true that Clinton has spent pretty much his whole life working to become president. Isn't that an awful thing? We in the media never forget it. He had to work hard at it, too: alcoholic stepfather, mom a piece of work, all the education from scholarships. The only "real" job he ever had was teaching constitutional law; aside from that, it's been politics all the way, and we all know how despicable that makes him, don't we? I mean, all the guy ever wanted to do was public service, so he stays in his home state (and we certainly all feel free to dump on Arkansas these days) at $50K a year instead of taking his Yale law degree to some big-money state and making a zillion dollars doing mergers and acquisitions. That sure means we should all look at him with contempt, right?

The trouble with being president is that the only thing you can do once you get there is the best you can. And I for one think they all do. Even Lyndon B. Johnson, who led us so deep into the Big Muddy that we're not out yet; even Richard M. Nixon, that poor paranoid expletive-deleted—I think they did the best they could.

And I'd say that Clinton's best is not bad at all. He had a good run his first two years—cut the deficit in half before the Republicans took over, saying a balanced budget was the be-all and end-all of government. Clinton blew health-care reform, but the money out to beat him on that was like nothing ever seen before in American politics. And for the last year and a half, he's staved off the worst of Newt Gingrich's nutty "revolution," which is just a take-from-the-poor-and-give-to-the-rich scheme.

What amazes me is the level of vituperative hatred aimed at Bill and Hillary Clinton. A lot of people hated Johnson because of Vietnam and civil rights; a lot of people hated Nixon, I think, because he was so full of hate himself. But what this reminds me of is John F. Kennedy.

Most people have forgotten it, but there was a substantial amount of intense, almost insane hatred of Kennedy. I always thought it was a class thing; in addition to being born on third, Kennedy embodied that aristocratic ideal (you see it in the Peter Wimsey character) of making excellence look easy. You're supposed to get a First at Oxford and play championship cricket all without appearing to work for it. With guys like Nixon, the sweat always shows.

But it doesn't seem to me that Clinton ever plays the aristocrat; he was proud of his mom, whom many of our snobbier citizens took for something close to trailer trash. (I thought she was a darling, myself; I like people who know how to have fun.)

Slippery is a word often applied to Clinton, and I wonder if it's because he's bicultural in the odd way that educated Southerners often are. If you go to Georgetown, Oxford, and Yale, you pretty much learn to walk the walk and talk the talk common in those places. But that doesn't mean you wouldn't really prefer to be eating barbecue in some joint back in the Piney Woods where no one cares which fork you use—or if you use one at all. It's not a matter of being two-faced; it's just being comfortable in two different worlds.

Clinton is an Arkansan, which an amazing number of sophisticated Washington reporters still think means being barefoot with a piece of straw in your mouth. Believe it or not, when George Bush was elected, there was a spate of alarmed articles about how "The Texans Are Coming," as though a bunch of barbarians were about to be unleashed to spit and cuss in the genteel precincts of D.C.

I think that Clinton's most salient traits as a politician are that he's a listener, he's a learner, and he's a deal-maker. When I hear talk about how "dirty" he is or about how he is, as one irate caller said, "the most corrupt man ever to occupy the White House" (may you rest in peace, Warren Harding), I'm at a loss to explain where the hate comes from.

**June 1994**

# Power Town

■

WASHINGTON, D.C. — I believe one should never pass up an opportunity to berate the Washington press corps, and so I did the other night.

Now that I've gotten all that spleen out of my system, it occurs to me I was a little unfair—just a trifle, you understand. I probably shouldn't've referred to the White House press corps as "a bunch of trained seals sitting around waiting for their four o'clock feeding."

And I guess I went too far in describing the level of political discourse in this city as "petty, pompous, and parochial." Not *all* political discourse here is petty, pompous, and parochial—just most of it.

Just because we read more about Hillary's hat than about homelessness was no reason for me to take on in that tacky fashion, was it?

In the calmer light of day, it occurs to me that my brethren and sistren in this trade are just trying to make up for lost time. Having blown every big story of the eighties—including the savings and loans, Iran-contra, Iraq-gate, Reaganomics, and the Housing and Urban Development scandal, just to mention a few—my colleagues are now determined to play "gotcha" journalism with the Clinton administration. Who am I to plead with the brethren, "Jeez, give the guy a break"?

I don't believe in breaks for the powerful, never have.

I think old Joe Pulitzer was right: "A free press should always fight for progress and reform, never tolerate injustice or corruption, always fight demagogues of all parties, never belong to any party, always oppose privileged classes and public plunderers, never lack sympathy with the poor, always remain devoted to the public welfare."

And by George, that inaugural hat of Hillary's *was* silly-looking. The reason I avoid Washington as much as possible is not because this is a city where everybody says what everybody else says. It's because whenever I'm here for ten minutes, I find myself saying exactly what everybody else says. Which is why I'm writing about Hillary Rodham Clinton and her hat.

What *is* the hangup this town has about Rodham Clinton? "No one voted for *her*," insist the sclerotic conservatives. *Hell*, no one ever voted for Jim Baker either, but he ran the country for several years without noticeable objection.

The latest flap over Rodham Clinton is that she won't open the policy-making process on health care to the press. Now, I'm confused about this. I thought I knew what secret government was. Ten years of covering Gib Lewis and I know a done deal when I see one. I just finished lambasting Bob Bullock for calling in the special interests to cut a deal on products liability. And now here's the Washington press corps agog because Rodham Clinton isn't calling in lobbyists for the American Medical Association to get their input on the health-care plan. Uh. Excuse me. But why should she?

Do we really think the poor, pitiful AMA is going to be shut out of this debate? The problem is that we're not to the debate stage yet. So far, we haven't even got a proposal. That's what Mrs. Clinton is trying to put together. Doesn't she get to work on her proposal without the press and the lobsters at the table? Isn't the usual deal that after she finishes this proposal and releases it, then the press and the lobsters pick it apart? I've no objection to the press picking on the Clinton administration—have at 'em—but I think the press has come down with a bad case of premature picking. I always thought you were supposed to wait until the folks in office had screwed up before you went after 'em.

I recall Abe Rosenthal, then editor of *The New York Times* and, Lord knows, not a man I often agreed with, once mildly suggesting that the new mayor of New York should be given a chance to mess up before we attacked him. In that particular case (Ed Koch), I thought we held off far too long, but I agreed with Abe's premise.

Quite a disconcerting number of the brethren here were claiming the Clinton administration was a disaster before the man had even been sworn in.

I am puzzled by the Washington press corps' reaction to affirmative action by the Clinton administration—not reverse discrimination, but affirmative action.

I thought it was a good idea to have an administration that "looks like America" instead of the usual suits. Look what's already happening on the Hill now that it looks a little more like the rest of America. When the family leave bill was being debated, Senator Patty Murray of Washington, the "mom in tennis shoes," put in her oar by recalling when she had to quit her secretarial job because she got pregnant. When they were discussing the Zoe Baird problem of people not paying Social Security taxes on their domestic workers, Representative Carrie Meek of Florida allowed as how she had been a domestic worker at one point in her life, her mom was a domestic worker, and so were all her sisters. Not a point of view normally heard in the corridors of power from the suits.

So why isn't it a good idea for Clinton to go out of his way to find a qualified woman attorney general (Zoe Baird not included)? How did this press corps get so conservative that they object to change on principle? Change is what this country rather stunningly clearly wants.

I am uneasily reminded of the last time this press corps failed to understand a president (for kindness' sake, we will draw a veil over the performance of this press corps during the Reagan years). Jimmy Carter was a president the press just never cottoned to. Like the senators during the Anita Hill/Clarence Thomas hearings, they just didn't get it.

Actually, it was pretty simple. Jimmy Carter has been out of office for thirteen years now. And every day for thirteen years, that man has gone out and behaved like a good Christian—for no money. Because that's who he is, and that's who he always was. But that was too simple for Power Town.

**July 1994**

# The New Regime I

■

THE MOST FUN GUY to watch in the New Regime is House Speaker-elect Newt Gingrich. The reason you want to keep an eye on Gingrich is that he plans to improve your morality, and he's just the fellow to do it.

You may not have had the improvement of your morality in mind when you voted to get the government off your back Tuesday, but here in the New Regime, many things are wondrous.

Gingrich explained to *The New York Times* the other day that the country has been in a state of moral decline since the 1960s and that he plans to root out the remnants of the counterculture and the Great Society. Said Gingrich: "Until the mid-1960s, there was an explicit, long-term commitment to creating character. It was the work ethic. It was honesty, right and wrong. It was not harming others. It was being vigilant in the defense of liberty."

Yep, you want to know right from wrong, you check with Newt here in the New Regime because Newt knows.

Gingrich spent the first part of the dread 1960s at Emory University in Atlanta, at a time when many who felt strongly about morality were involved in the civil-rights movement. He was not. Like President Clinton, being a graduate student—in Gingrich's case, already married with children—kept him out of Vietnam. He went to Tulane, where he was also not involved in the pre-eminent moral issue of the late 1960s. Like Clinton, the only nonpolitical job he has ever held was teaching college: Clinton taught constitutional law at the University of Arkansas; Gingrich taught history at West Georgia College.

Gingrich, the man who put term limits in the Contract with America, was first elected to Congress in 1978 after two earlier, unsuccessful races. He was, of course, strong on family values. In 1980, he filed for a divorce from his wife, Jacqueline, after eighteen years of marriage. While they were separated, she had her second operation for cancer. Gingrich went to see her in the hospital to discuss the terms of their divorce. In 1993, Jacqueline sued Gingrich for failing to pay his $1,300 monthly alimony on a timely basis and for failing to pay the premiums on a life-insurance policy for her. He settled the lawsuit by agreeing to give Jacqueline the first $100,000 coverage in his life-insurance policy. Gingrich remarried in 1981.

In the famous flap about the House bank, Gingrich was found to have bounced twenty-two checks, compared with Speaker Tom Foley's two.

But easily the most notable contribution to our political life made by Gingrich during his congressional career has been the level of rancor and vitriol with which he practices politics. So impressive were Gingrich's thrusts at the opposition that in 1990, the GOP issued a list of them—words that Republican candidates should use to describe their opponents so they could be successful, like Newt. The words are: *sick, pathetic, traitor, welfare, crisis, ideological, cheat, steal, insecure, bizarre, permissive, anti-(issue),* and *radical.*

Let's look at that list again because we're going to be hearing quite a lot from Mr. Gingrich, and not only in person. As he has announced, he will be using Rush Limbaugh and Christian-right radio and television programs to communicate his ideas. *Sick, pathetic, traitor, welfare, crisis, ideological, cheat, steal, insecure, bizarre, permissive, anti-(issue),* and *radical.*

Such language, here in the New Regime, will be helpful in solving problems, such as how to get health-care coverage for forty million Americans, how to get people off welfare, how to create decent-paying jobs and give people the skills to do them.

Mickey Kaus of *The New Republic* gives us a typical example of how Gingrich does politics. You may recall the flapette late in the mercifully over elections concerning a memo written by Alice Rivlin, one of the most consistently realistic deficit hawks in the Clinton administration. Rivlin outlined a number of options for further cutting the deficit and still finding ways to invest in programs, particularly job-skills programs. Among her options was cutting Social Security benefits to the wealthy. This was seized upon by Gingrich, who promptly raised an enormous furor about how Clinton was planning to cut Social Security. Clinton brilliantly riposted that he wasn't planning to cut it but that the Republicans were. Are not, are so, are not, they argued, which was the level of debate we got throughout the elections.

Kaus went and found Gingrich's 1986 Social Security proposal that advocates cutting off Social Security for everyone in the country under forty and then passing a national value-added tax of $200 billion per year. But—this is the beauty part—the accusation that Gingrich leveled at Rivlin and Clinton was hypocrisy. Which brings us to the First Rule of Newt-Watching: Whatever he accuses his opponents of, look for carefully in his own behavior.

Gingrich recently told a group of lobbyists he was, to put it crudely, shaking down that his election strategy was to portray Clinton Democrats as "the enemy of normal Americans" and proponents of "Stalinist measures." I'm fond of hyperbole myself. But when politicians start talking about large groups of their fellow Americans as "enemies," it's time for a quiet stir of alertness. Polarizing people is a good way to win an election, and also a good way to wreck a country. Stay alert.

**November 1994**

# The New Regime II

■

Aw, ARMEY! DICK, my man, what's wrong? Dr. No going soft! No fun, no fair.

Here I've been telling everyone how fabulous the new Texans at the top of Congress are going to be. Wait'll you see, I gloated. Bill Archer! Tom DeLay! And best of all, Dick Armey! This guy makes Newt Gingrich look like a fuzzy, cuddly bear.

I guaranteed it. The reason I guaranteed is because Newt Gingrich has already achieved the improbable effect of making Bob Dole seem cuddly. I've already started thinking of him as Uncle Bob. This is the same Dole about whom Jay Leno joked just last winter, "It's so cold in Washington, people are huddled around Bob Dole for warmth."

When Gingrich started muttering about putting millions of children in orphanages to be raised by a government that he believes can't do anything right, some of my compatriots here on what passes for the left were chilled to the bone. But no, I cried, you'll learn to love Noot! Just wait'll you get a good look at Armey.

I spoke with confidence, having followed Armey's career faithfully from his first campaign in the old mid-Metroplex, when he ran on a platform of abolishing Social Security. Not many people, even at that high tide of Reaganism, were advocating the abolition of Social Security, and I knew I had a live wire even then. Abolish farm subsidies! Torch the Capitol! Go, Armey!

One of my all-time favorite Dick Armey moments was when he looked at Hillary Rodham Clinton during a health-care reform hearing and said: "I have been told about your charm and wit, and let me say, the reports on your charm are overstated and the reports on your wit are understated." That was my man Armey—a noted authority, all agree, on both charm and wit.

But now, *now*, damned if we're not getting a kinder, gentler Dick Armey. He no longer advocates phasing out Social Security. He's not even going to fight for abolishing agricultural subsidies. Aaaawwww, Dick.

Where is the Dick Armey of yesteryear, the one who called the Family Leave Act "yuppie welfare"? The man who said the Clinton health-care program was "a Kevorkian prescription for the jobs of American men and women"? Heck, Armey used to say he was "embarrassed" ever to have been a college professor because so much education is "pure junk."

For a while, I was even working on the theory that Armey's scorched-earth approach to politics was genetic: He has a son, Scott, who has distinguished himself as a Denton County commissioner by pushing for prayer in the schools, an issue that some constitutional purists would consider outside the purview of county commissioners.

What do we get now? A kinder, gentler Dick Armey. Now we get Dick Armey telling *The Dallas Morning News* that in his early years in the House, he "risked being labeled a bomb-thrower, a loose cannon," but he learned that "you can be so ideologically hidebound you can cut yourself off from the process." He says that in 1990, when he was shut out of the budget summit, he learned that you have to have "a place at the table." And so he ran for the No. 3 spot in the Republican leadership and learned to play the game. And now, here he is at No. 2, just another perfectly good bomb-thrower we sent to Washington, only to have him turn into a politician. Sure, Armey insists that he has learned about Washington from being in the Congress since 1984. I say it's another reason for term limits.

At least Armey still believes in supply-side economics. It was such a success during the Reagan years that he wants to try it again. And he still believes in a flat tax rate. Why should Ross Perot pay any more in taxes than thee and me? But you can tell the old fire is gone from Armey. All this disgusting talk about being conciliatory and learning from experience—yuck. Sounds like Jim Wright.

Maybe Clarence Thomas will have some success in getting Armey back to his good old ways. The justice is Armey's good friend, and when they go fishing together, they catch supply-side fish.

**November 1994**

# Newt

■

WELL, HE IS a rare one, Mr. Gingrich is. But you have to admit, it takes a crew as gormless as the Washington press corps to take him seriously. The man is without question the single silliest public official east of the Texas Legislature.

The trouble with members of the D.C. press is that they are under the daffy impression they have to take him seriously just because he's been elected to high public office. Great gravy, poor Mencken.

Nincompoopery has never been a bar to high office in our nation. Newt Gingrich's sole claim to serious consideration is that he's great copy. He has no ideas, no principles, no integrity, and by and large, he's a damn fool.

On the other hand, what he does have is enthusiasm, and not just positive enthusiasm. Gingrich is just as positively negative as he is positively positive. He's not a lukewarm guy at all, much less one with any judgment. Enthusiasm is an endearing trait.

According to *Time* magazine, Gingrich's colleagues at West Georgia College called him Mr. Truth, because any time he finished a book, he'd come flying in, declaring, "This book is the truth! It's the best book I ever read!"

On the other hand, when Gingrich is negatively enthusiastic, he's just as positive. In January 1995 he declared, "There is no grotesquerie, no distortion, no dishonesty too great" for his political enemies to use against him. That remark echoed an earlier tirade in which Gingrich declared: "These people are sick. They are destructive of the values we believe in," he said. "They are so consumed by their own power, by a Mussolini-like ego, that their willingness to run over normal human beings and to destroy honest institutions is unending."

For those of you familiar with motivational speakers, Gingrich is the Zig Ziglar of Republican politics. In fact, there is an amusing parallel between the salesmen who drive between calls listening to Ziglar on "how to close" and

Republican candidates who drive between campaign stops listening to Gingrich on "how to win."

In addition to being an enthusiast, Gingrich is brazen. Isn't that a lovely old-fashioned word? Shameless. Without scruple. Possessed of brass-faced gall. A man for whom the word *hypocrisy* has no meaning.

There are a couple of easy pointers for the neophyte Newtist on how to read the Speaker. One is that Gingrich constantly accuses others of that which he himself is guilty. The shrinks call it projection, but I have no interest in his psyche or private life. Projection is simply a fact of his political life. It goes back at least to 1978, during his first successful congressional campaign, when he accused his opponent Virginia Shapard of preparing to leave her family behind if she went to Washington, while Gingrich's staffers were taking bets on how long his own collapsing marriage would last.

In Gingrich's career, the most famous of all the instances of projection is his destruction of Speaker Jim Wright. It is fashionable to write about how ironic it is that Speaker Gingrich had problems with a book contract and that he currently has ethics problems—both ordeals suffered by Speaker Wright. Actually, the irony is quite old. At the time Gingrich called Wright "the least ethical Speaker in the twentieth century" because Wright had exceeded the House's $20,000 limit on honoraria through bulk buying of his book, Gingrich himself had raised $105,000 from former campaign contributors to publicize his own book, *Window of Opportunity*. Gingrich's political friends formed a limited partnership to promote his book through advertising and touring. Gingrich's wife, Marianne, was paid $11,500 by the partnership and Gingrich made $24,000 off it. In Wright's case, his political friends helped him out by buying his book after it came out. In Gingrich's case, his friends helped by paying publishing-related expenses for his book. In both cases, special-interest money wound up in the authors' pockets.

Another easy take on Gingrich is that whenever he becomes offensively defensive, when he issues a flat, repetitive denial, you're on to something, and well advised to hone right in. For example, he said in March 1995, "Any liberal who tells you we are cutting spending and hurting children is lying. L-Y-I-N-G, lying!" The House Republicans then proceeded to propose cuts for Head Start, summer jobs for inner-city kids, prenatal care, education, Medicaid, assistance for poor and handicapped children, recreation programs for inner-city kids, school lunches, and, of course, welfare. According to a study by the Office of Management and Budget, the proposals could move 2.1 million children into poverty.

When asked about the Federal Election Commission's lawsuit against GOPAC, Gingrich's political action committee, he avoided details and called the charges phony. In fact, Gingrich used the word *phony* eleven times in the space of one minute. That's easy for him. He regularly floors House stenographers by spitting out 350 words a minute. Nevertheless, Gingrich headed GOPAC from 1986 until May 1995, and the FEC has several thousand pages of evidence showing that GOPAC helped candidates for federal office without registering as a federal PAC and without meeting reporting requirements. According to the Democratic National Committee, GOPAC has received between $10 million and $20 million in large, secret donations from corporate executives who had major interests pending before the government.

When a *New York Times* poll in October 1995 showed that almost two thirds of the American people did not favor the proposed Republican tax cut, Gingrich went ballistic. "This poll is a disgraceful example of disinformation. What we get are deliberately rigged questions that are totally phony." Gingrich wants to cut $270 billion from Medicare while giving out $245 billion in tax cuts that would significantly benefit those who make more than $200,000 a year. He is extremely sensitive about using the word *cut* in relation to Medicare. He says he is only slowing the rate of growth in order to "save" Medicare.

Frank Luntz, a Republican pollster, concluded in a memo that the only way to cut Medicare was to scare people into thinking it was going broke and then claim to save it. Of course, when Democrats objected to the proposed $270 billion cut, the Luntz strategy did not prevent our man Newt from saying, "Think about a party whose last stand is to frighten eighty-five-year-olds, and you'll understand how totally morally bankrupt the Democratic Party is."

Although many of Gingrich's critics would like to think he merely pops off all the time, in fact both his use of certain language and his repetition of certain ploys are quite deliberate. Connie Bruck, writing in *The New Yorker,* cites "polarization and oversimplification" as hallmarks of Gingrich's rhetoric.

Gingrich pays attention to language with a concentration that would do credit to a professor of semiotics. In a 1990 GOPAC letter to Republican candidates, he wrote, "I have also included a new document entitled 'Language: A Key Mechanism of Control,' drafted by GOPAC political director Tom Morgan. The words in that paper are tested language from a recent series of focus groups where we actually tested ideas and language."

Gingrich has a particular fondness for the words *grotesque, sick, bizarre,* and *twisted,* and regularly uses them in ad hominem attacks on his critics. He described a reporter whose question he didn't like as "an incredibly stupid person," and denounced another as "grotesque and offensive." Demonstrators protesting Medicare cuts along his book tour were "would-be fascists." Unfortunately, it's catching. Gingrich's critics respond with ad hominem attacks on him, and splendidly brazen as he is, he is not beyond posturing as a wounded innocent.

One of Gingrich's regular ploys is to associate "the opposition"—whether he defines it as Democrats, liberals, or counterculture McGoverniks—with the most heinous event of the moment.

In 1992 he said Woody Allen's affair with Mia Farrow's daughter "fits the Democratic Party platform perfectly." The Democratic Party has never recommended screwing your lover's adopted daughter.

When Susan Smith drowned her two sons in South Carolina in 1994, Gingrich said it "vividly reminds every American how sick society is getting and how much we have to change. I think people want to change, and the only way you get change is to vote Republican."

Actually, the Democrats have never recommended drowning your children either. But in reference to the above item, Susan Smith was in fact screwed by her stepfather from the age of fifteen on. He was a member of the state Republican executive committee and the Christian Coalition.

In September 1995 a three-year-old girl was accidentally killed during a gang-related shooting in Los Angeles. One of the suspects was out on parole, a circumstance in which Gingrich saw an opportunity. He called it "a glaring example of a liberal, New Deal approach that put up with violence, accepted brutality." The New Deal is not generally remembered either for putting up with violence or for accepting brutality.

In November 1995 a hideous crime caught the nation's attention: A welfare mother named Debra Evans, nine months pregnant, was killed along with two of her children. The killer cut the unborn child from her womb. Gingrich quickly tried to exploit the murders for political gain. "Let's talk about what the welfare state has created. Let's talk about the moral decay of the world the left is defending. It happened in America because for two generations we haven't had the guts to talk about right and wrong," he said. Evans, the victim, was, in fact, on welfare. She was also a regular churchgoer, known for opening her home and sharing what little food she had with others. She and her two children were each buried with Bibles on their chests. The left, no matter how loosely it is defined, has yet to encourage murdering pregnant women and cutting their babies out of the womb.

The latest round of journalistic efforts to take this unpromising specimen of political guttersnipe seriously includes de rigueur reflections on what *The Washington Post* calls "Gingrich's intellectual force." In *Time* magazine's hilarious Man of the Year profile, Lance Morrow hails his "first-class intelligence." According to Bruck's *New Yorker* profile, *Shōgun* is Gingrich's Bible. God save us, it isn't even a good book. On the other hand, it is a lot better than his own novel, *1945*, which is so appalling that anyone who admires Gingrich should be forced to read it.

It is now conventional wisdom that Gingrich's "ideas" dominate the Washington agenda, that he was somehow preternaturally in touch with the deepest yearnings of the American people. Actually, much of what Gingrich propounds stems from poll-driven politics and pollster packaging.

Conservatives, being conservative, object to Gingrich's ideological unsteadiness: He cannot be classified as a libertarian, an economic conservative, or a social conservative. From a thinking person's point of view, this is encouraging news: Surely only a dittohead could be so neatly pigeonholed. But the conservative critique of Gingrich is not that he is a synthesizer so much as he is a here-and-thereian. He frequently launches bozo ideas—orphanages, laptop computers for all, recognizing Taiwan, and Handicapped in Space are among the more memorable. (His Handicapped in Space program, described in his book *Window of Opportunity*, is based on the fetching notion that the handicapped will find it easier to work in a zero-gravity environment.)

Politics is normally considered hardball ("It ain't just beanbag," we all say cheerfully), but still a sport, and one with rules. For most of us. Tom Foley, by general consensus, will go down as one of the worst Speakers and one of the most decent human beings ever to serve in Congress. In 1989 a few Republicans were peddling the unsubstantiated rumor that Foley, married for years, was gay. An aide to Gingrich spoke to Lars-Erik Nelson of the New York *Daily News* and added, "We hear it's little boys." She also warned him that other newspapers were pursuing the story.

Nelson printed her words verbatim. Gingrich was furious and wrote a letter to Nelson's editors saying it never happened, that it was irresponsible reporting. He demanded that Nelson be fired. Then he apologized to Speaker Foley and said his aide's actions were "unforgivable and destructive." But he did not fire her.

In December 1995 Gingrich, citing an unnamed source during his appearance on *Meet the Press*, said that "up to one fourth of the White House staff have used drugs in the last four to five years." Gingrich, a master of the non-apology, said afterward, "It was a comment which produced a larger effect than I intended. In retrospect, I should not have said it. I've got to learn to be very specific about what I'm trying to accomplish. I stand by precisely what I said on *Meet the Press*."

Since becoming Speaker, Gingrich has called Democrats "sick," "corrupt," "thugs," and "liars." Also, a party "that despises the values of the American people," "cultural masochists" who enjoy bad news, "the enemy of normal Americans," and guilty of "multicultural, nihilistic hedonism." Various stories that have offended him are "socialist," "maniacally stupid" (that one was aimed at *The Wall Street Journal*), "a joke," "mean, spiteful, nasty," "a despicable hit piece by a person who has virtually no values."

But can he take it? In March 1995 he told the National Restaurant Association, anent the ethics charges against him, "Frankly, it hurts. It hurts to see people cheat, and it hurts to see the cheating reported as hard news."

In the same speech, he said, "I am so sick of the way the game is played by the news media and the way the game is played by the Democrats in this city that it is, frankly, all I can do to stand in there. They are misusing the ethics system in a deliberate, vicious, vindictive way, and I think it is despicable, and I have just about had it."

Last April he told *Face the Nation*, "I am very bitter about this. I am the only political figure of your lifetime who has been held to this incredible standard."

In October Gingrich reportedly said at a town meeting in Roswell, Georgia: "No one can get up every day and take the kind of totally dishonest cheap shots that we take and not wonder sometimes why you keep doing it. Frankly, I've thought about quitting because of the vicious, routine smears Marianne and I have to put up with." He loves to say "frankly."

Gingrich's tongue is almost as famous as Bob Packwood's. His funniest moments come when he takes a stand precisely contrary to an earlier stand (in some cases, only hours later) and is just as belligerent on the one side as he is on the other.

Before the 1994 election, Alice Rivlin, head of President Clinton's Office of Management and Budget, wrote a memo outlining a number of options for cutting the deficit while still finding ways to invest in programs such as job training. One option was cutting Social Security benefits to the wealthy. Gingrich promptly raised an enormous furor, claiming that the Clinton administration was planning to cut Social Security. Oh, what a heinous thing!

He was, of course, totally undeterred by the fact that he himself proposed a bill in 1986 that would have cut off Social Security for everyone in the entire country.

Great comic moments frequently follow his occasional vows to keep his tongue under control. In 1985, when *The Washington Post* said he was probably the most disliked member of Congress, Gingrich replied, "That was the old me—abrasive and confrontational. You'll see a change now. I am no longer the person I once was. I can be much quieter, much more positive."

That, of course, was before Jim Wright, Tom Foley, or Bill Clinton.

After being sworn in as Speaker in January 1995, Gingrich made a conciliatory speech, stating, "We are here as commoners together, to some extent Democrats and Republicans, to some extent liberals and conservatives, but Americans all. I would say to our friends in the Democratic Party that we're going to work with you."

Later the same day, he called Democratic tactics "dumb," "partisan," and "pathetically narrow."

Even more hilariously, after months of robustly Gingrichian rhetoric, he then turned and accused the press of dwelling on the negative and "trying to get a catfight started."

"In order to conduct a thorough and credible investigation, the special counsel needs unlimited subpoena power," said Gingrich during the investigation of Speaker Jim Wright. Now, of course, the special counsel who is investigating Speaker Gingrich must be carefully limited in authority.

Taiwan, term limits, and campaign finance reform are more issues Gingrich has seen from both sides, but Gingrich doesn't do anything so pedestrian as waffle or retreat. He is emphatic, no matter if he contradicts himself. Ambivalence is not Gingrich.

He can also be incredibly reckless in defining the differences between what he always posits as the conservative opportunity society versus the welfare state. An obscure and, by Washington standards, inexpensive program called Supplemental Security Income goes, literally, to poor, crippled children. It's not easy to attack a program that helps poor, crippled children. Were it not for the stipend that helps economically marginal families care for their children born with spina bifida, cystic fibrosis, and other diseases, the kids would have to be dumped into public institutions, where the cost of their annual care would run way over what their families now get to help pay for wheelchairs, ramps, etc. Gingrich told the U.S. Chamber of Commerce that poor people are not only coaching their kids on how to fake disabilities, but also beating them if they do not succeed. "They're being punished for not getting what they call crazy money or stupid money. We literally have children suffering child abuse so they can get a check for their parents."

There simply is no evidence for such a claim. Some shaky reporting based on unreliable sources had raised some questions about the SSI program, which also covers children with severe mental problems, and this was seized on by the right to discredit the program. Media reviews have since gone back and discredited both the reporting and the sources (who never alleged what Gingrich did to begin with).

One way to gauge Gingrich's commitment to "changing the way Washington works" is to look at what he has done with his own office. The budget for the Speaker's office has gone up 40 percent since Gingrich took over, to $600,000 a year. In addition to hiring a House protocol officer, Gingrich hired John Garbett, a Hollywood executive who formerly worked with Steven Spielberg, to coordinate media coverage for the House. His hire as House historian was "unfairly" criticized by the media for being pro-Nazi (a truly "bizarre" misunderstanding). He retained the $25,000 Speaker's slush fund that he had previously criticized and hired the coauthor of the miserable novel 1945, Albert Hanser, as a $60,000-a-year consultant performing ineffable services (or at least unidentifiable duties) for mankind.

In theory, Gingrich believes in devolution and the decentralization of power. In fact, the organizational changes he made in the House gave him an unprecedented degree of power: He has systematically broken down old independent centers of power, including the seniority system. Given that he's been in Congress for eighteen years, his reluctance to push for realistic term limits, the Contract with America notwithstanding, is understandable. On campaign financing, the root of the rot in American politics ("You got to dance with them what brung ya"), Gingrich has not sought reform but has cashed in.

The most striking evidence of Gingrich's allegiance to the old Washington concerns money. Baskets and buckets and trucks full of money. Majority Whip Tom DeLay, a former bug exterminator from Fort Bend County, Texas, is now Gingrich's lead moneyman. He's known as "The Hammer" for his tactics. Of which subtlety is not one. DeLay greets lobbyists with reports that show how much the lobbyists or their PACs have contributed to Democrats in the past. The message is that it's time to switch sides. One letter DeLay sent to PACs on behalf of a winning Republican candidate's postelection fund-raiser said, "You now have the opportunity to work toward a positive future relationship. Your immediate support is personally important to me and the House Republican leadership team. I hope I can count on you being on the winning team."

DeLay said: "We're just following the old adage of punish your enemies and reward your friends. We don't like to deal with people who are trying to kill the revolution. We know who they are. The word is out."

No one ever claimed the Democrats were simon-pure when in power, but veteran Washington observers agree they have never seen anything like the gold rush now taking place. The gusher of gelt now flowing to the Republicans comes from those who want to cut timber in protected forests, to drill for oil in environmentally sensitive areas, to get breaks on leasing or buying government land, to avoid taxes, and to avoid regulations for health and safety. Subsidies and tax loopholes for corporations, called corporate welfare, remain sacred while AFDC may be chopped into pieces. This is the old Washington with a vengeance.

Gingrich is not presiding over these festivities without some signs of stress. He has gained what appears to be in the neighborhood of thirty pounds since he became Speaker, and his political touch is occasionally wildly faulty. The most notable lapse was his juvenile snit about how "bizarre" it was that he had to exit by the back door of Air Force One after Yitzhak Rabin's funeral. Nor did shutting down the government prove to be a political plus for the Republicans.

In a now-famous speech given to college Republicans in 1978, Gingrich observed, "One of the great problems in the Republican Party is that we don't encourage you to be nasty." Or maybe not. The current nastiness of American politics has many fathers—political consultants and negative campaign ads among them. But Newt Gingrich is a leading force in the nastification of politics. More and more studies show that the upshot of the polarization and meanness of contemporary politics is that fewer and fewer people are willing to participate. And that is the death of democracy.

**May 1996**

# The Impasse

▨ .

WHEE! SPIN CITY. Who's responsible for shutting down the federal government and quite possibly sending the financial markets into a hopeless tizz?

"You hit me first."

"Did not."

"Did too."

"Did not."

"Did so."

We live in a great nation. Amen.

Actually, taking the popular, fail-safe, appearin'-as-wise-as-a-treeful-of-owls, plague-on-both-their-houses position here is as gutless as it is easy.

The who-to-blame conundrum is just not that tough a nut to crack, although it appears to have sent the Washington press corps back into the most timid form of objectivity: "We only report what other people say; we do not find the facts." For example, here's a dandy story from the Associated Press, reporting on how we got into this pickle: "Clinton said Gingrich promised in the spring to force a budget crisis, if necessary, to impose the GOP will." Now, how much effort does it take to determine that House Speaker Newt Gingrich said exactly that, at several times in several places? He did, he did, as we Texans say.

Don't know if you were privileged to hear Gingrich on Saturday blaming the entire impasse on President Clinton, but it was a bravura performance. He sounded exactly like Oliver Hardy saying to Stan Laurel, "Here's another fine mess you've gotten us into." Unable to restrain himself, Gingrich also took several cheap shots at Clinton for having gone off to play golf after announcing that he wouldn't sign a continuing budget resolution draped with extraneous matter, including a Medicare premium increase. The idea of Clinton golfing (!)

at such a time almost rendered the speaker apoplectic; the implication was that this president (a word that Gingrich manages to invest with contempt) is a lazy do-nothing.

Now, there are many things for which Clinton can be criticized, but not working hard enough is not one of them. His famous fifteen-hour days are a matter of both record and legend. As a matter of negotiating technique, when you have to resolve a critical issue with an unfriendly adversary, it is not wise to start out blaming everything on your opposite number and then to take cheap shots at same. This is ill-advised. Unproductive.

Clinton never gets credit for anything, so let me bravely swim against the entire Washington press corps and point out that Bill Clinton, faced for the past eleven months with the most hostile, nasty, relentlessly partisan Congress we have ever seen, has behaved like a real grown-up. In fact, I wish Virginia Clinton Kelley were still around so I could congratulate her on having taught that man good manners.

Newt Gingrich, who appears to have no sense of restraint whatever, has blamed Susan Smith's drowning her two children in South Carolina on the Democrats. He has blamed the death of a three-year-old in a drive-by shooting in Los Angeles on New Dealism, and he has called Democrats "morally bankrupt" while he himself has been embroiled in a series of ethical imbroglios, less than half of which were enough to drive Jim Wright from the same office.

It is true that while out on the campaign trail, at clearly political rallies, Clinton has taken some shots at the Republicans and engaged in a little ridicule of them. But when he is in Washington, speaking as president, he has been consistently mannerly, serious, and (in the opinion of this liberal populist) more than adequately ready to reach compromise. To blame Clinton now for the current budget impasse is outside of enough, and it's damn time someone said so.

Lee Howell, former press secretary to Gingrich, said: "There is the Newt Gingrich who is the intellectual, appealing and fun to be with. And there's the Newt Gingrich who is the bloodthirsty partisan who'd just as soon cut your guts out as look at you. And who, very candidly, is mean as hell."

On November 29, 1994, Gingrich said: "We don't particularly want to have a single ounce of compromise with those who still believe they can somehow improve and prop up and make work a bureaucratic welfare state."

My own modest contribution to Gingrichiana is the observation that the man regularly accuses others of that of which he is guilty himself. In a recent attack on Clinton, Gingrich said, "When you have a president who is capable of making up whatever fantasies fit his current position, I don't know how, as a serious person, you can do anything."

I am informed that this is a phenomenon well-known to psychiatrists; I've never seen it so clearly or so often in politics before. Pardon me, but I see no reason to pretend to objectivity on this. The facts are there, and the record is there—we can all fairly blame Newt Gingrich for this fine mess.

**November 1995**

# Pat Buchanan

∎

ETTING ASIDE THAT Pat Buchanan is a racist, sexist, xenophobic, homophobic anti-Semite, what wonderful news from New Hampshire! It's the nuts! It's the berries!

Yes, well, that is rather a large mound of manure there connected with his name, much of it justified, I'm afraid. There's even more—he defends old Nazis or something.

But since Buchanan has just sent the entire Republican Establishment and half the Democratic Establishment as well into a wall-eyed, blue-bellied snit, what can we do but rejoice?

The good news is that Pat Buchanan—aside from being a racist, sexist, xenophobic, homophobic anti-Semite—is a fairly likable human being. I mean, you'd much rather have a beer with him than Bob Dole or Phil Gramm.

Ask good liberals like Barbara Carlson of Minnesota or Al Franken, who works with Comedy Central—they can't help it, in fact. They'd rather not, but they like him.

Numero Two-o, being of the Irish persuasion, Pat Buchanan joys in a good fight, just loves biff-bam-pow, rejoices in a slugfest, gets off on a mudfight. Good thing, since he's in one now. What'll be really fun is watching his fellow Republicans attack him for being a racist, sexist, xenophobic, homophobic anti-Semite, which is not their native turf, as it were.

Somewhere in the Old Testament, it says, "I would that mine enemy had written a book," and Pat Buchanan has. In it, he notes that his father's heroes were Francisco Franco and Senator Joseph McCarthy, which is enough to frizz my hair right there.

On the other hand, I'd hate to have a lot of the stuff I wrote years ago taken out of context and twisted to represent my thinking. But Buchanan is in for it, so he might as well keep up his left.

As near as we can tell, Buchanan's victory in New Hampshire is a pretty much pure win for economic populism. Neither the Christian Coalition nor the anti-abortion movement count for much there, especially compared to Iowa.

What's even more interesting is that the state is not in an economic recession. That vote is a direct reflection of just how worried people are about their future in this two-tier economy. And there's what Bob Herbert calls "a cosmic disconnect" between what people are actually worrying about and what the Republicans are doing in Washington.

There are two problems with Buchanan as a populist.

One is all the divisive garbage he brings with him. It's exactly what has been used to destroy populist surges in the past—setting whites against blacks, natives against immigrants, men against women, straights against gays, Christians against Jews—divide, divide, divide—and lose. Look, Hispanic farm workers are not responsible for the savings and loan mess, blacks on welfare are not moving factories to Taiwan, lowering the tax on capital gains is not part of the "gay agenda," and Jews, having been historically discriminated against, by and large support raising the minimum wage.

The second problem is that Buchanan's economic populism is rudimentary. It's one thing to recognize that the gap between the rich and everybody else is growing like a cancer; it's another thing to come up with useful solutions. It's fine to jump on trade and economic globalization, but that's only part of the problem, and not a very big part at that. Nor is git-tough jingoism the solution. Buchanan still favors trickle-down economics—he wants to cut inheritance taxes, the capital gains tax, and taxes on the rich.

The only people I see in public office trying to address what's wrong with this economy are Labor Secretary Robert Reich and Massachusetts senator Ted Kennedy. Reich has been valiantly struggling to get raising the minimum wage on his boss' agenda and coming up with one improvement and suggestion after another on worker training. Kennedy came out with a multipronged plan earlier this month to attack what he calls "the quiet Depression," which contains a lot of carrots as well as sticks to get corporations to Do the Right Thing. (Someday even conservatives are going to notice that Ted Kennedy is the most effective senator in Washington: He has a wonderful habit of getting Republicans like Nancy Kassebaum and even Orrin Hatch to cosponsor good legislation.) Kennedy's plan covers the Federal Reserve Board, proposes a two-tier corporate tax plan to favor those that treat workers well, closes lots of stinky corporate tax loopholes, puts brakes on mergers and acquisitions, helps small business, helps labor, helps secure pension plans, and more. Buchanan would do well to study it.

Meanwhile, the Republicans in Congress are so lost in loonyland that they're now cutting off their nose to spite our face.

President Clinton nominated Felix Rohatyn, a guy so smart that Wall Street is in awe of him, to the Federal Reserve Board, where it was expected he would counter the right-wing monetarist Alan Greenspan. The Republicans wouldn't even let the nomination out of committee because it might reflect credit on Clinton.

**February 1996**

# The Newtzis

■

$A$ND NOW, LET'S have a round of applause for that fun-loving, slap-happy gang in the U.S. House of Representatives: Newt Gingrich and the Newtzis!

What impresses me most about the Newtzis is their imagination. Time after time, this merry gang comes up with some measure that makes me stand back in all honesty and admit, "You know, I never would have thought of that."

Just last week, they offered the country something it really needs. Now, just try to guess what it was.

Let's see, our country desperately needs . . . a much more efficient system for dealing with child abuse, some help for working moms who are losing their minds trying to find reliable day care, uhhh, a higher minimum wage, of course, ummm, more Meals on Wheels, annnd . . .

No! Not even close! Give up? What they offered us was more assault weapons! Yes, just what we needed and wanted: more assault weapons. Now, admit it—you're really surprised too, aren't you?

Yes, indeed—by voting to repeal that weenie ban on seventeen types of assault weapons, Newt and the Newtzis have sought to improve the lives of every drug dealer in America, not to mention loony militia types holed up in the mountains. Now, that's imagination.

And, coming up this week, a truly exciting way to improve the family! Yep, pro-family legislation from the Newtzis. This time, you only get three guesses.

They're going to support the Earned Income Tax Credit for working poor families? No. They're going to quit trying to cut Medicare so you don't have to go broke taking care of your aging parents? No. They've decided that they love the Family Leave Act even though it was President Bill Clinton's idea? No. Get ready . . .

The Newtzis are going to drastically cut the Legal Services Corp.! Isn't that great?

What do you mean—how will that help the family? Don't you see? Poor women won't be able to get divorced anymore! They'll just have to stay married to men who knock them around and beat their kids to a pulp. Great news, eh? If some poor woman marries a guy and then finds out he's sexually abusing her daughters, there won't be a thing she can do about it. Isn't that grand? They'll just have to go right on being a happy family.

And the fifty-two thousand cases that Legal Services pursued last year, getting deadbeat dads to cough up the money they owe for child support? Hey, no divorce, no problem with child-support payments, see?

As Anthony Lewis of *The New York Times* reminds us, the Legal Services Corp. was instituted in 1974 by President Richard Nixon to give some reality to the American concept of Equal Justice Under Law. To hell with that—if you can't afford to pay a lawyer yourself, why should you have any rights at all? Been cheated by a landlord, injured on the job, held prisoner in a labor camp, working day labor for less than minimum wage? Tough. The law doesn't apply to you, buddy.

See? It's just like that song, "I-maag-i-naaaa-tion!" Creative lawmaking, that's our Newtzis.

And here comes another creative move by the Newtonians: how to screw up someone else's perfectly good legislation. You may have read about an impressive piece of legislation—written by Senators Nancy Kassebaum (R-Kan.) and Ted Kennedy (D-Mass.)—to plug up one of the most notorious and harmful holes in our health insurance system, such as it is. The bill would make it possible for workers who lose their jobs to keep their health insurance coverage—a rather critical problem, as you know, when the headlines announce almost weekly that tens of thousands of workers have been "downsized." The bill would not only require insurance companies to sell policies to workers who lose their jobs, but it would also prevent them from dropping those with "pre-existing conditions." Some analysts say that twenty-five million Americans would benefit from having portable health insurance; up to eighty million have "pre-existing conditions."

The Kennedy-Kassebaum bill would have fixed these problems—until the Newtzis fixed the bill. They decided to lard it up with special-interest provisions. The most glaring example is medical savings accounts, a device that allows health insurance companies to skim the cream off the low-risk pool and leave everyone else with higher premiums. This insurance-company dream is the brainchild of the Golden Rule Insurance Co., which—according to Representative Cynthia McKinney—contributed $1.4 million to Republicans. And, according to the Associated Press, J. Patrick Rooney, an executive at Golden Rule, has contributed $103,000 to Gingrich and GOPAC. Imagine that.

**March 1996**

# The 1996 Vote

∎

C HICAGO — As someone who is seriously considering, for the first time in my life, simply not voting for president (I don't need a line that says, "None of the above"—I need a line that says, "It makes me vomit"), I am still finding sweet consolation in the belated appearance of some intelligent defenders of President Bill Clinton.

I honestly do not know if I will vote for the man—in part because I don't think I need to; he's going to win anyway. But I remain chapped over four years of watching Clinton absorb more unmitigated garbage—both from right-wingers who wanted him to fail before the git-go and from the media—than any human being short of Adolf Hitler should ever have to endure. Garrison Keillor said in *The Washington Post*, "If Clinton had been president in 1863 and had gone to Gettysburg and given that speech, the press would have written, 'Clinton Seeks to Burnish Image at Cemetery Dedication: Hopes Talk Will Distract Public from Whitewater Rumors.'" (Which reminds me: On the actual occasion of the Gettysburg Address, one newspaper reporter wrote, "President Lincoln also spoke.") To misquote Linda Ellerbee: And so it has gone.

It's awfully hard to pick the lowest moment. Vince Foster's suicide—now, there was a gem. An absolute stampede by paranoid conspiracy-mongers and would-be Woodwards-and-Bernsteins to take a not-unusual tragedy—archetypal gifted perfectionist, unable to bear his failure to meet his own impossible standards, slides into depression and kills self—into whatever seamy tale would most damage Clinton (make that "the Clintons").

Then, there was the froo-fraw over how Clinton was exploiting—yes, milking—Commerce Secretary Ron Brown's death for political mileage. I mean, all that mourning stuff went on for *a whole week*. Bound to be politically motivated! Right—the whole deal could have been cut down to three days if the folks in Bosnia had just been a little quicker about scraping whatever was left of Brown's body off the side of that mountain. It was definitely Clinton's fault.

Next came the stupendous scoop by the actual Bob Woodward about how Hillary had an imaginary conversation with Eleanor Roosevelt—revealed to an astonished world only months after the first lady wrote all about it in her widely syndicated newspaper column. Quel daring journalism.

Of course, one could go on for pages with examples of equally fair and balanced coverage by the same Washington press corps that was declaring Representative Newt Gingrich a political genius just eighteen months ago. (If you really want to hear all of it, nestle down and listen to James Carville for a few hours.)

Hey, I'm no wizard; I'm a good little conformist at heart. I probably would have thought Newt "Beach Volleyball" Gingrich was a political genius myself if the Washington press corps had not trespassed beyond the border of sanity by writing admiring profiles of his henchpersons from Texas—Representatives Dick Armey of Irving, Tom DeLay of Sugar Land, and Bill Archer of Houston. *Nobody* (outside the Beltway) is that dumb.

Then, there is the Mother of All Scandals, that teeny-tiny drop in the Old S&L Bucket, Whitewater. Gene Lyons, the Arkansas reporter who is no more gaga about Clinton than I am, has been fighting a valiant rear-guard action on Whitewater for years now. With commendable patience, using textbook methods of journalism, he has relentlessly exposed every nutty conspiracy theory, every exaggeration, every carelessness, and every distortion by saying over and over again: "Here are the facts; this is what the record shows." For an example of Lyons at his best, see the August 8 issue of *The New York Review of Books*, which debunks yet another Clinton-is-a-sleaze bookette. (There's money in them thar bookettes.) This one sounds like the best Clinton bookette since ex–FBI agent Gary Aldrich so brilliantly demonstrated why no one should believe what's in an FBI file. And that, in turn, raises one of those rare Clinton screwups where the press did not get excited enough.

I don't have Lyons' patience. I watch the reporters go down to Arkansas, which they all assume is Dogpatch with L'il Abner geeking around at Moonbeam McSwine, from Washington, that stainless bastion of sea-green incorruptible politics. They remind me of the French cop in *Casablanca*, who was *shocked* to find gambling in the back room. I think the word I want is *hypocrites*.

Also entering the list of intelligent Clinton defenders is Taylor Branch, chiefly known as the superb biographer of Martin Luther King Jr. (*Parting the*

*Waters*). His piece in the current issue of *Esquire* is written with the almost painful scrupulosity that marks all his work.

Soon to be out: Martin Walker, the ridiculously smart correspondent for *The Guardian* of Britain, looks at Clinton's record from an international point of view, which you would never catch anyone in our provincial media corps doing.

So, if Clinton is all this much better than the American media have ever hinted, how come I'm such an unhappy camper? Read the welfare bill.

**August 1996**

# Clinton's Report Card

■

**N**O ONE," THE EDITORS of *The New York Times* argue, "can doubt [the president's] commitment to using government to spur the economy, protect the environment, defend the cities, promote racial justice, and combine compassion with fiscal prudence."

Fine. Here, then, are a few notes from no one.

Perhaps the best gloss that liberals and progressives can put on the first Clinton administration is that the president would have liked to use the government for the purposes outlined above, but only if no one with power and influence objected overly much. It's not that Clinton won't fight for anything but that each issue represents a precise mathematical calculation: popularity of an issue times its political importance minus the number of enemies it has, divided by the power of those enemies to disrupt the rest of Clinton's agenda. For liberal causes to make any progress in the second Clinton administration, their proponents must first subject themselves to the same disciplined analysis.

It ain't pretty. A whopping 16 percent of Americans now admit to the label "liberal." According to the musings of some senior administration advisers, the campaign issues that have at least a fighting chance of enactment in the next four years include:

• Political Reform. Clinton promised in his first inaugural address to "reform our politics so that power and privilege no longer shout down the voice of the people." He lied. This time, however, having recognized the potential explosiveness of the issue, as well as Al Gore's vulnerability in 2000 regarding it, advisers swear that Clinton means it. Indonesia-scam aside, Republicans will be loath to look like shills for corporate corrupters if Clinton takes the issue center stage.

• Poor Kids. If the welfare reform bill is to be in any way defanged, it will happen because of "the children." Clinton is genuinely eager to ameliorate the bill's harsh treatment of immigrant kids and further beef up its child care provisions. If he is truly ambitious, he will challenge Congress to invest not only in "empowerment zones" but in transportation resources, to allow former welfare recipients who don't have cars and can't afford trains and express buses to travel to areas that need workers. If he were someone else entirely, he might even challenge the private sector to invest in the worker training programs that Congress gutted in his 1993 budget. But never mind that.

• Health Care. Kids rule here as well. A movement is afoot to pass a new tobacco tax to pay for universal health coverage for children. Given all the money Philip Morris spread like manure on Bob Dole's candidacy, Clinton might want to do it simply for revenge. Gore would probably go along just to prove he hates tobacco as much as he said he did when he made everybody cry in August. And of course Hillary's on board—unless she's behind bars. Tobacco pushers are even less popular than liberals.

• Workers' Rights. This is the progressives' sleeper issue. Americans hate sweatshops and they hate child labor. They hate the idea of foreigners taking away jobs with exploitative practices and they could be driven crazy over the idea of, say, Indonesian influence-peddlers buying themselves sweetheart deals that put U.S. workers out of business. With labor rejuvenating itself and Gore's campaign vulnerable to a Perot/Buchananite explosion around the issue of workers and wages, Clinton could be forced to see the wisdom of vigorously enforcing the GATT rules already on the books. That means, in the case of, say, Indonesia, a country's special trade preferences could be withdrawn until it allows collective bargaining and discontinues its practice of ending worker disputes with bullets and prisons. Much could also be done to put the fear of The Market into the minds of the leaders of China, Colombia, Mexico, and Pakistan as well. The issue works particularly well in conjunction with political reform. Do the calculations yourself: Without campaign contributions, how many votes does Indonesia have?

# Your Cheatin' Heart Surgeon

TWO SOLID WEEKS on the road talking about nothing but the president's dick. Not that I haven't tried to change the subject. Valiantly, if I say so myself, I keep trying to point out that with all due respect to the president's private parts, we do have bigger problems in this country. No go. The media are just obsessed. Happily, the rest of the country is taking all this in stride, making useful distinctions to which the media are oblivious.

When in the course of human events, fate throws a girl like I into a book tour at the very moment the media have gone into their worst feeding frenzy since the Dead Diana, the consequences are fairly gruesome. My least favorite form of televised bear-baiting is when they put me on some program with other women who are bound to disagree with my contention that political skills and an upright private life are not necessarily connected. "Let's watch the girls have a catfight!"

Two days in Washington, D.C., convinced me that the entire city has gone bonkers. The folks at the White House say Kenneth Starr is an obsessive maniac; Starr's people say Clinton is the moral equivalent of pond scum, that he has gotten away with God-only-knows-what by dint of vast conspiracy, cover-up, intimidation, and bribery.

These two immense powers sit pulsing hatred toward one another across the entire city. If a person tries gently to suggest that perhaps the truth lies somewhere in between, both camps begin booing and hissing.

OK, disgusting as it is, let's look at the "character" issue. The gross abuse of this important word is a large part of the problem. Character does not mean sex. It is possible to have an unhappy home and still conduct the rest of one's life with perfect probity. Likewise, it is just as possible to be a person of impeccable moral character, say Jimmy Carter, and still not be much of a politician. Of course, we have a right to look for both in our elected leaders—a dimension of moral leadership along with a shrewd, practical politician. But how often does an Abe Lincoln come along?

Thirty years of covering politics have given me a healthy respect for political skills, for the art and craft of finding that tiny sliver of daylight in the huge wall of obstruction that prevents anything from getting done about anything.

I submit to you that Lyndon Johnson was a superb politician. Had it not been for the fatal error of Vietnam, I believe Johnson would have gone down as one of the greatest presidents in our history. Think of government as a gigantic Rube Goldberg contraption, perhaps the most complicated, least straightforward piece of machinery ever devised: Lyndon knew which buttons to push, which levers to press, which handles to crank, and where to kick the damn thing to get it to whirl around and turn out something that would actually help people. But as a human being, he was a miserable specimen. Who but Lady Bird ever could have put up with him?

I've known a lot of exceptionally decent people in politics, and I've known a handful of great politicians: The two are not mutually exclusive, but it is also true that they rarely overlap.

What to do?

Say it's a life-or-death situation: You need open-heart surgery, and you're looking for the best doctor you can find. This doctor is going to be cutting your heart: You want to know where he or she got his training, what his success rate is, what his peers think of his skills. I submit to you that you don't particularly care if he cheats on his wife.

All I'm trying to say here is that I don't think the press corps is particularly well qualified to go around passing judgments on other people's private lives. (In fact, most of us are singularly ill qualified to do so.) I think we should stick to what we do know, which is looking at a politician's record and reporting what's there. And Clinton's record is damn peculiar.

Sometimes politicians can be divided into those who are good at running for office and those who are good at governing. Clinton is obviously amazingly good at the former, not so great at the latter. Yet he is an intelligent man and genuinely knowledgeable: a true policy wonk. His greatest strength in governance is persistence.

An Arkansas state senator once told me Clinton reminded him of one of those broad-bottomed children's toys: You tump it over, it pops back up; you tump it over, it pops back up again. He'd propose some grand scheme to make Arkansas a better place, and the Lege would peck it to death—costs too much, leads to new taxes, more bureaucracy, etc. They'd all vote no and assume the scheme was dead. But Clinton would always come back next session with a new way to achieve the same goal: George, I took care of that part you didn't like; Mary, look what this will do for your district; Sam, you're gonna like this amendment. And lo and behold, it would get done: not in the best or most efficient way, but in the way that was politically possible.

That's an art, and I think it deserves respect.

Look at Clinton trying to get the public schools fixed. One third of American schools are somewhere between dilapidated and flat falling apart—holes in the roof, broken windows, kids tripping on broken linoleum and bad stairs. Estimates as high as $100 billion to fix them, new schools also needed, no way the local districts can handle this. First, Clinton asks Congress for a $5 billion appropriation to fix the schools. Typical Clinton—way too little, a mere gesture at the problem. R's immediately reject the proposal—costs too much, balanced budget, local control sacred. Goes down in flames.

So he comes back this year: new approach on same problem. He wants $20 billion worth of bonds with a special tax break. Buy these bonds, you pay zero in federal taxes. Use private capital to fix the schools. Money is to be handled by the states and school districts: George, I took care of your problem with local control. Districts can use the federal bonds to leverage their own. Now we're looking at $40 to $50 billion to fix the schools. We're talking real progress.

If you can't get it done one way, get it done another. That's a smart politician. That is not a faithful husband.

If we can't have both, take your pick.

**May 1998**

# Look Beyond the Blather
# to the Political Buyouts

FROM HERE IN THE have-no-mercy-liberals camp, the political weather continues delightful. What could be more fun than watching Republicans turn on one another, snapping and snarling, throwing left hooks, right jabs, and mud pies? Splendid doings.

From a strategic point of view, I suppose I should want House Speaker Newt Gingrich to stay where he is, considering that he's both hateful and incompetent. But I must admit to a mild case of Greater Good here: I'd really like for America to see Gingrich in its rearview mirror, because I think he's a nasty piece of work who has brought American politics even lower than it would otherwise go. It's a good-of-the-nation moment.

The same might be said for our Texans in the House leadership, Majority Leader Dick Armey and Majority Whip Tom DeLay. Personally, I've always wondered what it says about Republicans that those two were chosen for leadership positions in the first place. Armey is an ideologue of no noticeable political skill, and DeLay has been so clumsy and heavy-handed in his abuse of power that it's been painful to watch, whether you're for him or against him. Let the caucus decide.

In the meantime, a wonderful corrective has appeared on the horizon—an astonishing piece of journalism so timely and so much more important to what is actually going on than all this political blather that I'm tempted to announce it in terms of "Lo, a star in the East."

In a typical item from the blather front, *The New York Times* sees internal Republican politics as leading to "still larger victories for minimal government and taxes, unfettered free enterprise and a return to conservative Christian values." That's almost a mantra (along with the fashionable new cliché, "conservatism with compassion"—the Bush brothers' theme song) that somehow

Republicans need to "get back" to their core values of less government and lower taxes. What's wrong with this picture?

The answer is to be found in the current and forthcoming issues of *Time* magazine, in which the superb investigative team of Don Barlett and Jim Steele is unleashed on the subject of corporate welfare. Holy mackerel—what a story.

While the R's and the D's sit here having this silly pretend-debate (education, the environment, and Social Security, chant the D's; less government and lower taxes, chant the R's), what's really going on is being ignored by everyone. They're all giving away the store—to big corporate campaign donors, of course.

Even for those of us who regularly follow corporate welfare, the Barlett-Steele investigation is mind-boggling. To what depth, breadth, and height can corporate welfare reach? And how much is it costing every one of us? Barlett and Steele not only dug out the answers, they dug out still more astonishing information. The system doesn't even work; it's not producing jobs. All these taxpayer rip-offs, subsidies, tax abatements, low-cost loans—all for nothing.

While state and local governments have caved in to this folly to an extent that's beyond stupid and well into acutely embarrassing, the feds are still the biggest Uncle Sugar of them all, handing out $125 billion in corporate welfare during a time of robust economic growth and corporate profits. It's insane. Barlett and Steele's conclusion is that the corporate welfare system exactly mimics the most criticized aspects of traditional welfare programs: It "is unfair, destroys incentive, perpetuates dependence, and distorts the economy." But instead of rewarding the poor, it rewards the powerful.

Corporate welfare also penalizes the rest of us; for every tax advantage given to a corporation, the tax burden shared by the rest of us is that much greater. Just in federal taxes, it is the equivalent of all the income tax paid by sixty million individuals and families. Lower taxes, anyone?

At the state and local levels, the folly knows no bounds. The investigators found cases in which governments gave away $323,000 in taxes and services to secure a $50,000 job that couldn't yield that much in taxes over several lifetimes.

And as usual, the system is weighted toward the biggest (and biggest contributors): "Ten million jobs have been created since 1990. But most of those jobs have been created at small- and medium-sized companies, from high-tech start-ups to franchised cleaning services. Fortune 500 companies, on the other hand, have erased more jobs than they have created this past decade, and yet they are the biggest beneficiaries of corporate welfare."

This is my idea of extraordinary political journalism—investigating the real effects of politics on our lives. True, it has nothing to do with spin, counterspin, or Monica Lewinsky, but it sure does make a lot of difference to the people of this country. I think they'll appreciate knowing about it.

**November 1998**

# Remembering the Sixties

■

Y OU MUST ADMIT, this is the most curious political phenomenon of our lifetimes: After five years of investigation by Kenneth Starr, one solid year of media frenzy, and three months of impeachment proceedings, President Clinton's job approval rating is 72 percent, and Republicans now rank below Larry Flynt in public esteem. And their response to all this is: "More! More!" Kind of hard to know what to say to them.

And here am I in concert with Pat Robertson: Please, stop!

Incidentally, journalist Lars-Erik Nelson rather uncharitably noted that aside from impeachment, the Rs' major legislative accomplishment of 1998 was renaming Washington National Airport after Ronald Reagan.

The latest wrinkle in right-wing spin is to claim that this is not a political phenom at all but rather the final battle in some culture war that I didn't know was going on. I have my doubts about this culture war—can you be in one and not know it? Did our side actually vote for Flynt as our standard bearer? What is our side?

My last effort to grasp what the right wing is on about here was reading Robert Bork's latest book—an experience so horrifying that I have not yet recovered and cannot bear to read any more in the genre. If Bork was the beginning of the political-culture war, as is sometimes claimed ("payback for Bork" being an occasionally heard battle cry), all I can say is: I didn't know it was war at the time, but I'm sure glad I was on the right side.

An alternative theory is that the culture war dates back to the 1960s, and this is where I get totally lost reading right-wing cultural interpretations. The old joke is that if you can remember the sixties, you weren't there. I was there, and I can remember it.

I remember the decade as being about the Peace Corps, the civil-rights movement, and the anti-war movement. As Margo Adler writes in her memoir of the period, it was quite possible to be an activist in the sixties and miss sex, drugs, and rock 'n' roll in their entirety. "We Shall Overcome" remains the song of the decade for many.

That is, until 1968, the year of assassinations, when it all turned very, very dark.

I could be wrong, but I still think the berserker element of the 1960s was largely the consequence of Vietnam—the drugs, the craziness, the sense that the world made no sense because that war certainly made no sense. And that war was not the fault of those who fought it or opposed it. Your famous World War II generation presented that little gift to us: Eisenhower, Kennedy, Johnson, and Nixon. Long time passing.

Another right-wing interpretation of the sixties is the bizarre notion that black rage was fomented by white liberal social programs. Bill Kristol has been alone among right-wing intellectuals, I believe, in consistently and gracefully conceding that liberals were right about civil rights and that conservatives (a word often synonymous with "racist" in those years) were wrong. That's most generous of him, but I think it leaves a wrong impression (a bit like that odd film *Mississippi Burning*) that somehow white people were the key players in the civil-rights movement.

It was a movement of, by, and for black Americans; those few whites who took part—and there were mighty few of us in the South—were just bit players. As Taylor Branch's wonderful King biography and many other books make clear, the whites in power, whether they reacted for good or ill at the time, were just reacting—reacting to one of the most astonishing, beautiful, and spontaneous uprisings for justice the world has ever seen.

The movement split in '64, when Stokely Carmichael's "Burn, baby, burn" stood in contrast to "We shall overcome someday." But to blame that on anything that white liberals did is ludicrous. Race riots had been part of American history for one hundred years; they were not unusual before the civil-rights movement, and the roots of the rage underlying them are obvious.

These silly books blaming the sixties for various social evils are pathetically truncated in their viewpoint. Were there symptoms of decline in black family structure? According to anthropologists, the black family is one of the most durable social structures in history; it survived both slavery and Jim Crow and finally was visibly damaged only by the Depression, which of course fell more harshly on blacks. Incidentally, the Depression had the same effect on white families—those who yearn for hard times to bring us together might keep that in mind.

Was there an increase in sexual activity outside marriage in the sixties? If so, don't you think it had more to do with the invention of the birth control pill than with "permissive attitudes"?

Don't get me started. But perhaps what I object to most is the use of war as a metaphor for political differences. That way lies folly and worse. Call it a spirited discussion, a disagreement, or an all-out slinging match, but don't call it war. That's how you get murdered abortion doctors and bombed buildings in Oklahoma.

**January 1999**

# Let's All Play
# Hunt the Hypocrites

■

THERE'S A BEAUT OF a media story happening right in front of our eyes, and if you want to have a good time, you can start tracking this one yourself. The game is called "Hunt the Hypocrites," or "What's Wrong with This Picture?"

A few weeks ago, I kept running into civilians (nonjournalists) who all had the same question: Why isn't this Newt Gingrich story a bigger deal?

The story, in case you missed it (and you may well have), is that the former Speaker of the House is getting a divorce because he has been having an affair with a much younger woman. I think that story got exactly the play it deserved—almost none.

Gingrich seems to be a spent cartridge as a politician. All that speculation about whether he would run for president is long gone—no more *Time* magazine Man of the Year, no more "defender of civilization" or lectures on how liberal policies cause moral decay in America. However, Gingrich is still huge on the fund-raising circuit. Since he left office in January, he has raised $1.3 million for his new political action committee. So he is still a public figure to some extent, and under the new rules of journalism, his private life is a story.

Of course, there is the oddball angle to the story. It turns out that Gingrich was having this long-running affair with the much younger woman all during the time the government of the United States all but came to a crashing halt over Monica Lewinsky.

This is the man who promised that Republican leadership would "improve the moral climate of the country." So this presents us with an epochal moment in the history of hypocrisy. As Gingrich led the Republicans in full hue and cry concerning the moral sleaze, the sordid tawdriness, the unbearable, brazen shameless conduct of Bill Clinton, he was having something more than a flingette himself. We could be looking at a new world record for being two-faced.

But note the deafening silence from the media. It's the same problem they have dealing with George W. Bush and drugs. (I am proceeding on the new media premise that he must have done coke because he sure as hell would have denied it by now if he hadn't. I like these new journalism rules—it's so much easier than having to go dig up evidence.)

And of course, Bush got into the Texas Air National Guard instead of having to go to Vietnam because of who his father was. How bright do you have to be to figure that out? As cartoonist Ben Sargent put it: "Find me a rich, Yale-educated congressman's son in 1968 who DIDN'T get help staying out of the draft—now THAT would be a story."

Note the astounding difference between the way the media covered Hillary Clinton's interview in *Talk* magazine—the one in which she did NOT excuse her husband's infidelity—and a far more interesting piece in the same issue of the same magazine about Bush, in which he cruelly mimics an imaginary plea for life from the executed Karla Faye Tucker.

Acres of air time on Mrs. Clinton's supposed effort to excuse her husband, hours of tutting and judgmental commentary and psychological parsing of the Clinton marriage; almost nothing (honorable exception to George Will) on the appalling vulgarity of W. Bush.

And then there is the even messier problem of Dubya's business dealings.

You thought Whitewater was a story? Wait'll you read this one. Where's Kenneth Starr now that we need him? And yet, you notice, the media reaction to all this is curiously . . . muted. Gone are the full-scale scrums of yesteryear, when packs of baying reporters surrounded Bill Clinton, the badgering about the draft, the screaming front-page tabloid headlines, the saturation television coverage. So what's the deal?

Two things.

One, the media have been so hideously unfair to Clinton that they are now in an incredible box. They can't savage this nice, young Bush boy the way they did Clinton, or the sheer ugliness and unfairness of it will turn everyone against the media, not against Bush. On the other hand, if they dismiss Bush's "youthful indiscretions" as he wants them to, they abandon all hope of appearing even-handed.

Numero two-o, what's missing here is the right-wing echo chamber and amplification system. There is a fascinating study in the spring issue of *The Public Eye*, put out by Political Research Associates in Boston, of the right-wing media chain that often starts with some story or nonstory dug up by an outfit funded by Richard Mellon Scaife.

But before we get ourselves off into "vast right-wing conspiracy" territory, may I make a suggestion? Both the media and the nation will be spared enormous travail if we stop pretending that politicians are here to provide moral leadership. That way, we won't have to listen to little Georgie Bush, the frat boy, lecture us all about responsibility and purpose and family values and moral uplift and chastity and abstinence and all the rest of it. Instead, we can sit down and try to figure out whether he's smart enough to run the country.

You want moral leadership? Try the clergy. It's their job.

**September 1999**

# Off Your Duff

■

**H**ERE'S A STORY FOR all you nonvoters who won't have anything to do with politics because it doesn't make any difference to you who wins.

A few weeks ago, I lost my prescription sunglasses. Can't do without 'em in Texas. I went out to the jiffy optical place to order a new pair. Nope, they said, no can do—the prescription for your eyeglasses is too old.

I see just fine with the glasses I have now, but it had been in the neighborhood of five years since I'd last had my eyes checked, so whatthehey, I toddle off for an eye exam. Turns out that no change in the prescription is needed, so they ask why I came in. Oh yeah, reports the ophthalmologist, they passed a new law: You can't get glasses made on any prescription that's more than a year old.

I have to admit, that little piece of special interest legislation went right by me. I don't even want to think about the lobbying on that one, but rest assured that our legislators did this for our own good, because we should have annual eye exams even if we're seeing fine, and you can bet that the campaign contributions track so well on this one that we can see 'em without glasses.

So I'm out 110 bucks even before paying for new glasses. I look forward to a frequent reoccurrence of this happy event, since I either lose a pair or the dog chews one up at least once a year. Even if you have health insurance, yours may not cover the standard eye exam unless you've purchased separate vision insurance.

The moral of this story is: Don't sit on your glasses, and don't sit on your duff come election time—find a candidate in favor of campaign-finance reform.

Further evidence of the wisdom of this excellent advice: Our fearless Republican leaders in Washington were wanting to give us a $792 billion tax break. Actually, they wanted to give the $792 billion to rich people and to a whole lot of special interests that give big campaign contributions.

They seem to have forgotten that there's more than one way to take the burden off the shoulders of taxpayers. For example, we could charge the oil companies the going market price for drilling on federal land, which happens to be owned by you and me. Instead, we let the oil companies set their own payment for drilling on our land. Is that a sweet deal or what?

According to a former oil-company executive who testified before Congress on this, the companies always set that payment $4 to $5 per barrel below market. Interior Secretary Bruce Babbitt has been trying to get this changed, but Babbitt doesn't make big campaign contributions. Our own Senator Kay Bailey Hutchison, whose campaign contributions from oil companies in the past five years total $1.2 million, has successfully fended off Babbitt by passing midnight riders on appropriations bills to stop any change in this sweetheart deal.

Last week, the Senate—despite a noble effort at filibuster by Barbara Boxer of California—passed Kay Bailey's rider yet again by a vote of 51–47. Senator Russ Feingold of Wisconsin, who does favor campaign-finance reform, stood there and read aloud the oil company contributions to various senators before the vote, and you should have heard them howl. How dare Feingold suggest their votes are for sale, uncollegial conduct, bad taste, you're a fink, Russ, etc. These honorable members felt that Feingold should be ashamed of himself for doing such a tacky thing. This bunch clearly knows dog about shame, so I suggest that Feingold pay them no attention.

And speaking of the honorable members of Congress, I trust it did not escape your attention that they have once again given themselves a raise: $4,600, on top of the $3,100 cost-of-living "adjustment" they got last year. They are at $141,000 a year, putting them in the top 5 percent of all earners, not counting their almost free health care, haircuts, etc. But you'll be happy to know that they're still whining about the cost of maintaining two homes, the cost of living in D.C., etc. Before you waste any sympathy on them, check out how many of them took their spouses to the Paris air show at our expense or went to "fact-finding" golf tournaments at lobbyists' expense.

On the theory that gritching alone will not improve anything, here's a positive suggestion for world betterment: I move that we pay members of Congress precisely the median wage in this country. Fifty percent of Americans will earn more than they do, 50 percent less. The median goes up, they get a raise. What could be fairer? Median is currently a little under $50K for a family of four. Welcome to the real word, honorable members.

In closing, may I say I am heartbroken to hear that my man Dan Quayle is dropping out of the race for presadent.

**September 1999**

# Clinton's Merits

DON'T KNOW HOW many of you heard President Clinton's speech at the World Trade Organization. Except for C-SPAN junkies, I doubt anyone was watching. But it is high time somebody said the obvious out loud: The son of a gun is good.

How long has it been since you heard Clinton make a whole speech? I've been catching him on the tube in snippets for so long that I'd forgotten just how effortlessly persuasive he actually is. There he stood, the No. 1 Free-Trader in the Whole World, facing all the opposition. By the time he finished, he was on their side and they were on his side. He is a superb politician.

Anyone volunteering a kind word for Clinton nowadays has to issue the obligatory disclaimer. In my case, it's easy, since I barely agree with him 50 percent of the time.

He's not my kind of Democrat and never has been. But at least I have the sense to recognize the man's merits, whatever his failings.

He is an amazingly skilled pol at the top of his game. I know—everybody hates politicians so much that to say someone is a great one is a form of cussin' him out. Nevertheless, I do admire real political skill, and Clinton has it in spades.

I'm not sure I've ever seen anyone better. Maybe Lyndon Johnson on a roll, or Bob Bullock in good health. Too bad that Clinton had to spend most of his presidency on defense. I would have liked to see him quarterback a Democratic Congress for the sheer interest of the exercise.

Don't ask me to explain what went wrong between Clinton and the Washington press corps. I've never understood it. I don't want to drag anyone through the Late Unpleasantness again, but as near as I can tell, about half the

D.C. press corps is totally wiggy on the subject of Clinton. Otherwise rational people—like Chris Matthews, Chris Hitchens, George Will, there's an army of them—are so obsessed by Clinton's moral failings that they cannot see his performance, what he actually does with the job.

I'm sorry that Clinton is so flawed. That's truly a shame. As Mr. Shakespeare said, ". . . and the elements / So mixed in him." But I still don't see why that prevents people who presume to have some grasp of objectivity from seeing what's right in front of them. Clinton is such a master that he has played a Republican Congress to a dead standstill for six years now—and often with no cards at all in his hand (mostly due to his own stupidity during the Late Unpleasantness).

And what a set of Republicans. It's not as though he's had to deal with constructive citizens who happen to differ with him on the issues—your Robert Tafts, your Bob Doles, your Margaret Smiths, or such as that. Newt Gingrich and the Republican Revolution—God save us.

Lord knows, the Republicans have saved Bill Clinton. Time after time after time, they are so blinded by their hatred of Clinton that they do themselves in. I'm sure it's a mercy, but it's also a peculiar phenomenon.

I've already said my piece on the Clinton-haters. I suspect it has something to do with sex or sexual envy, which always makes people irrational. But there has already been far too much parlor psychoanalysis and idiot psychobabble about Clinton. When the content-analysis mavens at the schools of communication go through coverage of the Clinton administration, my bet is that they find a lot more psychobabble than they do actual reporting on what he's done:

- A seven-year economic boom (and some of the credit for that should go to George Bush the elder), marred by a terrible maldistribution of wealth, mostly caused by stupid tax policies. If Clinton had had a better Congress, it wouldn't be such a problem.
- Some nice peace work here and there—Northern Ireland, the Middle East.
- One bozo military adventure. Clinton's bombing of the drug factory in Sudan ranks right up there with the time that Ronald Reagan invaded Grenada to save us all from some Cuban construction workers. Kosovo is a disaster, but Kosovo was going to be a disaster no matter what we did.

• Almost certainly should have done better with Russia; there was an awful lot of capitalist hubris in this country after the cold war ended.

• Some very graceful and deft diplomatic work. The Republicans keep complaining that Clinton apologizes for our foreign policy mistakes when he goes abroad. We had a lot of mistakes to apologize for. What, you thought the Greek junta was a swell bunch?

• A big failure on health-care reform, though I still think that lobby money is what really killed that bill. But note the interesting way that Clinton works as a pol. He really is an incrementalist. He got a full children's health insurance program through a Republican Congress (much credit to Ted Kennedy and Orrin Hatch). He signed a lousy welfare reform bill and then quietly went back and fixed many of the worst provisions in it. The guy just keeps chipping away.

Given the amount of personal abuse the man has taken, his resilience is just extraordinary. Apparently, he really does get up every day and start over.

We've never seen him get mad in public, and I have often wanted to congratulate his late mother on his manners. Would that Trent Lott's momma had done half that well. Given the circumstances of his presidency, Clinton deserves a medal just for being generally cheerful.

On the sleaze factor, I don't know that one can blame Clinton so much as the whole system of campaign financing. By 1996, the floodgates were wide open; it was ally-ally-in free on the money.

The Republicans didn't look any better. Who can forget the immortal testimony of former GOP chairman Haley Barbour that while sitting on the deck of a junk in Hong Kong harbor, he had no idea he was being offered foreign money?

This administration's indictment count is still well under the glorious benchmarks set by Nixon and Reagan. (Although I think we're going to have to put Nixon in a permanent separate category. Did you read the transcripts of the tapes they just released? What a despicable human. In the long history of rationalization, have you ever seen anything more bizarre than someone as intelligent as William Safire carrying on about the moral leprosy of Clinton while still defending Nixon?)

Whatever Clinton's mistakes, they don't seem to have stemmed from malice. I may be wrong, but I don't see much mean in him.

Whoever wins the election next year, I give him six weeks and one good screwup before someone in Washington has the simple honesty to say, "You know, Clinton coulda handled that with his eyes shut."

**December 1999**

# Comrade Donald Trump

COMRADE TRUMP'S DANDY IDEA — "Soak the rich!" saith the Donald, that l'il lefty—has raised The Issue That Dare Not Speak Its Name. To wit, the obscene maldistribution of wealth in this country, also known as the Income Gap.

While Comrade Trump proposes a onetime 14 percent tax on everybody with more than $10 million to his name—thus raising more than enough to pay off the entire national debt in one foul sweep—Brother Bush is marching militantly in the wrong direction. Governor Dubya wants more tax breaks for the rich. Sigh. Does not get it.

The biggest break for the rich in the Bush package is the elimination of the estate tax, which Republicans have now taken to calling "the death tax" in one of those public-relations ploys they think will fool us all.

(One envisions a pod of Republican shrewdies brainstorming: "Let's call it 'the death tax!' Then they'll think everyone has to pay it, and that will make it really unpopular!" What kind of mushrooms do those people eat?)

It's still an estate tax, and it still applies only to those who leave more than $2 million per couple, so Junior gets his first $2 mil without paying anything. Then the government takes 37 percent of everything over that, sliding up to a top rate of 55 percent on truly major estates.

This is a sizable problem for all the Wifford Wasp Witherspoon IVs out there, but not noticeably burdensome to the rest of us. Besides which, you may have noticed that the flowering field of "estate planning" contains an astounding array of loopholes by which the very rich shelter their gelt from the tax man.

Next Bush proposes to flatten the income tax by moving from five progressive rates to four—keep in mind that "flatter" means less progressive, which means less fair—and then adds insult to injury by lowering the rate for the richest taxpayers even more than he lowers the rate for the lowest-income taxpayers, thus making the total system even less fair. According to Citizens for Tax Justice, two thirds of the total tax relief in the Bush package will go to the wealthiest 10 percent of Americans. How Republican.

Now let's look at this suffering top 10 percent and see just how terribly much they need a tax break. Keep in mind that they have been getting tax breaks steadily since Ronald Reagan was elected in 1980, with the following consequences: By 1997, the top 10 percent of the population owned 73.2 percent of the nation's net worth, up from 68 percent in 1983. The figures keep moving rapidly, so by now it's fair to guess that less than a fourth of the nation's wealth is shared by the other 90 percent of us.

Even more staggering, a 1995 study by the Federal Reserve says the top 1 percent of American households (that's everybody with more than $2.3 million) own about 35 percent of the nation's wealth, and that figure gets worse every year, too.

Looked at from the other side of the Income Gap, we find that those in the bottom 20 percent have actually lost ground in the nineties, while those in the middle have benefited only very slightly, while simultaneously piling up a staggering degree of debt. Why would anyone deliberately aggravate what is already a ridiculous imbalance?

We've just finished with a Congress that couldn't bring itself to raise the minimum wage by a whopping $1 over three years. And I remind you that the R's loaded even that pitiful gesture with $40 billion in tax breaks for the rich. Senator Don Nickles of Oklahoma, that nasty man, even tried to use the minimum-wage bill to sneak in an additional tax write-off for the three-martini lunch—what a highly developed sense of class justice he has.

(I call Nickles nasty because, according to *The Washington Post*, he is one of the senators behind a whispering campaign against John McCain, claiming that McCain is unstable because of the years he spent in a North Vietnamese prison camp. If that doesn't strike you as nasty, what does?)

Back to our man Trump. Being new to Marxist thought, the Donald has not fully grasped the finer points and wants to eliminate the estate tax himself. The bottom line for Comrade Trump is that his one-shot 14 percent wealth tax on those with more than $10 mil would cost him personally somewhere in the neighborhood of $350 million, but abolishing the estate tax would save him twice that. He may be a tyro leftie, but he's not stupid.

However, the notion of a tax on wealth bears close examination. Eleven European countries already have such a tax, including those devoted capitalists in Germany and Switzerland. As you know, in this country we tax only income, not wealth; but in Europe, they put a low tax (between 1 percent and 3 percent) on wealth in addition to income taxes.

According to Professor Leon Friedman of Hofstra Law School, writing in the current issue of *The Nation*, if we put a 1 percent tax on the total assets of the richest 1 percent of Americans (now there's a simple tax plan), it would net us $70 billion a year (more than half of what we take in now from all other sources), giving the feds a total of $200 billion per year with which to shore up Social Security and maybe even give a tax break to people who actually need one. Just 1 percent on the 1 percent.

Friedman points out one slight hitch in the getalong here: We'd have to amend the Constitution to impose a tax on wealth, just as we did to impose the first income tax back in 1913. Personally, I think it's worth doing. And I'm curious to know how many of those worth more than $2.3 million think a 1 percent tax is too high. Pollsters, can you help?

**December 1999**

# Bill Bradley

■

IT'S TAKEN ME QUITE a while to make up my mind about the Democratic presidential contest. I find Al Gore as discouraging as everybody else does. Even if you agree with him, imagine trying to work up enthusiasm for Gore.

I once spent a day with Al Gore off the record, so I know there's a real human being in there somewhere. Lord knows what happened to it.

Meanwhile, Bill Bradley has been coming up and coming up. It's always been clear that the man is a class act, without a phony bone in his body.

The trouble is, class acts are a problem in this country. Adlai Stevenson was a class act, and he lost twice. I've had my political heart broken by class acts more times than I care to remember. I'm class-act-shy.

Almost every cycle we get some candidate greatly esteemed by those who know and care a lot about government—John Anderson, Bruce Babbitt, Paul Tsongas—some brainy, professorial type who appeals to some of the media, all the college kids, and practically nobody else. No lunch-bucket appeal.

I long since decided that if the candidate doesn't have some Elvis to him, he ain't gonna make it. Bradley has zip in the Elvis department.

What he does have, and it takes a while to explain this, is Midwesternness. Not to paint with a broad brush or anything, but Midwesterners tend to be incredibly practical and incurably down-to-earth. (I base this opinion on the three years, including eighteen winters, I spent in Minnesota.)

Bradley represented New Jersey in the Senate, but he was raised in Missouri and it shows. He can be going along explaining some complicated policy—it's like listening to a good teacher—when it suddenly occurs to him to explain why we should be doing whatever-it-is in the first place.

"I think we should fix the roof while the sun is shining," he offers—as homely a metaphor as one can find, but precisely the actual reason we need to make some changes in Social Security, Medicare, education, etc. Everybody nods, and then we go back to the gory details, which he explains so well that everybody then feels like an expert on the subject.

But will it sell in a thirty-second sound bite? No question, Bradley is not a thirty-second kind of guy. But if you listen to him for even ten minutes, what you get is a sense of his depth, unflappability, seriousness, and knowledge.

He also has very good manners, even inducing the notoriously over-caffeinated TV host Chris Matthews to calm down. If I may be crudely political here, he's the perfect candidate to put up against George W. Bush, who does have some shallow-twit tendencies.

Without being at all witty (I would guess he gets off a good line about once every ten years), Bradley is capable of a wry take on things, including himself. For a man running for president, he's amazingly mellow, which is what comes of spending years of your life under the incredible pressure of playing in championship games—state high school, college, Olympics, pros.

If you're used to twenty thousand people screaming hysterically at you while you go for a free throw with a championship on the line, Chris Matthews is not likely to rattle you. This is a guy who knows how to play under pressure.

Bradley has one of those eerily perfect biographies: grew up in a small Midwestern town, top student, top athlete, Eagle Scout, committed Christian, Princeton, captain of the 1964 Olympic team, Rhodes scholar, Knicks star, U.S. Senate. Bradley was so strikingly mature and extraordinary even as a boy that John McPhee, the great *New Yorker* writer, did a profile of him as a college freshman that became the book *A Sense of Where You Are.*

The ten years that Bradley spent playing pro ball gave him a rare understanding of what it is like to be black in America, the subject of the best and certainly the most passionate speech he ever made in the Senate. Those years also give us all the character clues. Everyone who ever watched Bradley play knows he made it on brains and hard work rather than great natural talent.

My favorite basketball story is from the Olympics, when Bradley was keen to beat the tough Soviet team. He knew that it would be a rough game and that the Soviets liked to call out their plays in Russian, expecting no one to understand. So Bradley went to Princeton's Slavic languages department and got them to teach him a Russian street phrase meaning roughly, "Watch it" or "Be careful."

The first time he got an elbow thrown in his ribs, he used the phrase. The Russians got flustered, stopped calling out their plays, and lost some of their harmony. The Americans won the gold.

His Senate career is also characteristic of the man in that Bradley took on a few tough issues, mastered them, and in many cases got something done about them. His most notable contribution was the tax reform act of 1986, simplifying the code and lowering the top brackets. Brains and hard work—never any flash or grandstanding or posturing. A lot of Bradley's Senate record is surprisingly conservative, however.

Bradley is a man of truly unusual stature; he seems to have been a grown-up all his life, and a man concerned with the most serious issues. He also talks to voters as though we're grown-ups, too.

True, he suffers from low-watt charisma. He will not dazzle you with his oratory or his nimble wit. He will, however, just impress the pants off of you with how much he knows and how serious and determined he is to get some big problems fixed. And he's the man who can do it.

**January 2000**

# Class Warfare, Anyone?

■

W E   C O N T I N U E   T O   enjoy the faux-naïf routine offered by Republicans and their media flunkies: What could Gore mean by "the people against the powerful"?

Dubya was so confused about it that he called it "class warfare." I especially enjoy watching Washington pundits affect to be unable to figure out the fuss. They cover Washington, D.C., and they never in their whole lives have seen or heard of a case in which special interest money influenced legislation against the people and in favor of the powerful.

They missed communications deregulation (a bill written by lobbyists), utilities deregulation, bankruptcy "reform," banking deregulation, the S&L disaster, the killing of the patients' bill of rights, the pittance in royalties from public lands paid by the oil companies, the sugar subsidy, the ethanol subsidy, and the auto industry's lobbying against higher pollution standards and a rating system for SUV rollover hazard.

What could Gore mean by "powerful special interests"?

They missed the drug industry's continuing rip-off of the public above and beyond the already wretched pricing system by sneaking drug-patent extensions through Congress, never noticed the insurance industry spending $10 million to kill health-care proposals, didn't see the corporate tax write-off for obscene executive salaries, haven't wondered why a $1-an-hour increase in the minimum wage can't get through Congress, and never saw the Forest Service subsidizing logging roads for the timber industry.

So, why in the world is Gore trying to incite "class warfare"?

By the way, I'm fascinated by the fact that Dubya far outpolls Gore among men. One guy played football, went to Vietnam, and is notoriously emotionally distant. The other guy was a cheerleader who got into a National Guard unit through family influence, lost money in the oil business, traded Sammy

Sosa, and is now sliding through a presidential race on his charm. Do I not get American men, or what?

I JUST finished with nine months of treatment for cancer. First they poison you, then they mutilate you, then they burn you. I've had more fun. And when it's over you're so glad, you're grateful to absolutely everyone. And I am.

The trouble is, I'm not a better person. I was in great hopes that confronting my own mortality would make me deeper, more thoughtful. Many lovely people sent books on how to find a deeper spiritual meaning in life. My response was, "Oh hell, I can't go on a spiritual journey—I'm constipated."

Being sick actually narrows your world, I'm afraid—makes you focus more on yourself. Maybe when it's over and you don't feel like crud all the time, then your spirit soars.

I vomited in the office, couldn't sleep, lost fifty pounds. I don't recommend the diet. I was like, help, I'm flunking cancer.

Of course, I laughed a lot—who could not laugh? I got my first hair a few weeks ago. It came in right next to my mouth—that little mustache I've always hated. That God—what a sense of humor!

Cancer is good for priorities. Traffic, for one thing, is not worth getting upset about. As my pal Spike Gillespie says, you look at those fools honking, getting steamed, cutting in front of you, and you just think: "Hey, it's not a malignant tumor, you know?"

Despite my request, untold numbers of people wrote wonderful cards, notes, letters. My friends sent funny stuff by e-mail. I'd save it up, and about once a month when I couldn't sleep at 3 A.M., I'd be sitting in front of the computer, laughing and laughing. And I'm most grateful of all to the women who went out and got mammograms. It's going to take me longer to write all the thank-you notes than it took to get over cancer.

Cancer is not easy, it is not pleasant, and given a choice, I would just as soon have skipped it. But I now know what all survivors know, and I am grateful. So grateful.

**October 2000**

# Credit Where It's Due

■

THE TIME HAS COME to bid farewell to President William Jefferson Clinton. Been a lot of wasted time and wasted talent these eight years. The politics of personal destruction. A level of vituperation so intense and so stupid that it shut down the federal government twice.

And through it all came the Unsinkable Clinton, ever bobbing up again cheerfully in a fashion that maddened his enemies. As near as I can tell after eight years, the man gets up every single day in a state of cheerful anticipation, ready to set about whatever's on the plate.

We have never once seen him in a temper or a sulk or being vindictive or holding a grudge. Closest we ever saw to an upset Bill Clinton was right after we had watched him discussing the most intimate details of his private life for four hours on national television, and to this good day I have no idea what public purpose was served by that exercise in humiliation.

But I continue to be amazed by the man's good manners.

When Clinton arrived in Washington, there were two untouchable lobbies: the National Rifle Association and the tobacco industry. They are not untouchable today. This is not the result of inevitable social change; it is the result of real political leadership by Clinton and many others.

Clinton is a master incrementalist—he gets a little bit done, then a little bit more, then a little bit more. Because he knows and cares about the details of policy, he has often gone back and fixed or improved things that were initially passed in unsatisfactory form.

The two great failures of his administration are the domestic wealth gap and Russia.

We are now facing a destabilized nuclear power many times more dangerous than the former Soviet Union. Life expectancy in Russia is crashing, 75 percent of the people live in poverty, health care is a disaster, and the country is being run by gangsters pretending to be capitalists.

There will eventually be a terrible price for all this misery—and the country still has thousands of deteriorating nuclear weapons. Its early warning system is in such disarray that last summer the Russians came within a hair of nuking a Swedish weather balloon.

The first thing that George W. Bush might usefully do is spend a few billion rebuilding the Russian DEW line. By expanding NATO, bombing Serbia, and horsing around with the oil pipeline on Russia's southern border, we have managed to hit every paranoid button that the Russians possess—and if there is one clear strain in the Russian worldview over the centuries, it is paranoia. Further talk of putting the Baltic republics in NATO is frankly nuts.

In this country, we still have trickle-down economics, but mighty little is trickling down. Although it is not Clinton's fault, Congress becomes ever more the tool of corporate special interests. Because Clinton is such an enthusiastic free-trader, the tendency toward gigantism continues—mammoth, international corporations with more wealth than most governments and subject to only one imperative: higher profits.

Meanwhile, I don't think you can argue that we are better off today than we were eight years ago, despite the long boom. Even after wages in the lowest quartile finally, finally started to go up, it wasn't enough in constant dollars even to get people back to their standard of living thirty years ago.

*The Wall Street Journal* headlined last week: "Raw Deals—Companies Quietly Use Mergers and Spin-offs to Cut Worker Benefits." Duh.

The wealth gap is worse than ever, and the mechanisms slowly and painfully created to check capitalism—government regulation, lawsuits, and unions—have all been eaten away.

I grant you, it would have been worse without Clinton, especially his expansion of the earned income tax credit. Goodness only knows what Newt Gingrich and his merry crew would have done without Clinton there to outplay them at every turn. That was a masterly political performance and a real joy to watch—too bad the media missed it because they were so focused on Monicagate.

As for Clinton's private life, even though it's none of my business, I think we had a right to expect him to keep it zipped for eight years. Shame on him.

But having to listen to the likes of Henry Hyde, Bob Barr, and Newt Gingrich lecture Clinton on personal morality took shamelessness to new heights. What a bizarre hypocrisy festival that was. I wound up preferring Clinton to his enemies.

The Clinton-haters have been an odd and troubling part of these past eight years. In *The Hunting of the President,* Gene Lyons and Joe Conason traced most of it back to a sorry posse of old enemies in Arkansas.

The distressing part was how so much of that baloney got picked up by Establishment media and taken seriously. We wasted years on Whitewater. Some of it, I believe, has nothing to do with the Clintons but is simply a reflection of the viciousness of their enemies.

Clinton probably has as much sheer political talent as any player I've ever watched. But he got dealt a very odd hand as president, perhaps aptly compared to that of Andrew Johnson.

At least he never whined in public. It is commonplace to say that the Clintons led others into trouble and then left them to hang; actually, it can be argued that they were singularly ill-served themselves by those who had cause to be loyal to them.

It seems to me that most of the media have a very odd take on the Clintons. You look at all those "scandals," and there is no there there. It's nonsense.

Clinton was smart, able, articulate, graceful, and humorous, and he busted his tail for a Middle Eastern peace and a lot of other important things, some of which he didn't get. Life will be duller once Elvis has left the building.

**December 2000**

# Texas
# Animals

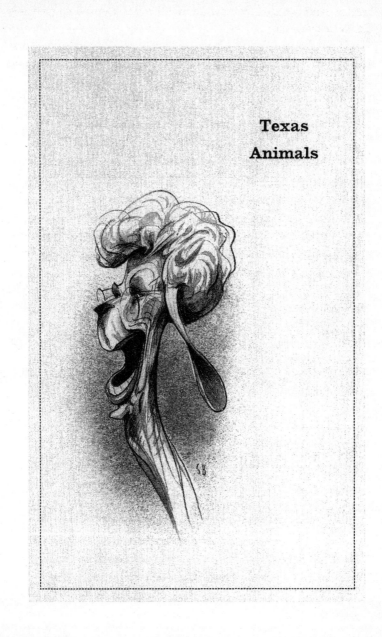

# Is Texas America?

⬛

**W**ELL, SHEESH. I DON'T know whether to warn you that because George Dubya Bush is president the whole damn country is about to be turned into Texas (a singularly horrible fate: as the country song has it: "Lubbock on Everythang") or if I should try to stand up for us and convince the rest of the country we're not all that insane.

Truth is, I've spent much of my life trying, unsuccessfully, to explode the myths about Texas. One attempts to explain—with all good will, historical evidence, nasty statistics, and just a bow of recognition to our racism—that Texas is not *The Alamo* starring John Wayne. We're not *Giant*, we ain't a John Ford western. The first real Texan I ever saw on TV was *King of the Hill*'s Boomhauer, the guy who's always drinking beer and you can't understand a word he says.

So, how come trying to explode myths about Texas always winds up reinforcing them? After all these years, I do not think it is my fault. The fact is, it's a damned peculiar place. Given all the horseshit, there's bound to be a pony in here somewhere. Just by trying to be honest about it, one accidentally underlines its sheer strangeness.

Here's the deal on Texas. It's big. So big there's about five distinct and different places here, separated from one another geologically, topographically, botanically, ethnically, culturally, and climatically. Hence our boring habit of specifying East, West, and South Texas, plus the Panhandle and the Hill Country. The majority of the state's blacks live in East Texas, making it more like the Old South than the Old South is anymore. West Texas is, more or less, like *Giant*, except, like every place else in the state, it has an incurable tendency toward the tacky and all the cowboys are brown. South Texas is 80 percent Hispanic and a weird amalgam of cultures. You get names now like Shannon Rodriguez, Hannah Gonzalez, and Tiffany Ruiz. Even the Anglos speak

English with a Spanish accent. The Panhandle, which sticks up to damn near Kansas, is High Plains, like one of those square states, Nebraska or the Dakotas, except more brown folks. The Hill Country, smack dab in the middle, resembles nothing else in the state.

Plus, plopped on top of all this, we have three huge cities, all among the ten largest in the country. Houston is Los Angeles with the climate of Calcutta, Dallas is Dutch (clean, orderly, and conformist), while San Antonio is Monterrey North. Many years ago I wrote of this state: "The reason the sky is bigger here is because there aren't any trees. The reason folks here eat grits is because they ain't got no taste. Cowboys mostly stink and it's hot, oh God, is it hot. . . . Texas is a mosaic of cultures, which overlap in several parts of the state, with the darker layers on the bottom. The cultures are black, Chicano, Southern, freak, suburban, and shitkicker. (Shitkicker is dominant.) They are all rotten for women." All that's changed in thirty years is that suburban is now dominant, shitkicker isn't so ugly as it once was, and the freaks are now Goths or something. So it could be argued we're becoming more civilized.

In fact, it was always easy to argue that: Texas has symphony orchestras and great universities and perfect jewels of art museums (mostly in Fort Worth, of all places). It has lots of people who birdwatch, write Ph.D. theses on esoteric subjects, and speak French, for chrissake. But what still makes Texas Texas is that it's ignorant, cantankerous, and ridiculously friendly. Texas is still resistant to Howard Johnsons, interstate highways, and some forms of phoniness. It is the place least likely to become a replica of everyplace else. It's authentically awful, comic, and weirdly charming, all at the same time.

Culturally, Texans rather resemble both Alaskans (hunt, fish, hate government) and Australians (drink beer, hate snobs). The food is quite good—Mexican, barbecue, chili, shrimp, and chicken-fried steak, an acquired taste. The music is country, blues, folk mariachi, rockabilly, and everything else you can think of. Mexican music—norteño, ranchero—is poised to cross over, as black music did in the 1950s.

If you want to understand George W. Bush—unlike his daddy, an unfortunate example of a truly Texas-identified citizen—you have to stretch your imagination around a weird Texas amalgam: religion, anti-intellectualism, and machismo. All big, deep strains here, but still an odd combination. Then add that Bush is just another li'l upper-class white boy out trying to prove he's tough.

The politics are probably the weirdest thing about Texas. The state has gone from one-party Democrat to one-party Republican in thirty years.

Lyndon said when he signed the Civil Rights Act in 1964 that it would take two generations and cost the Democrats the South. Right on both counts. We like to think we're "past race" in Texas, but of course East Texas remains an ugly, glaring exception. After James Byrd Jr. was dragged to death near Jasper, only one prominent white politician attended his funeral—U.S. Senator Kay Bailey Hutchison. Dubya, then governor, put the kibosh on the anti-hate crimes bill named in Byrd's memory. (The deal-breaker for Bush was including gays and lesbians. At a meeting last year of the Texas Civil Liberties Union board, vicious hate crimes against gays in both Dallas and Houston were discussed. I asked the board member from Midland if they'd been having any trouble with gay-bashing out there. "Hell, honey," she said, with that disastrous frankness one can grow so fond of, "there's not a gay in Midland would come out of the closet for fear people would think they're a Democrat.")

Among the various strains of Texas right-wingism (it is factually incorrect to call it conservatism) is some leftover loony John Birchism, now morphed into militias; country-club economic conservatism, à la George Bush père; and the usual batty anti-government strain. Of course Texas grew on the tender mercies of the federal government—rural electrification, dams, generations of master pork-barrel politicians, and vast subsidies to the oil and gas industry. But that has never interfered with Texans' touching but entirely erroneous belief that this is the Frontier, and that in the Old West every man pulled his own weight and depended on no one else. The myth of rugged individualism continues to afflict a generation raised entirely in suburbs with names like "Flowering Forest Hills of Lubbock."

The Populist movement was born in the Texas Hill Country, as genuinely democratic an uprising as this country has ever known. It produced legendary politicians for generations, including Ralph Yarborough, Sam Rayburn, Lyndon, and even into the 1990s, with Agriculture Commissioner Jim Hightower. I think it is not gone, but only sleeping.

Texans retain an exaggerated sense of state identification, routinely identifying themselves when abroad as Texans, rather than Americans or from the United States. That aggravated provincialism has three sources. First, the state is so big (though not so big as Alaska, as they are sure to remind us) that it can take a couple of days' hard travel just to get out of it. Second, we reinforce the sense of difference by requiring kids to study Texas history, including roughly ten years as an independent country. In state colleges, the course in Texas government is mandatory. Third, even national advertising campaigns pitch brands with a Texas accent here and certain products, like the pickup truck, are almost invariably sold with a Texas pitch. (Makes sense: Texas leads the nation with more than four million registered pickups.)

The founding myth is the Alamo. I was raised on the Revised Standard Version, which holds that while it was stupid of Travis and the gang to be there at all (Sam Houston told them to get the hell out), it was still an amazing last stand. Stephen Harrigan in *The Gates of the Alamo* is closer to reality, but even he admits in the end there was something romantic and even noble about the episode, like having served in the Abraham Lincoln Brigade during the Spanish Civil War.

According to the demographers at Texas A&M (itself a source of much Texas lore), Texas will become "majority minority" in 2008. Unfortunately, we won't see it in the voting patterns for at least a generation, and by then the Republicans will have the state so tied up by redistricting (recently the subject of a massive standoff, now over, in the Legislature), it's unlikely to shift for another generation beyond that. The Christian right is heavily dominant in the Texas Republican Party. It was the genius of Karl Rove/George W. Bush to straddle the divide between the Christian right and the country club conservatives, which is actually a significant class split. The politics of resentment plays a large role in the Christian right: Fundamentalists are perfectly aware that they are held in contempt by "the intellectuals." (William Brann of Waco once observed, "The trouble with our Texas Baptists is that we do not hold them under water long enough." He was shot to death by an irate Baptist.) In Texas, "intellectual" is often used as a synonym for "snob." George W. Bush perfectly exemplifies that attitude.

Here in the National Laboratory for Bad Government, we have an antiquated and regressive tax structure—high property, high sales, no income tax. We consistently rank near the bottom by every measure of social service, education, and quality of life (leading to one of our state mottoes, "Thank God for Mississippi"). Yet the state is incredibly rich in more than natural resources. The economy is now fully diversified, so plunges in the oil market can no longer throw the state into the bust cycle.

It is widely believed in Texas that the highest purpose of government is to create "a healthy bidness climate." The Legislature is so dominated by special interests that the gallery where the lobbyists sit is called "the owners' box." The consequences of unregulated capitalism, of special interests being able to buy government through campaign contributions, are more evident here because Texas is "first and worst" in this area. That Enron was a Texas company is no accident: Texas was also ground zero in the savings and loan scandals, is continually the site of major rip-offs by the insurance industry, and has a rich history of gigantic chicanery going way back. Leland Beatty, an agricultural consultant, calls Enron "Billie Sol Estes Goes to College." Economists call it "control fraud" when a corporation is rotten from the head down. I sometimes think Texas government is a case of control fraud too.

We are currently saddled with a right-wing ideologue sugar daddy, James Leininger out of San Antonio, who gives immense campaign contributions and wants school vouchers, abstinence education, and the like in return. The result is a crew of breathtakingly right-wing legislators. This session, Representative Debbie Riddle of Houston said during a hearing, "Where did this idea come from that everybody deserves free education, free medical care, free whatever? It comes from Moscow, from Russia. It comes straight out of the pit of hell."

Texans for Lawsuit Reform, aka the bidness lobby, is a major player and has effectively eviscerated the judiciary with a two-pronged attack. While round after round of "tort reform" was shoved through the Legislature, closing off access to the courts and protecting corporations from liability for their misdeeds, Karl Rove was busy electing all nine state supreme court justices. So even if you should somehow manage to get into court, you are faced with a bench noted for its canine fidelity to corporate special interests.

Here's how we make progress in Texas. Two summers ago, Governor Goodhair Perry (the man has a head of hair every Texan can be proud of, regardless of party) appointed an Enron executive to the Public Utilities Commission. The next day, Governor Goodhair got a $25,000 check from Ken Lay. Some thought there might be a connection. The guv was forced to hold a press conference, at which he explained that the whole thing was "totally coincidental." So that was a big relief.

We don't have a sunshine law in Texas; it's more like a partly cloudy law. But even here a major state appointee has to fill out a bunch of forms that are then public record. When the governor's office put out the forms on the Enron guy, members of the press, that alert guardian watchdog of democracy, noticed that the question about any unfortunate involvement with law enforcement looked funny. The governor's office had whited out the answers. A sophisticated cover-up. The alert guardian watchdogs were on the trail. We soon uncovered a couple of minor traffic violations and the following item: While out hunting a few years earlier, the Enron guy accidentally shot a whooping crane. As a result he had to pay a $15,000 fine under what is known in Texas as the In Danger Species Act. We print this. A state full of sympathetic hunters reacted with, "Hell, anybody could accidentally shoot a whooper." But the press stayed on the story and was able to report that the guy shot the whooper while on a goose hunt. Now the whooper is a large bird—runs up to five feet tall. The goose—short. Now we have a state full of hunters saying, "Hell, if this boy is too dumb to tell a whooper from a goose, maybe he shouldn't be regulatin' public utilities." He was forced to resign.

As Willie Nelson sings, if we couldn't laugh, we would all go insane. This is our redeeming social value and perhaps our one gift to progressives outside our borders. We do laugh. We have no choice. We have to have fun while trying to stave off the forces of darkness because we hardly ever win, so it's the only fun we get to have. We find beer and imagination helpful. The Billion Bubba March, the Spam-o-rama, the time we mooned the Klan, being embedded with the troops at the Holiday Inn in Ardmore, Oklahoma, singing "I'm Just an Asshole from El Paso" with Kinky Friedman and the Texas Jewboys, and "Up Against the Wall, Redneck Mother" with Ray Wylie Hubbard laughing at the loonies in the Lege—does it get better than this? The late Bill Kugle of Athens is buried in the Texas State Cemetery. On the front of his stone are listed his service in the marines in World War II, his years in the Legislature, other titles and honors. On the back of the stone is, "He never voted for a Republican and never had much to do with them either."

We have lost some great freedom fighters in Texas during the past year. Billie Carr, the great Houston political organizer (you'd've loved her: She got invited to the White House during the middle of the Monica mess, sashayed through the receiving line, looked Bill Clinton in the eye and said, "You dumb son of a bitch"), always said she wanted her funeral to be like her whole life in politics: It should start half an hour late, she wanted a balanced delegation of pallbearers—one black, one brown, two women—and she wanted an open casket and a name tag stuck over her left tit that said, "Hi there! My name is Billie Carr." We did it all for her.

At the funeral of Malcolm McGregor, the beloved legislator and bibliophile from El Paso, we heard "The Eyes of Texas" and the Aggie War Hymn played on the bagpipes. At the service for Maury Maverick Jr. of San Antonio, and at his request, J. Frank Dobie's poem "The Mustangs" was read by the poet Naomi Shihab Nye. The last stanza is:

*So sometimes yet, in the realities of silence and solitude,*
*For a few people unhampered a while by things,*
*The mustangs walk out with dawn, stand high, then*
*Sweep away, wild with sheer life, and free, free, free—Free*
*of all confines of time and flesh.*

**November 2003**

# Smart as a Shrub

■

GEORGE BUSH THE Younger ("Shrub" we call him) is running for governor of Texas and shapes up as a promising source of electoral entertainment. Shrub was recently in the Rio Grande Valley at a Republican function where two actual brown persons were in attendance. He headed toward them with his hand out, saying, "HitherehitherehowareyouI'mGeorgeBushgladtomeetyouhow'sitgoingthere." Shrub is a fast talker.

He next inquired what these gentlemen did and one replied that he works for Mexican-American economic development.

"That'sgreatthat'sgreat," said Shrub, and then leaned over to confess in greatest confidence, "If you're for making the pie bigger—I'm for that. If you're for making the pie smaller—I'm not for that." And they say this boy is not ready to be governor.

Our public servants have been busy contributing to the general joy lately: Mayor Lee Cooke of Austin had this to say about why the city has been negotiating in secret for a new city manager: "I wanted to have all my ducks in a row so if we did get into a posture we could pretty much slam-dunk this thing and put it to bed."

Dallas justice added yet more lustre to its national renown by attempting to hang on to Randall Dale Adams, an innocent man sentenced to death for a murder he didn't commit, long after it was clear to all but the meanest intelligence there was no way he could even be tried again.

And the Legislature is almost too embarrassing to contemplate. Turns out the Parks and Wildlife Department has obligingly been stocking the Speaker's ranch with deer, elk, bass, and turkey, for which he has not paid. When this was pointed out to him, the Speak promptly offered to round-up the beasties and send them back.

One solon has introduced a bill to lop off the fingers of repeat drug offenders, joint by joint and then digit by digit for each offense. Another senator wants to make it a felony for anyone knowingly to spread AIDS.

The Texas Lege has long had a tendency to notice grievous social problems and then pass laws against them. But the city of San Diego seems to have carried this trend to an apogee even the Texas Legislature hasn't yet contemplated: In San Diego, they ticket the homeless just as if they were illegally parked cars. The practice raises questions, of course. If a homeless person won't move along, can the cops put a boot on him? Can a homeless person say, "I'd rather not take the ticket here, just send it to me?"

Thank heavens we can turn to Washington for comic relief. Shrub's daddy's dog had puppies and that's it for the good news: drugs, S&Ls, the environment, Third World debt—all of these get worse by the day while Bush the Elder continues to impress us with the news that he rises at seven and stays awake through cabinet meetings.

Newt Gingrich, now there's a gladsome tiding. Great hair, no integrity. He's the real Bob Forehead. The reason Republicans elected this repellent little demagogue to the whipship is that they thought it would annoy Democrats. That's the Donald Segretti school of politics. With any luck, Robert K. Dornan of California will be next.

If the Republicans keep putting these right-wing fruitloops out front as spokesmen for their party, Democrats won't have to do dog.

Meantime, I'm pushing a new right-wing Dallas billionaire. This specimen's name is Harold Simmons, and he's a corporate raider by trade. He supports conservative Republican senators because "I feel I get more bang for my buck dealing with senators than I could anybody else. In the last five years I've headed up numerous fund-raising events here in Dallas for out-of-state Republican senatorial candidates. As a result, I can now call on a first-name basis about thirty Republican senators."

Isn't that nice? And to what ends does ol' Harold put his influence?

"I will lobby for things I believe in, primarily to keep Government off our backs, to keep them from passing laws to stop hostile takeovers and junk bonds and things like that."

I like the boy's candor. I like the equation of "keeping the Government off our backs" (where is Harold on drug testing?) with the use of junk bonds for hostile take-overs.

There should be an ad campaign on television. Some announcer with a four-balls voice will say, "Freedom to use junk bonds—one of our fundamental constitutional rights."

**May 1989**

# Too Wussy for Texas

$\blacksquare$

**B**IGGEST FIGHT WE'VE had all summer here in the Great State is over what motto to put on our license plates. The Highway Commission voted early this summer to put TEXAS—THE FRIENDSHIP STATE on our plates. This was unanimously condemned as Too Wussy for Texas, and it took Bubba a couple of months to get it turned around.

Historians will recall that we had the same flap a few years ago when some unusually demented Highway Commissioners decided TEXAS—THE WILD-FLOWER STATE would look good on our plates. This caused the ever-vigilant guardians of Texas machismo to declare that we might as well call it The Gay Rights State.

Now, The Friendship State is not nearly as wussy a motto as The Wildflower State—and it does have cultural roots. Our state motto is Friendship, and our state safety slogan is Drive Friendly, which is ungrammatical but perfectly clear.

And it wouldn't be false advertising—Texans actually are friendlier than normal people—at least outside the big cities, which you can prove any day by driving into a Texas town and saying "Hidy."

But we do have a shitkicker image to maintain, so the papers have been rife with suggestions like Yankee Go Home, and Fuck Alaska, and Texas: Kiss My Ass.

If we were to go for honesty instead of public relations, we'd wind up with something like Too Much Is Not Enough or Texas—Land of Wretched Excess. Or, perhaps, Home of the FDIC.

If honesty were a national license plate policy, we'd see:

- RHODE ISLAND—LAND OF OBSCURITY
- OKLAHOMA—THE RECRUITING VIOLATIONS STATE

- MAINE—HOME OF GEORGE BUSH
- MINNESOTA—TOO DAMN COLD
- WISCONSIN—EAT CHEESE OR DIE
- CALIFORNIA—FREEWAY CONGESTION WITH OCCASIONAL GUNFIRE
- NEW JERSEY—ARMPIT OF THE NATION
- NORTH DAKOTA—INCREDIBLY BORING
- NEBRASKA—MORE INTERESTING THAN NORTH DAKOTA
- NEW YORK—WE'RE NOT ARROGANT, WE'RE JUST BETTER THAN YOU

IT WAS a slow summer for scandal here until Bo Pilgrim, an East Texas chicken magnate, walked onto the floor of the state Senate and started handing out $10,000 checks with no payee filled in. He said he wanted to encourage the senators, then meeting in special session on the workers' compensation issue, to do right by bidness.

Turns out it's perfectly legal to walk onto the Senate floor and start handing out checks for $10,000 made out to no one in particular. Just another campaign contribution, folks. Bo Pilgrim is a familiar sight on Texas television, where he dresses up in a pilgrim suit and pitches ads for his fowl. He adds a certain je ne sais quoi to our communal life. His chicken factory is a major source of pollution in East Texas so, of course, the governor put him on the state Water Quality Board.

THE DEATH of Houston congressman Mickey Leland made so many hearts ache that poor Mick like to got buried under a mountain of hagiography. But you can't make a saint of a guy who laughed as much as Mickey.

My favorite Leland stories go back to the early 1970s, when he came to the Texas Legislature, one of the first blacks ever elected right out of a black district without having to get white folks' permission to run at-large. He showed up wearing an Afro and dashikis, and the Bubbas thought he was some kind of freak-radical Black Panther, and it meant the end of the world was at hand.

His first session Leland carried a generic-drug bill to help poor, sick, old people. He couldn't believe anyone would vote against poor, sick, old folks, but the drug companies and the doctors teamed up to beat his bill. After the vote, he stalked up to the medical-association lobbyists at the back of the House and in a low voice that shook with fury he hissed, "You are evil motherfuckers."

They almost wet their pants on the spot. He got the bill passed in the next session.

During the 1975 Speaker's race, members of the Black Caucus made a shrewd political play—they deserted the liberal/labor candidate and threw their support to Billy Wayne Clayton, a West Texas redneck, in exchange for some major committee chairmanships and heavy clout. Leland came out of the meeting with Clayton waving a tiny Confederate flag and announced, "We done sold de plantation."

I remember wondering early on if guys like Mickey were going to make a difference in the Lege. One day during his first session I saw him standing in the middle of the Capitol rotunda, which is a natural amplifier, trying to get Craig Washington and Paul Ragsdale, who were peering down at him from the third-floor gallery, to come along. In a voice that stopped traffic he yelled up, "Gottdammit, are you niggers comin' down to get lunch, or what?" Yep, gonna make a difference.

And he did. He made a much bigger difference in the world than all the damned old racists who used to vote against him.

**October 1989**

# A Fairly Normal Spring

■

THE TRANSSEXUAL TORCH murderer who's in a runoff for chairman of the Harris County (Houston) Democratic Party here in the Great State was my man (well, OK, so she is my woman now) until I found out more about her politics.

Hey, I've got nothing against torch murderers—she's paid her debt to society. Besides, she was a different person then. As for the gender change, people have a right to choose alternative sexual identities; at least she stayed Hispanic. But now I find out that after switching candidates several times in the recent special congressional election in Houston, she wound up supporting Al Edwards. Al Edwards, for you outlanders, is the state representative who favors lopping off the fingers of drug dealers, joint by joint, digit by digit, conviction by conviction. That's too weird for me, even if the torch murderer's opponent is Lloyd Bentsen's nephew.

(Speaking of the late, great Houston congressional race won by Craig Washington, if we could get the new congressman to give the commencement address at my alma mater, I could write an article about it headlined, MR. WASHINGTON GOES TO SMITH.)

The recent plebiscite offered many snacks for thought. We've got a guy who's seriously dead running in Tarrant County (Fort Worth). But the convicted drug dealer lost his legislative race, if not his fingers, in the Rio Grande Valley. On the other hand, the state senator accused of murder won handily. So did the fellow who was accused of being a pornographer and a henchman of organized crime.

But the real triumph over electoral handicap was the reelection of Frank Tejeda of San Antonio, who stood accused not only of wife-beating, child neglect, adultery, and whoring for the insurance lobby, but also of stealing from the Little League. Stealing from the Little League is low. But Tejeda successfully denied all charges and is back in the state Senate.

And some races are still in doubt: We may yet turn out to have nominated a monkey or a car for public office. We regularly put inanimate objects on the public payroll.

The big news was our peppy race for state executioner. Gosh, what a lot of fun the voters had trying to decide which candidate would fry the most felons if he or she became governor. Each and every one of them vowed to outfry the others; the gubernatorial race became a fry-off. Actually, we no longer fry felons in the electric chair: We now put them to sleep, like dogs, by lethal injection. Not in the least deterred by this symptom of creeping humanism, our gubernatorial candidates made a fetish of the death penalty.

Treasurer Ann Richards was judged the least bloodthirsty, but made it into a run-off anyway against Attorney General Jim Mattox, who watches people die for the fun of it.

On the Republican side, Clayton Williams, a rich guy from Midland, bought himself the nomination for a pricey $8 million, twice as much as was spent by his three opponents combined. Williams promised to teach those who try drugs "the joys of bustin' rocks." He plans to double the number of prison cells in the state without raising taxes by saving on the air-conditioning bill. We all had to admit, it was innovative.

Meanwhile, the Lege is back in Gridlock City over the question of how to finance the public schools fairly. Some good hands tried to head 'em off at the impasse, but it was like drawin' shovel duty in a feedlot. The state Senate passed a bill that calls for $1.2 billion in new spending, the governor threatens to veto anything over $300 million, and the house just voted no. Their ox is in the proverbial ditch.

All in all, a fairly normal spring here in Texas—tornados, floods, killer bees, primary elections, and the Legislature.

**May 1990**

# Happy Days for
# Armchair Rambos

■

Y OU MAY HAVE noticed that many of our fellow citizens have slipped into wretched excess on the patriotism front. Yellow ribbons tied around the necks of pink plastic yard flamingos. A bumper sticker on a huge gas-hog that says, WHIP THEIR ASS, THEN TAKE THEIR GAS.

Eight veterans groups in Pittsburgh, Pennsylvania, endorsed a decision not to let an anti-war group use the county-owned Soldiers & Sailors Memorial Hall. The chairman of the hall's board explained the anti-war group is opposed to "the flag, martial music, and everything else that is patriotic."

All in all, festive days for armchair Rambos.

For those of you who relish life's little ironies, Saudi Prince Alwaleed bin Talal has just bought $590 million worth of Citicorp, America's largest bank, thus becoming its largest shareholder. I personally enjoyed President Bush's presentation of his energy policy in midwar: He said he wouldn't do anything to conserve energy because he didn't want Americans to have to make such a sacrifice.

Here in Texas, Bonker Central as always, we're yellow-ribboned out the wazoo. Happily, the Lege is in session to give us comic relief from the war news. State Senator Rodney Ellis recently found himself in a minority of one on a committee vote. He looked around and said, "When I look at Senator Lucio, I see bilingual [Lucio is Hispanic]. When I look at Senator Leedom, I see bipartisan [Leedom is Republican]. When I look at Senator Whitmire, I see biracial [Whitmire is white, Ellis is black]. But when I look at me, all I see is by myself."

TEXAS WAR humor: Mrs. Saddam Hussein is seriously pissed off. She says, "Saddam, you are the dumbest guy in the world. You could have talked your way out of this, but now we're in a war. You are the stupidest person in the world." He says, "You really think so?" She says, "Go ask the mirror." So he goes into the bathroom, looks into the mirror, and says, "Mirror, mirror on the wall, who's the dumbest one of all?" Comes out a minute later and asks, "Who's this Clayton Williams person?"

Q: What's the difference between America and Kuwait?

A: Kuwait is a banking system without a country.

WELL, WE do have some other news. Our Speaker has been indicted. I know, I know, all you Gib Lewis fans around the nation are groaning and saying, "Ah, nah, not the Gibber!" What can I say? It's traditional to have the Speaker of the Texas House indicted. The Gibber is the third in a row to have someone roll over on him. (Actually, we did have one Speaker in there, 1973 to 1975, who was not indicted: He was murdered by his wife instead.)

Gibber's problems stem from this vacation he took in Mexico with a woman-not-his-wife. They stayed in an $850-a-night hotel room (and I'd like to point out that it's damned hard to find an $850-a-night hotel room in Mexico), paid for by a lobbyist who wanted a certain piece of legislation killed. The Gibber, that sly devil, registered as "Don Lewis."

The good news is that so far it's only a misdemeanor, because the D.A. can't prove the Speaker killed the bill. So the Demosthenes of the Texas Lege remains at the helm in the House, still confusing sin tax with syntax, humility with humidity, asking people in wheelchairs to stand and be recognized, and otherwise contributing his own special je ne sais quoi to our political life.

LEGISLATIVE JOKE:

Q: What's the difference between an anus and an asshole?

A: An anus can't put its arm around you.

The New Texas under Governor Ann Richards is otherwise progressing nicely, thank you. She's put a black woman on the board of regents of Texas A&M, so we know the world will never be the same again. In fact, if we weren't all obsessed by the war, half the press in the country would be down here whomper-jawed at the revolution. As it is, it barely makes page 17-D in the Texas press.

Still, it is amazing how much difference one governor who cares can make even in a "weak-governor" system. Trouble is, Ann can't be funny anymore—at least not in the same way. It's not considered "gubernatorial." Which means that the funniest line at a roast of Representative Jake Pickle a few nights ago turned out to be Liz Carpenter's. She said she'd known Jake so long she knew him when he was still a cucumber.

**April 1991**

# A Scientific Explanation
## of Texas

A LOCAL TELEVISION station here in Lubbock, Texas, recently ran a three-part investigative series on pantyhose entitled "Born to Run."

And some people wonder why I love Lubbock.

After a local farmer mowed an anti-Clinton message into his wheat field, another television station reported that he had "mowed it with his concubine."

Meanwhile, culture in Lubbock is stepping right along: A local feed and seed dealer named Godbold put up the money for the Godbold Cultural Center, which features an Espresso & Cappuccino Bar, so there.

Lubbock is, alas, now so conservative that even the city clerk, who has been getting elected as a Democrat since shortly after the Earth's crust cooled, has now switched to the Republican Party. Mark Harmon, a professor at Texas Tech who is running unopposed for Democratic county chairman, says he's thinking of switching parties so he can get elected, too.

Meanwhile, Texas politics is roaring along while no one in the state pays any attention. I think maybe we should start scoring our pols and awarding medals. In the last Democratic Senate candidate debate, Evelyn Lantz, who represents the Lyndon LaRouche cult, held out firmly for colonization of Mars. I'd give her 5.8 for artistic impression.

"Hey, Kay Bailey Hutchison, what're you going to do now that you've been acquitted?"

"I'm going to Disney World!"

And, indeed, Senator Hutchison was triumphantly acquitted in Fort Worth after the prosecutor refused to present his case against her just because the judge said he couldn't use his evidence.

I am working on a theory that there may actually be a scientific explanation for why this state is so strange. We know there's helium in the air around

Amarillo and lithium in the water in El Paso. In West Texas, the water has so much naturally occurring fluoride that everyone has strong yellow teeth, and it sometimes kills off African violets and goldfish. (This is the subject of Robin Dorsey's semi-famous country song, "Her Teeth Was Stained but Her Heart Was Pure.") Don't you think it's likely fluoride affects the old psyche as well? Of course, in East Texas, where fluoride is still considered a communist plot, we'll just have to admit that the problem is genetic. And if there's a natural element responsible for South Texas, we probably don't want to know what it is.

Texas justice threatens to join Texas politics as a synonym for "would drive buzzards off a roadkill." We're having this spate of Rodney King-lets, in which law enforcement officers videotape themselves brutalizing suspects and then charge the suspects with assault. We were especially impressed with the imagination it took to charge the citizen who was shot twice in the back.

But I have a dream. A dream that someday Phil Gramm, the world's meanest Republican, will be joined in the United States Senate by Jimmy Mattox, the world's meanest Democrat. And then the rest of the country will give us back to Mexico.

**April 1994**

# David Richards

∎

I'VE BEEN PUTTING this column off, hoping if I didn't write about it, it wouldn't happen. Makes me so glum to report it. David Richards, one of our greatest freedom fighters, is leaving Texas. But maybe only temporarily, we think he'll be back, he's bound to come back, really, who'd want to live in Santa Fe forever when Waco beckons? I give him a year before he hollers "uncle" and comes back to freedom-fight where it counts. Meantime, we'll have to stagger along without one of the best civil-rights lawyers and one of the best all-purpose battlers for justice this state has ever produced. (He promised he wouldn't let my writing his political obituary affect his decision to return.)

David's ex-wife has gotten more publicity in recent years, but if you want to know the truth, David Richards has done more to make Texas a fair and just place to live than Ann has (term's not over yet, Annie, keep working). One man–one vote, school desegregation, freedom of speech—the list of cases with David Richards' name on them as attorney for those getting shafted by unfair and unconstitutional laws goes on and on. So many of them seem self-evident by now—the shame of legal segregation is so clear to us at this point, we forget when it was worth a person's life to work to change it. One man–one vote, who could be against that? Oh, just an entire class of powerful, entrenched politicians who benefited under the old system of gerrymandered districts: In the old days when the Lege was "rural-dominated," the rule was one cow, one vote.

One of my favorite David Richards' cases was the tuba player who taught at the community college in Dallas. He had one tuba student for one hour a week and was paid all of $3.50. In those days, we had a lot of wiggy, leftover laws from the McCarthy era—in order to teach at, or even attend, a Texas college you had sign a pledge saying you were not now and never had been a member of the Communist Party, despite the fact that the Communist Party was perfectly legal. Now Richards' tuba player was not a communist (I think he was a Methodist), but he felt strongly that he shouldn't have to make any kind of political commitment to teach tuba. (Given our Lege in those days, we're lucky they didn't outlaw being a Republican: Come to think of it, not a bad idea.) The college wouldn't give the tuba teacher his $3.50 because he wouldn't sign the pledge, so David took the case (I assume for a handsome contingency fee, like half of the $3.50). And lo, at long last, at the end of the legal process, Richards triumphed and got this silly little menace to freedom of thought removed.

David Richards started as a lawyer in the Dallas firm Mullinax, Wells, which specialized in labor law and has produced so many freedom-fighting attorneys over the years. But he was not destined to be a happy camper in the rigidly conservative Dallas of the fifties and sixties. So David and Sam Houston Clinton, now on the Court of Criminal Appeals, started their own firm in Austin. They worked chiefly as attorneys for the AFL-CIO. One of the wonderful things about being in a state as backward as Texas, where we normally run twenty to thirty years behind most places (thank God for Mississippi), is that no element of our tiny progressive coalition has ever had time to become fat, complacent, and part of the Establishment—including Texas labor. The labor movement in this state remained for a long time more like the labor movement of the thirties, scrappy fighters for justice rather than defenders of their own turf. The AFL-CIO filed the first school desegregation suits (Corpus Christi, on behalf of a Mexican-American meat-cutter's daughter). The key one man–one vote case in this state was *White v. Register*, subsidized by the AFL, that finally integrated the state Legislature. It took years. Richards developed one man–one vote cases as a specialty, trying them all over East Texas—county commissions, school boards, city councils. As Sam Houston Clinton says, if you were to hold a meeting of all the folks who first got elected because of David Richards, it would fill a hall. "He practically invented that kind of litigation," said Clinton. "The thing about him is he wasn't just marching in the streets to protest discrimination, he went into the courtroom and got it changed. He absolutely made it all happen. He'd come into the court and produce the evidence in front of you so you couldn't deny it."

It's fashionable to bash lawyers as a bunch of greedy SOBs these days. The number of cases David Richards has taken pro bono would fill a book. In one of his most recent adventures, he tried to help the Save Our Springs coalition in Austin protect the city's jewel, Barton Springs, from the depredations of developers and the city council. Richards has not only fought for freedom him-

self, he has inspired a generation or more of young lawyers to go and do likewise. During Jim Mattox's first term as attorney general, Richards was his top
hand, and that office almost crackled with energy and idealism. Everyone who
was there seems to remember the speech Richards made at the farewell party
they gave for him. He closed with a favorite line from one of the Mexican revo-
lutionary leaders, who had been offered a share of the spoils, a big hacienda,
when it was over: "I did not join your revolution to become a haciendado."

As much as David Richards loves the struggle—he's a born battler—he
also has an equally outsized gift for relishing life. He loves softball and camping and canoeing and beer and singing and good books and running rivers and
his wife, Sandy, and all his kids. So have a wonderful year in Santa Fe, David,
but for God's sake, come back: You know we need you more here.

**May 1992**

# Charlie Wilson

※

THE TREE IS down, the bills are due, the weather's lousy, we're all on Rye Krisp and cottage cheese, the Texas Legislature is upon us, and Charlie Wilson has gone to save the Bosnians. Katy, bar the door.

Wilson, Texas' answer to Hunter S. Thompson, the Uncle Duke of Congress, is off on one of his save-the-freedom-fighter missions. When last we checked in on Representative Wilson's foreign policy, he was working as Lawrence of Afghanistan, with his girlfriend Miss World in tow. For a while there, he took up Angola, as though the poor country didn't have enough trouble with Jonas Savimbi running around loose.

But now Wilson's bound for Bosnia and is so serious about the assignment that he has announced "no chicks." Those who misunderstood him to mean "no checks" were also relieved (Charlie was a high scorer in the Rubbergate scandal).

Personally, I think Wilson should be declared a state treasure, if not an actual national monument, and protected like the snail darter. If it weren't for Charlie, Henry B., and Jack Brooks, the Texas congressional delegation would be perilously close to boring—a bunch of earnest strivers, Bob Foreheads, and uninterestingly wrongheaded right-wingers. (And that's another bone I have to pick with the right wing: You people used to produce a lot of entertainingly loopy public servants, but lately you've been letting down the side. Dick Armey is only marginally qualified.) It's my belief that the nation depends on Texas to provide genuine, certified, bona fide characters as players in the political drama. We have a responsibility in this regard. You can't count on South Dakota or Iowa to send anyone interesting to Washington. The place needs a bunch of hell-raising Texans, and Charlie is one.

He's the only man in Congress with an M-16, which he has personally fired at actual commies, mounted over his office door. When he was in Afghanistan, he taught the freedom fighters to yell in English what he told them was an old Texas war cry, "Kill the commie @ %&-suckers!"

As a feminist, I am duty-bound to deplore Wilson's perpetually adolescent attitude toward women, but since he has an excellent voting record on women's issues, I see no reason to get into a stew about it. In the old days, before he lapsed into relative respectability, Wilson had a standing order to his office manager concerning the hiring of secretaries: "You can teach 'em to type, but you can't teach 'em to grow tits." On the other hand, he's always had a crackerjack staff, noted for outstanding constituent casework.

Given the level of hideousness the situation in Bosnia has achieved, I suppose we should View With Alarm the prospect of our favorite loose cannon from East Texas careening around over there. But the Bosnians seem to be increasingly feisty these days, and if that's their mood, Wilson's their man. He specializes in government-sponsored gunrunning, which is what I think we should have been doing for the Bosnians all along.

Meanwhile, back at the Capitol, the poor old place is starting to look like postwar Berlin. The roof was leaking, the walls were cracking, and they'd found asbestos all over it, so our Capitol is now undergoing a giant redo. Workmen putter around the place continually, finding more things to take down and tear apart. The House will be meeting in its regular chamber, but the Senate has been shunted over to a former branch bank, which isn't doing anything for the majesty of the Senate.

The underground extension of the Capitol is now open, and if you have to build a building underground, this one is state of the art. A central courtyard and lots of ground-level skylights keep it from being too gloomy: Most of the state toilers even have windows that open onto sort of moatlike runs between the walls. I rather miss the quaint, Dickensian squalor that ensued from having everybody squashed in on top of everybody else at the Capitol: The new subterranean roominess is slightly eerie.

Another form of gloom is already hovering over the seventy-third session. As we all know, the state has been close to broke ever since the oil crash of '85. Every year, we've barely scraped by, cutting this and that, failing to take care of urgent needs, hoping to bail ourselves out with a lottery, raising sin taxes yet again. A combination of obdurate idiocy ("no state income tax, no state income tax": talk about shooting yourself in the foot over and over out of sheer stubbornness) and gumptionless leadership means we still have this pathetic, regressive tax structure. We not only don't have enough money to do anything well, we have grossly unfair taxes.

This time, after crying "wolf" and then staving off the wolf with some sorry, jerry-built patch, we are looking at the wolf. Knocking old folks out of nursing homes, dropping mothers and babies from nutrition programs, closing the schools. Oh, this is just going to be lots of fun.

*January 1993*

# Ann Richards vs. Shrub

GRACIOUS DEARIE ME, who would have thought the sensibilities of Texas Republicans had become so delicate? They are in a tizzy, having the hot fantods, close to swooning because Governor Ann Richards indirectly referred to Shrub Bush as "some jerk."

I distinctly recall having heard Republicans refer to their opponents as commies, queers, traitors, drug addicts, and murderers during past campaigns. And of course, what Texas Democrats have called one another cannot be repeated in a family newspaper. Those were the days, my friends, when Texas politics earned its national reputation for hardball. And now we're having the vapors over "jerk"?

I especially appreciate the fine flush of indignation rising from Republican Party chairman Tom Pauken, the man who taught Jim Mattox how to be mean. During two memorable Pauken-Mattox matches in Dallas in the early eighties, even grizzled veterans of Texas politics found the level of vituperation actually awesome. This is sissy stuff.

Of course, it does require us to examine the timely question: *Is* Shrub Bush a jerk? In fairness to Richards, it must seem as though Bush is a jerk. If you had spent much of your first term building prisons and doing law-'n'-order stuff—especially at the price of not getting a raise for schoolteachers and other things you really wanted to do—of course it would annoy you if some jerk came along and said that a drop in crime rates is unimportant. The jerk who actually said that was George W.'s campaign adviser, Karl Rove, and I confess that *jerk* is not the word that came to mind when I heard him—although *jackass* does also start with a *j*.

Shrub's new TV ad only *implies* that the drop in the crime rate is unimportant by announcing in a voice of doom that "the number of violent crimes is up." (Actually, even the number is up only in some categories. The rates are down across the board.) So I guess that makes Shrub Bush a jerk only by implication—or, as Richards' campaign so genteelly put it, it was not a personal remark but was made "in a generic fashion." That's one of the funniest distinctions in the history of politics.

Actually, this raises a profound semantic question: Can one act like a jerk or sound like a jerk without being a jerk? Can we hate the jerkiness, but not the jerk? I leave this to theologians.

The fact is that Shrub is not a jerk. It would be nice to dismiss him as a hopeless lightweight because he has no credentials. Ted Kennedy's first opponent used to go around saying, "If this man's name was Smith, nobody would vote for him." Kennedy has since gone on to amass the third-longest legislative record in American history—not, one suspects, a precedent that the Republicans are happy about. But young Ted Kennedy, like Shrub Bush, was especially galling to his opponents because all he had was a famous name, and he hadn't even earned it himself. It's not as though Bush were Tom Landry or Willie Nelson or even Ronald Reagan, who at least earned his own fame before he went into politics. Had Bush's name been Shrub Smith, he wouldn't even have gotten the nomination.

On the other hand, I don't think it's smart for the Richards campaign to try to dismiss Shrub as though he were some political pygmy, to be brushed off just because he's never held office before. In the first place, pointing out that you have political experience and your opponent has none is not exactly shrewd politics these days. For veterans like Richards and Lieutenant Governor Bob Bullock, who know how hard it is to get anything done and who carry a lot of scars from the fights they've been in, the temptation to dismiss some puppy who's yapping "Vote for me—I've never done anything" is understandable. But folks are so fed up with politicians these days that anyone who can claim outsidership has a built-in advantage. It's the same impulse that drives the term-limitation movement: The people who are in office have made such a mess, let's put in a bunch of people who have no experience—they can't possibly do worse. (Although this flies in the face of a time-tested theorem: Things can always get worse.)

Besides which, as anyone who has met Shrub Bush will attest, he's not a lightweight. He's a lot brighter than some people who already hold public office, he's working like a dog at this campaign, and it's real hard to dislike the guy. Now, I don't think his ideas about state government amount to much. The very fact that he's running around saying he'll do this and that and the other if elected is proof that he doesn't know how state government works. (Welcome to the weak-governor system, Shrub.) But when did you ever hear of anyone running for public office without making promises impossible to keep?

In sum, let us put this teapot tempest where it belongs in the long view of Texas politics: Referring to your opponent as a jerk—in the generic rather than the personal sense, of course—is gentility personified.

**August 1994**

# Ann Richards vs. Shrub II

O K, O K, I'M so partisan that after seeing the debate between Ann Richards and George W. Bush, instead of saying it was 2–1 in Richards' favor or 3–2 or whatever all those other commentators said, I find myself asking, "WHAT ARE YOU, OUT OF YOUR TINY MIND THAT YOU WOULD EVEN CONSIDER VOTING FOR SHRUB BUSH?!"

I really don't get it. Is this some total failure of imagination on my part? Am I missing some sparkling quality of Shrub's that's apparent to others? I've said from the beginning that Bush is a guy you could take anywhere. He's not going to tell rape jokes in public or drop his trou in his office or have a paranoid episode on *60 Minutes*.

I still don't see anything particularly wrong with him. He's nice. He's not dumb. He works real hard at making people like him. True, he is awfully . . . privileged, but that's not his fault. It's a little creepy to hear him say that the schools are his top priority when you know that he went to prep school and his kids go to prep school. It's fine for him to say he's going to clean up welfare . . . do you think he's ever actually known anyone who was stuck on welfare?

Of course, he inherited money and has been given a lot of breaks in business by his daddy's friends, but no one ever said this was a level playing field. He's had some business losses; lots of people did in the 1980s, including Claytie Williams, if you'll recall. Being born lucky is not a character flaw, and folks in business do take risks.

The problem is not Shrub Bush; it's the comparison with Ann Richards.

Richards really is one of a kind. Just unique. She's a great politician who also happens to be remarkably good at governing. The two things do not always come in the same package. Richards is an "OK, let's work this thing out" kind of governor rather than a "Do it my way or I'll break you" kind. All over the country, people comment on Richards' "star quality," but what strikes me most about Richards—first, last, and always—is that she's a hard worker.

I cannot remember Richards when she was not doing something, not out of nervous energy but just plain efficiency. For years, she has had a Christmas Eve party for family and old friends, which always includes singing Christmas carols around the piano. The highlight is the patented Richards version of "The Twelve Days of Christmas" in which everyone imitates lords a-leaping, geese a-laying, and so forth. Toward the end of the evening, as old friends settle down for quiet chats, Richards is always to be found in the kitchen, doing dishes. Even at the mansion. Dish towel tucked into her belt, sleeves rolled up, a steaming sink of soapy water in front of her, handing spotless plates to a team of wipers while they all discuss some way to make Texas work better.

Richards has always been interested in how to make things work better; she's one of the most practical people I've ever met. I'm confounded when I read that Richards is "too liberal." I am a liberal. I'll talk theories of social justice all night while Richards finishes the dishes, peels potatoes for tomorrow's picnic salad, sews a child's Halloween costume, and figures out how to make the House and Senate agree on the appropriations conference bill.

State government is fairly simple in some ways: roads, schools, prisons, and what Allan Shivers called "eleemosynary institutions"—help for the blind, deaf, disabled, and mentally ill. Richards started in politics as a county commissioner, doing roads. This is a woman who knows her road graders. And she knows everything else about state government in the same from-the-ground-up way, including how to run bureaucracies. (Don't get her started on bureaucracies unless you really want to hear a forty-five-minute lecture on just how many ways bureaucrats have of not doing anything about a problem.)

Her real passion is kids and education. I guess that's why Bush struck me as so flat when he said that schools would be his top priority. Of course, Richards started out as a teacher ("spent her entire adult life in politics" is just one of those charming little election-year lies we're all so used to) and also spent twenty years raising four terrific kids.

Anyone who has ever seen Ann Richards with a bunch of schoolkids knows the magic of a great teacher. I'll never forget Richards with a group of forty or so Anglo, black, and brown kids from Dallas visiting the Capitol. She uses the Socratic method: She asks the questions; they figure out the answers. "Who owns this building?" she asked. It took several steps for the kids to realize they're taxpayers, too, and finally shout out in delight: "*We* own it. It's *ours.*"

Ann Richards is not a perfect person. In the first place, she has serious perfectionist tendencies; in the second place, she gets crabby when she's tired. But you'll never find a former employee of Richards' telling tales about what a stinker she is, the way Senator Kay Bailey Hutchison's do. Because on top of the smarts, the discipline, and the fact she works harder than anyone around, she has warmth, wit, and charm. They are genuine, and she is generous with them.

It's not that there's much wrong with Bush; it's the comparison to Richards that makes one want to refer to him as "little," "young" (as though forty-eight were young), "callow," and, frankly, sort of a jerk. When you compare the two of them in wisdom, life experience, understanding and liking of people, and knowing how to get things done for Texas, he *is* a shallow little twerp who's too dumb to realize how much he doesn't know.

He may well beat her. It's up to you.

**November 1994**

# Adios, Annie

■

AVE ATQUE VALE, Miz Ann. Hail and farewell, Governor Richards. Adios, Annie. Keep your wagon between the ditches. May your days be full of laughter. Good on ya.

Ann Richards' electoral loss to George Dubya Bush will keep political scientists studying for years. By all the conventional measures, she should have walked back into office. Her approval rating was and is over 60 percent— practically golden. The state's economy is ginnin', crime rates are down, school scores are up, she never raised taxes, and never had a scandal.

The short, easy version is that Richards lost because of President Clinton. In Florida, where Clinton was at 42 percent in the approval ratings, Governor

Lawton Chiles pulled it out. In Texas, where Clinton hovers around 36 percent, there just wasn't a shot. Another short, easy version is that she won by 100,000 votes last time against a gloriously inept opponent, and in the meantime, 120,000 people have moved into the state and registered Republican.

The more complex and more accurate version is that George Dubya ran a helluva campaign and Annie ran a dud. Their race became a peculiar black-and-white negative of the 1992 presidential race between George Dubya's daddy and Clinton, with Richards as the stay-the-course, no-vision candidate and Bush as the proponent of change, change, change. George Dubya's campaign was full of ideas and plans (of dubious merit, but whatthehey), while Richards neither successfully sold what should have been limned as a brilliant record nor projected any enthusiasm for a wonderful future. The New Texas disappeared. The television ads were lousy.

A lot of they-sayers believe Richards & Co. underestimated George Dubya, who ain't no Claytie Williams. I thought she took him seriously from the git-go, which is why she flip-flopped on federal protection for Caddo Lake, thus royally annoying the enviros. But dismissing him as a "jerk" set off the now-famous angry-white-male vote. I'm not sure what Richards could have done to win over that vote; my personal opinion is that some men feel threatened by a strong woman, especially one with a quick tongue.

Of the hundreds of distinguished appointments that Richards made, which will surely include the black, brown, and female leaders of the coming years, only a literal handful were gays or lesbians. But the Christian right, using the fear-mongering hyperbole for which it is so noted, managed to imply that the capital had become a sink of iniquity. Richards' veto of the concealed-weapons bill set off the gun nuts. I still think it was statesmanship of a high order.

As for Richards' real record in office, to the extent that the governor of Texas is really nothing more than a salesman for the state, I'm not sure we've ever had better. Ann Richards is as popular outside Texas as she is inside. And although her sense of humor may have cost her votes with the angry white males, I think she has definitely proved again that it is possible to hold high public office and be witty, too.

Her biggest mistake in my book was early on, when Bob Bullock had the guts to come out for a state income tax and Richards left him out there, slowly twisting in the wind. (So did the bidness community, which has quietly been in favor of same for many years.) That was gutless.

In the bidness community's books, Richards' appointments in insurance, environment, and nursing home regulation were "too militant." They felt they were perceived as the enemy when they went in to deal with those folks, and no one likes that. There's an extent to which it was a real problem with some of Richards' more purist appointments and an extent to which it was nothing more than willful misperception. Besides, anyone who doesn't make enemies in office isn't worth spit.

Richards said in a farewell interview with the press corps that if she'd known she was going to be a one-term governor, she would have "raised more hell." I wish she had. But these are relatively minor quibbles with what is, overall, a distinguished record. My political memory of Texas governors goes back to Allan Shivers, and I know that in that time we have not had a governor who worked nearly as hard as Ann Richards. Who was nearly as gracious as Richards. Who made more good appointments than Richards. Who set a higher standard of honesty than Richards.

A special thanks is due Richards from recovering alcoholics and addicts all over the country. Her grassroots work in this field, done in addition to her duties as governor, has been tireless, inspirational, and quite simply extraordinary. From mansions in Dallas to prisons all over the state, she has changed lives. To see the governor of Texas sitting in a circle with convicted criminals saying simply, "My name is Ann, and I am an alcoholic," is to learn a great deal about recovery.

What our notoriously weak governors actually do is set a tone for the state. So let it be recorded that for four brief shining years, Ann Richards gave the joint some class.

Good on ya, Annie. So now go camping and have some fun.

**January 1995**

# The Lege

■

**W**E DIDN'T ASK for it, we don't want it, we're not ready, and we haven't done anything to deserve it; nevertheless, the Texas Legislature is about to start again.

Veteran Texans know that the only solution is to hunker down and laugh, since the one thing we can count on our Lege for is Pure D, top-grade, high-octane entertainment. Better than the zoo, finer than the circus, pratfalls, fist-fights, clowns, animals—what could be better? It's representative democracy, Texas-style, in full-blooded action. As former state senator Carl Parker used to say, "If you took all the fools out of the Legislature, it wouldn't be a representative body anymore."

A brief recap on some of our major players:

- The Gov, George W. Bush, is somewhat short of running room on account of he's playing to a two-tier audience. The national press corps will be watching his every move, analyzing how it will play not only in Iowa and New Hampshire but even among general voters beyond the primaries. Meanwhile, he has to keep the red hots in his own party from doing anything that will embarrass him nationally, and that may not be easy.
- The Lite Gov, Rick Perry (a new player at this level), has not started out in a sure-footed manner.

A lite gov can, both by the Texas Constitution and by force of personality, be far more powerful than the gov, as Bob Bullock has been. Perry hired some good staff people, and all were hopeful. Then word hit the Capitol that Perry proposed to replace Senator David Sibley of Waco as chairman of the powerful Economic Development Committee.

Sibley is widely regarded as one of the best and brightest of the Republican senators, a class act, and Bullock (never one to waste talent) gave him some big jobs. A perfect storm of rumors attended the alleged effort to remove Sibley, including one that Bush intervened.

The whole thing led to a come-to-Jesus session between Perry and the Republican senators, and now no one says anything for the record. Speculation is that Sibley keeps his chairmanship but that some of his power is stripped by moving jurisdiction on tort questions to another committee.

In general, Perry is regarded, both by philosophy and by campaign contributions, as entirely a creature of the business community, especially big business.

- Democratic House Speaker Pete Laney normally runs a benign and nonpartisan operation, giving major committee chairmanships to Republicans and pretty much letting everyone have a run with his or her bills. But the Speak is now down to a six-vote margin in the 150-member House, and furthermore he is reportedly more than a little chapped over the tactics used by Republicans to defeat Democratic members.

    It's not that easy to make Laney mad, but the R's have done it. He will probably recover his usual equanimity before the session starts, but it may take a lot less than it once did to turn him into an angry Democrat.
- She's baaaack! The least popular member of the Legislature, Representative Arlene Wohlgemuth of Burleson, was reelected, proving that Wohlgemuth may have learned something since last session but the voters of Bosque, Johnson, and Somervell counties sure haven't. Good luck to all y'all.

Wohlgemuth distinguished herself last session by killing off about fifty bills with a parliamentary maneuver because she hadn't gotten her way on an unrelated matter. That means several dozen bill sponsors will be out gunning for anything she puts up.

We can also count on some of those jolly hot-button issues being brought up. The anti-abortion forces are determined to push parental notification through this session. School vouchers will be a big issue; they are supported not only by Republicans but also by many Chicano reps who support Roman Catholic schools and some black reps who have been convinced it will improve inner-city education. The generous campaign contributions of James Leininger, the San Antonio millionaire who favors vouchers, are also a factor.

Personally, I favor Jim Pitts' old idea of handing the death penalty to eleven-year-olds—as long as we give them hot milk and a teddy bear before we slip 'em the needle.

Tax relief is in sight, but the gov's proposal to give it all in property tax relief will get a fight. The state doesn't even have a property tax. Sales tax relief makes more sense, especially since the sales tax weighs more heavily on poor people. And you must admit that there is a certain contradiction between saying you want to improve the public schools and making all your cuts in the tax that supports the schools.

The most promising and important initiative that the state could take (aside from putting some serious money into the schools) is in health care for poor children. This is not only high payoff in terms of cost savings down the line, but there's a 3-to-1 federal matching program (as rich as it gets), so we could cover every poor child in the state for as little as $150 million. That's out of a projected $2 billion surplus.

**January 1999**

# Sympathy for the Shrub

∎

**S**TRANGE PEACHES IN the media world. As one who rarely identifies with Governor George W. Bush, I find myself in odd sympathy with the Shrub these days just because media people keep turning up in Austin to ask me about him. I seem to be on the list because I'm one of the few people who will say anything negative about the man on the record. What chaps me is the kind of questions I'm asked.

I offer to explain how Bush flubbed the tax-reform proposals last session—couldn't even get his own party to go along—and the visiting journalists want to know if he ever used drugs.

I describe his one legislative triumph—a tort reform bill that has so completely reversed the state's old reputation as a trial lawyer's paradise that we have now become an insurance company's paradise—and the visitors want to know if I've heard any gossip about his love life.

Give us a break!

I reluctantly agreed to do one more TV interview the other day because this crew said it had come to cover the issues. They said they were particularly concerned that Bush was so vague on so many important questions, and they were here to pin him down. Great, says I—this is public service.

It's one thing to try to straddle the abortion issue when you're governor of Texas and have no power to do anything about it; it's another matter to straddle on abortion when you're running for president and will be naming people to the Supreme Court. It becomes necessary to clarify what has been a singularly muddled bunch of mush, on this and other topics.

So in comes the happy TV crew to report that Bush has just addressed a group of young people and told them not to make the mistakes he made when he was young. *But what mistakes did he make, specifically and in great detail,* the television reporter wants to know. This is what he means by clarification of the issues.

Next, a print journalist asks in all seriousness: "But why does Bush keep bringing up this supposed misbehavior when he was young? Why does he dwell on it?" I was completely boggled; you could have knocked me over with Drew Nixon's brain. Why does *Bush* bring it up? Why does *he* dwell on it?

This is a national press corps that has obsessed about the president's sex life for fourteen months; while much of the world's economy collapsed, our political press corps was completely caught up in a tawdry soap opera. Now, they come to Texas and bombard Bush and everybody else with questions about his private life, and they want to know why *Bush* is dwelling on it? Now that's chutzpah.

If the media want to address Bush's character, then they should address his character, not his sex life. The main thing about Bush is that there's not much there there.

This is not a person of great depth or complexity or intelligence; he does not have many ideas. (Actually, aside from tort reform, I've never spotted one.) I don't think he knows or cares a great deal about governance. Nevertheless, he is a perfectly adequate governor of Texas, where we so famously have the weak-governor system. Bush was smart enough to do what Bob Bullock told him to for four years, and it worked fine.

Bush is also a pretty nice guy. I really think you would have to work at it to dislike the man. His best trait is self-deprecating humor.

He's above average; he's more than mediocre. He has real political skills. If you separate the political part of public life (i.e., running for office) from the governing part (i.e., what you do after you get there), Bush is much better at the politics. This is true of many people in public life—in fact, a genuine interest in governance is relatively rare among politicians.

As proof of his political shrewdness, I submit two pieces of evidence: first, his careful wooing of the Hispanic community in Texas (such a refreshing contrast to that fool Wilson in California); and second, an extremely difficult balancing act keeping the Christian right, which controls the Texas Republican Party, from being perceived as the face of the party. (Most of Bush's money comes from precisely the kind of rich Republicans who are horrified by the Christian right; anyone who has covered Texas Republican conventions during the past ten years knows how deep that split is.)

The single worst thing I can say about George W. Bush after five years of watching him is that if you think his daddy had trouble with "the vision thing," wait'll you meet this one. I don't think he has any idea why he's running for the presidency, except that he's competitive and he can. On the other hand, most Republicans don't want government to do much anyway, so Bush is perfect for them.

Anyone who thinks Bush's sound-bite slogan "compassionate conservatism" actually means something programmatic should study the latest reports on poverty in Texas. Hint to national media people (courtesy of the Center for Public Policy Priorities):

- Texas has a much higher percentage of poor *working* families with small children than other states.
- More poor Texas families have a full-time, year-round worker than similar families in other states.
- Texas' poor families are more likely to rely on earnings for a majority of their income, and less likely to rely on welfare, than similar families in the nation.
- Poor working families in Texas are much less likely to be covered by health insurance. They are less likely to receive unemployment benefits. More than half the poor families are headed by a married couple. One out of six Texans is below the poverty level. The child poverty rate is 24.2 percent, compared to 20.4 percent nationally.

In other words, poor Texans are doing everything Bush thinks they should—they work, they marry, they rely on themselves, they don't get help from the government—and the upshot is that the state has more poor people, and those poor people are much poorer and less healthy than poor people elsewhere. Now *that's* an issue.

And another good issue is Bush's business record, where he very clearly did *not* take his own advice that we shouldn't look to the government for help.

As for the rather silly argument that if George W.'s last name were Smith, no one ever would have heard of him—that's quite true, but so what? His last name isn't Smith. Get over it. Yes, he is ahead now on name recognition, and no, most people don't know a single thing about where he stands. And whose fault is that?

**April 1999**

# "No Position" Bush

A FEW WEEKS ago, a consoling clip from an Arizona newspaper arrived on my desk informing me that one member of the Arizona Legislature had said to another, "Gee, I didn't know you were Jewish. You don't look Jewish. You don't have a big hook nose." There was even a picture of the Jewish member helpfully labeled: DOES NOT HAVE BIG HOOK NOSE.

A pal sent me this snippet because the last time I was in Arizona this sensitive state representative had managed to conflate homosexuality and cannibalism into a single menace, a confusion so remarkable I felt impelled to write about it. It's always nice to know not all the morons are in the Texas Lege.

Trouble is, I can't think of anything else encouraging about the seventy-sixth session of the Texas Lege. I'll put our morons up against theirs, anytime.

Representative Arlene Wohlgemuth, one of our top contenders, opposed a resolution noting that 1.5 million Texas children do not have health insurance. She said they might not have health insurance because their parents are so rich they can afford to pay cash for medical care. "Their parents might be making $1 million a year. It is still our right in this country not to have health insurance," she said.

The right not to have health insurance is one of the most undercelebrated rights we have in this great nation, and we are all grateful to Arlene for pointing it out to us.

Perhaps the high point of the session was the day the Democratic minority in the Senate left the chamber en masse, decamped to the rotunda of the Capitol, and there proceeded to hold hands and pray. Led in prayer, I might add, by Senator John Whitmire of Houston, who has not heretofore been much noted for Christian leadership. (Whitmire has taken offense at my astonishment over his new incarnation as a spiritual leader and informs me he is known as "John the Baptist.") The proximate cause of this Democratic re-course to The Lord was that they couldn't get the hate crimes bill out of com-mittee. And the reason they couldn't get it out is because gays and lesbians were included in the bill, and that presented a huge problem for George W. Bush, who is running for president. Because, you see, it would upset the many fundamentalist Christians who would vote in Republican primaries if killing "sinners" was somehow especially illegal. I know this because Senator Drew Nixon explained it to Senator Rodney Ellis, sponsor of the hate crimes bill. Senator Nixon knows his onions when it comes to sin, he being our leading convicted perp in the Senate, having done time for the unfortunate sin of solic-iting a prostitute last year. He served his sentence in a halfway house and, may I add, is in point of actual fact one of the more useful and intelligent members of the Texas Senate.

I am in some danger of becoming fond of Senator Nixon, who has populist instincts. You may think incipient fondness for him reflects poorly on my judg-ment, but that's only because you don't know the other Republicans in the Senate.

Senator Florence Shapiro, one of the other Republicans, said the entire hate crimes bill was about one man, George W. Bush—all an effort to embar-rass the governor. Actually, the hate crimes bill was about one man, and his name was James Byrd Jr., who was dragged to death behind a pickup truck near Jasper, Texas, last year because he was black. His corpse was recovered in chunks. In this year of Our Lord 1999, the Legislature of the state of Texas is still not ready to condemn hate crimes because that includes crimes against "queers." A lesser person might be discouraged by that. The governor, inciden-tally, had no position on the hate crimes bill: That's the governor's usual posi-tion—he has no position. He has said, "All crimes are hate crimes." As Representative Senfronia Thompson, House sponsor of the James Byrd Jr. Memorial Bill, asked sarcastically, "Is forgery a hate crime? Fraud? Prosti-tution? Armed robbery?"

The other big fight of the session was over whether to use federal money to give health insurance to the children of the poor (about 165,000 kids would be covered). The governor had no position. The House, the one that still has a Democratic majority, prevailed.

Governor Bush, the crown prince of the Republican Party, had one big goal this session: He wants to give $2 billion in property tax relief back to the people who own property in this state. Texas has an extraordinarily regressive tax structure; it weighs most heavily on those who are poorest. Poor people rarely own property. Nevertheless, property tax relief was the goal. And it was certainly aided by the fact that we in Texas have a handsome budget surplus this year. What better to do with it than give a property tax rebate to those who own property? They will get a cut worth as much as a Big Mac and fries every month! Meanwhile, Texas ranks fiftieth among the states (that's last) in per capita spending, and that includes highways, the one thing we do well. If you were to exclude highway spending, Texas would rank where it so often does—behind Puerto Rico and Guam.

So what could we have done instead of a tax cut? Kindergarten. We thought it would be nice to have kindergarten in Texas. We keep reading all these studies about how important early childhood development is. Hillary Clinton—you should forgive I mention her name—has made a big deal about this, all this new research shows the early development stuff is critical. So we thought maybe kindergarten. But no. The Education Governor is not *that* keen on education.

**July 1999**

# The Real Question for Bush

U<small>NDER THE OLD</small> rules, before we wrote about something, we were expected to have some evidence that it was true. Under the new rules, the fact that there is gossip about someone is news, whether the gossip is true or not.

In the case of George W. Bush, the fact that he refuses to deny that he used cocaine has seemed to the entire press corps sufficient evidence—a charming latter-day version of "Have you stopped beating your wife?"

The media, as happens so depressingly often, are asking the wrong question. Bush himself stands there and begs us to ask it. "I have learned from my mistakes," he says over and over. The question is: *What* did he learn?

Until 1973, Texas had the most draconian drug laws in the nation. Whether they stopped Bush or not, they didn't stop me, didn't stop people now serving in the Legislature, and didn't stop most of a generation of Texans from trying marijuana.

What did Bush learn from that? Nothing.

Harsh laws do not stop young people from trying illegal drugs. So what does Bush do when he gets to be governor? Increases the penalties and toughens the system so it's harder on young people. Signs a memorably stupid bill making possession of less than a twentieth of an ounce of cocaine punishable by jail time.

Are there people who are now in Texas prisons for making "youthful mistakes"? There are thousands of them. At least 5,000 people are in for marijuana possession alone. Twenty percent of the state prison population of 147,000 is there on drug-related charges.

The truth is, if Bush *had* been caught using marijuana or cocaine twenty-five years ago, he would not have been sentenced to prison. He was rich and white, and his daddy was an important guy. That's the way the system worked then; that's the way the system works now.

When Bush became governor, he had a world of opportunity to try to make the system more fair. What did he do? He vetoed a bill (passed unanimously by both sides of the Republican-controlled Legislature) that would have given poor defendants the right to see a lawyer within twenty days. Twenty days, big deal: In most of the country, an indigent defendant gets a lawyer within seventy-two hours, or they have to let him go. We have poor people in Texas who spend months in jail just waiting to see a lawyer, who may be drunk or asleep at trial.

Bush vetoed that bill. He learned nothing.

When Bush came in as governor, this state had committed to the most extensive in-prison drug-and-alcohol rehabilitation program in the country—the joint legacy of Ann Richards and Bob Bullock, both recovering alcoholics. Eighty percent of the people in Texas prisons are diagnosed by the system as having substance abuse problems. The entire program is gone now, completely repealed.

Bush learned nothing. That's the story.

THE REPUBLICAN Party expects to find at least one hundred supporters who will give $250,000 a year over four years in soft money. Just what we need: a club of $1 million donors. In one of the funniest statements in years, Julie Finley, chair of the Republican Team 100 program (these are the pikers who give only $100,000), explained to *The New York Times* what the $1 million donors will get for their money: "What they get is they are left alone. They don't get calls to buy a table at the gala. They don't get calls to give to the media program. They have a pass that lasts all year."

And, by George, if that's not worth a million bucks, what is?

Oh, they also get private meetings with the people who write the laws for all of us.

MY GUN-NUT friends often tell me that mass shootings like the one at the Jewish community center in Los Angeles wouldn't happen if more people carried concealed weapons. How right they are: If those five-year-olds in L.A. had just been packing, none of 'em would have gotten hurt.

I wrote that line right after the shooting but didn't use it on the grounds that it was too flip. But I'm using it now because Thomas Sowell, a right-wing columnist from the Hoover Institute, actually wrote a column in all seriousness saying, yep, the solution to these mass killings is more guns. Incredibly, he argues that the mass killings that have been taking place in white, middle-class settings wouldn't happen in the ghettos or barrios because more folks there are packing.

I hate to tell him this, but if the murder rate in white, suburban America were the same as that in the ghettos and barrios, we'd be confiscating guns by now.

**October 1999**

# Political Advertising

■

Houston — My favorite thing at the Texas Republican Convention was the advertising in the back of the hall that constituted an almost perfect record of the major scandals, conflicts of interest, and bad public policy that have occurred during the W. Bush gubernatorial administration. There they all were, proudly displaying their gratitude to Bush and the party. It was a near-perfect metaphor for American politics today.

Chemical had several of the small billboards for each part of the hall. Dow and the rest of the chemical industry were given one third of the seats on the Texas equivalent of the Environmental Protection Agency when Bush got into office.

He appointed a lobbyist for the Texas Chemical Council to the Texas Natural Resource Conservation Commission. This citizen had spent thirty years working for Monsanto. He used his position as one of the top environmental officials of Texas to go to Washington to testify that ozone is benign and to oppose strengthening federal air-quality standards. Being in Houston during the lovely summer ozone season reminds us all how grateful we must be for this kind of zealous watchdoggery of our air quality.

Also advertising its gratitude to Bush was TXU, formerly Texas Utilities, which under Bush's deregulation scheme is trying to stick consumers with $3.7 billion in "stranded costs"—aka dumb management decisions. Enjoy that on your summer utility bill.

And how nice to see an ad from a grateful Metabolife.

According to the May 22 issue of *Time* magazine, Texas was fixing to regulate ephedrine, an amphetamine-like stimulant widely used for weight loss. Ephedrine products had been linked to eight deaths and fourteen hundred health problems in Texas, so the health commissioner was ready to regulate. But according to *Time*, Metabolife International of San Antonio hired a San

Antonio law firm headed by some of Bush's closest political associates, and instead there was a meeting with the commissioner, who then decided to bring in an outside lawyer to negotiate a settlement with ephedrine producers.

Metabolife's Washington lobbyist, who had given $141,000 to Bush's gubernatorial campaigns and raised at least $100,000 for his presidential campaign, was also a player. Stricter limits on ephedrine were dropped.

Next up, an ad for Pilgrim's Pride, the chicken company of Lonnie "Bo" Pilgrim of East Texas. Some of you may remember Lonnie-Bo from the famous time, pre-Bush, when he strolled onto the floor of the Texas Senate and started handing out $10,000 checks to senators in the midst of a hearing on workers' comp law.

Lonnie-Bo was also a big funder of Texans for Public Justice, a tort reform outfit, and gave $125,000 to Bush for his gubernatorial campaigns. As you know, tort reform under Bush has gone so far that the state is now paradise for insurance companies.

Next up, Promised Land Dairy, owned by James Leininger, who crusaded first for tort reform and is hot on school vouchers and other Christian-right causes. Leininger gave $1.5 million in contributions and loans to Lieutenant Governor Rick Perry, helping to provide the razor-thin margin by which he defeated Democrat John Sharp. Leininger also provided a huge loan to Comptroller Carole Keeton Rylander in 1998, as well as $65,000 to Bush in '98.

How nice to see an ad for Philip Morris Co., Inc. Philip Morris provided employment for Karl Rove, the man running Bush's campaign, from 1991 to 1996. Rove was paid $3,000 a month to lobby for Philip Morris while also working for Bush. This was during the time that Texas was suing the tobacco companies.

What a pleasant stroll down memory lane these little billboards provided.

Meanwhile, various Republican orators were at the mike describing the coming election as "a struggle for the soul of the American people" (U.S. Representative Tom DeLay) and a battle between our values and the "indecency" of Al Gore. (Everyone was on the virtues-and-values theme, usually referred to as "our virtues" and "our values.")

And I was just strolling along that wall of ads, studying those virtues and values.

# Henry B.

IN MAY 1957, one of the ugliest times in Texas history, the Legislature was debating a long series of bills designed to reinforce the legal structure of segregation.

Henry B. Gonzalez opposed the bills for twenty-two hours straight—still the record in the Texas Senate. Ronnie Dugger of *The Texas Observer* reported:

> A tall Latin man in a light blue suit and white shoes and yellow hand-kerchief was pacing around his desk on the Senate floor. It was eight o'clock in the morning. An old Negro was brushing off the soft sena-torial carpet in front of the president's rostrum. Up in the gallery, a white man stood with his back to the chamber, studying a panel of pictures of an earlier Senate. The Latin man was orating and gestur-ing in a full flood of energy, not like a man who had been talking to almost nobody for three hours and had another day and night to go.
>
> "Why did they name Gonzalez Gonzalez, if the name wasn't hon-ored in Texas at the time?" he asked. "Why did they honor Garza along with Burnet? My own forebears in Mexico bore arms against Santa Anna. There were three revolutions against Santa Anna—Texas was only one of its manifestations. Did you know that Negroes helped settle Texas? That a Negro died at the Alamo?"
>
> The angry, crystal-voiced man stopped in his pacing and raised his arms to plead, "I seek to register the plaintive cry, the hurt feelings, the silent, the dumb protest of the inarticulate. . . ."
>
> For 22 hours he held the floor, an eloquent, an erudite, a genuine and a passionate man; and any whose minds he didn't enter had slammed the doors and buried the keys.

What you have to remember about a twenty-two-hour filibuster, still the record, is that it requires more than enormous physical stamina. You have to have twenty-two hours' worth of knowledge in your head—and having heard many a shorter filibuster, I can testify that many people do not. They just don't know enough to talk that long, not to mention talking that long at such a level of historical, constitutional, legal, and judicial knowledge, in addition to the extraordinary passion for justice that animated the whole.

Henry B. read widely his whole life and spoke four languages. That he was dismissed on the floor of the Texas Senate as a "lousy Mexican" was just a tiny part of the contempt and hatred that he experienced because of his skin color. Henry B.'s filibuster finally killed all but two or three of the whole hateful package.

When someone like Henry B. dies, as Gonzalez did Tuesday, I sometimes think those platitudinous tributes "fearless champion of the underdog, honorable and principled" actually get in the way of those who did not know the late, sainted whoever. Henry B. was not a saint. He was a boxer.

When he was seventy years old, some fool called him a communist, so Henry B. decked the guy. At the time, Henry B. claimed that although he was provoked, he had still acted in a restrained manner. "If I had acted out of passion, that fellow would still not be able to eat chalupas."

Henry B. once observed of a long-ago bit of political correctness that someone calling himself "Latin American" was just "a Mexican with a poll tax." As high-flown as his rhetoric could be—Senator Phil Gramm once called him "the old blowhard"—it was often laced with mordant humor. He was always being outspent in his campaigns and would tell his supporters, "You can drink his beer and eat his tamales, but when you go to the polls, vote for Gonzalez!"

As you look back on his career, what's astonishing is how principled, consistent, and right he was. In his thirty-seven years in Congress, he lived entirely on his salary and refused to take contributions from the special interests affected by the committees on which he served, including all his years as chairman of the Banking Committee.

The man never sold out to anyone, from his early service on the San Antonio City Council—where he fought to desegregate public swimming pools—to the great stand on the hate bills in the Senate, through the thirty-seven years in Congress.

He was right about deregulating the S&Ls—he was one of a handful who opposed that lobby-engineered disaster. He was right about Mexican banks not being strong enough for NAFTA.

He was right about Ronald Reagan's HUD secretary's misusing his office. Because Henry B. had long been a champion of public housing, he saw the department being twisted. It took Henry C.—i.e., Cisneros—several years to untwist it.

Henry B. told us how often PAC money turned our own representatives against us. He warned us about the concentration of power in ever-larger banks.

Henry B. was a powerful man for a long time. But he never forgot where he came from and what it was like. His best friend's mother went blind from hand-sewing baby clothes at five cents a piece.

Dugger told a story of him that I cannot forget.

Henry B.'s parents were from Durango, but he was born in San Antonio. He started haunting the public library when he was eight, but when he started junior high, his accent was still so thick that they made fun of him.

He had read that Demosthenes of Athens developed his oratory by shouting at the sea with pebbles in his mouth. So Henry B. would read Thomas Carlyle aloud with pebbles in his mouth "until Poppa thought I was nuts and told me to stop."

He had a friend correct his enunciation as he read Robert Louis Stevenson. And on some nights, his sisters and brothers would creep up to his bedroom window and watch him declaiming to a mirror, and then they would run off giggling.

**November 2000**

# Shrub-watch

∎

EVERY NOW AND again Shrub W. Bush will stop you faster than pullin' on the whoa reins. You can go along for long periods thinkin' to yourself, "Don't agree with him about dog, but he seems like an amiable fellow." And then he says something that sort of makes your teeth hurt.

One time W. got to describin' the first time he ran for office—the Boy Bush was an unsuccessful candidate for Congress in 1978 out in West Texas—George Mahon's old seat, district runs from Lubbock to Midland/Odessa to hell and gone. Dubya allowed the race had startled his friends: "They were a little confused about why I was doing this, but at that time, Jimmy Carter was president, and he was trying to control natural gas prices, and I felt the United States was headed toward European-style socialism."

So there you are, trying to envision the very Baptist Brother Carter as a "European-style socialist." Well, Carter does build homes for poor folk without charging, and if that doesn't prove it, what would? Besides, West Texas oilmen, of which W. was one at the time, think everyone to the left of Trent Lott is a socialist. Reminds me of a story. One time in those very same years the ineffable Good Time Charlie Wilson and Bob Krueger, a Shakespeare scholar last seen in a political ad imitating Arnold Schwarzenegger—two of the finest minds the Peculiar State has ever sent to Congress—cooked up a scheme to deregulate the price of natural gas in such a way that everybody in West Texas would get stinking rich and all you Yankees would have to pay through the nose. They were delicately tap-dancing this masterpiece of reverse socialism through the Commerce Committee one afternoon by the time-tested ploy of sending everyone to sleep (the ploy works best right after lunch) with excruciatingly boring testimony. Wilson swears every Yankee on the committee was snoring when, to his horror, the late Jim Collins, a Dallas Republican, came to and caught the fatal words *gas prices*.

"Gas prices?! Gas prices?!" shrieked Collins, waking up all the napping Yankees. "We wouldn't have gas prices this high if it weren't for all this school busing. It's school busing, busing all these Nigras and all these little white children for integration, that's what's driving up gas prices!" And he was off on an anti-busing rant that would not quit. By this time, both Wilson and Krueger were on their hands and knees under the table trying to unplug Collins' mike, but it was too late. The Yankees promptly voted to squelch deregulation of natural gas under the impression that they were carrying on the legacy of Martin Luther King Jr.

Collins is the man who once moved me, in the days when I wrote for *The Dallas Times Herald*, to observe, "If his IQ slips any lower, we'll have to water him twice a day."

Probably the best known of the "whoa" moments with W. Bush comes from an interview with Tucker Carlson printed in *Talk* magazine, concerning the execution of Karla Faye Tucker. Bush has now signed more than one hundred warrants of execution, but, as you may recall, the born-again Tucker drew attention both for being female and for having an extensive prison ministry.

> In the weeks before the execution, Bush says, Bianca Jagger and a number of other protesters came to Austin to demand clemency for Tucker. "Did you meet with any of them?" I ask.
>
> Bush whips around and stares at me. "No, I didn't meet with any of them," he snaps, as though I've just asked the dumbest, most offensive question ever posed. "I didn't meet with Larry King either when he came down for it. I watched his interview with [Tucker], though. He asked her real difficult questions, like, 'What would you say to Governor Bush?'"
>
> "What was her answer?" I wonder.
>
> "'Please,'" Bush whimpers, his lips pursed in mock desperation, "'don't kill me.'"
>
> I must look shocked—ridiculing the pleas of a condemned prisoner who has since been executed seems odd and cruel, even for someone as militantly anticrime as Bush—because he immediately stops smirking.

Tucker also reported that the exchange mimicked by Bush never took place; Bush made it up.

Well, that was a moment.

Another came during one of Bush's rare appearances on a Sunday chat show. (Ann Richards used to call him "the phantom candidate"; political reporters on his national campaign say he is "in the bubble," rarely let out for an unscripted performance.) Tim Russert asked Bush who on the Supreme Court he most admired. "Scalia," said Bush promptly. And after a second's thought, "and Clarence Thomas."

He sure can pick 'em. If you are a heavy-duty right-winger, as opposed to the moderate, compassionate conservative, Scalia is a good pick. First-rate mind, hideous politics. But no one covering the Court, regardless of politics, has ever chosen Clarence Thomas as a standout. The best I've ever seen written about him, by people who consider Scalia a great justice, is that he's adequate. Everyone else, including those of no noticeable ideological persuasion, considers "adequate" far too kind.

Thomas, of course, was W.'s daddy's pick. I don't do Siggie Freud myself, being completely unqualified. I leave that to such great minds as Gail Sheehy. But W. does have a daddy problem. Pretty much the entire record of his life is daddy, but it's not his fault. His name is not George W. Smith: What the hell was he supposed to do? Be a big enough fool to throw it all away? Nevertheless, it does sometimes trap him into ridiculous positions.

Twice in the past few weeks we've seen Bush, as we so rarely do, outside the bubble in "debate" with fellow Republican candidates. Myself, I think mah fellow pundits have been entirely too polite. In the first Republican debate in New Hampshire, Bush was, at best, "adequate." In the Arizona debate, he was just bloody awful. Call a spade a spade, troops. If you will pardon a personal note here, I was in hospital, facing a delayed surgical proceeding, during the entire hour-and-a-half debate, and by the end of it, I was screaming, "Put me under the knife! I can't take any more!"

A note here for those of you who will be following "Shrub-watch" in the coming weeks. I am a Texan, and we are notoriously soft on our own: I drew the line at Phil Gramm (who wouldn't?), but I can still give a lecture on the virtues of John Connally (when he was a Democrat) on occasion. Texas liberals (screw you, it's not an oxymoron) are persons of large political tolerance. I may intervene from time to time to explain certain political/cultural phenomena—such as why W. Bush keeps leaning into people and touching them—but I plan to limit myself mostly to the geopolitical terrain with which I am most familiar. I know what kind of governor this guy has been—if you expect him to do for the nation what he has for Texas, we need to talk.

**Shrub**

# Gems of Opacity

∎

YOU MAY THINK A person would bring up the subject of political rhetoric in our day only to dis it, to mourn the decline of the once-noble art, to compare the puny babble of our modern pipsqueaks to the magnificent cadences of Jefferson, Lincoln, and Churchill, and so lament anew. Not me.

What I mourn is that none of the current candidates measures up to the glory years of the Ineffable Big George Bush and the Immortal Dan Quayle, who shall be forever revered for setting new standards in political language.

My personal favorite in the oratory sweepstakes is George W. Bush, who is rapidly developing a style that may yet become comparable to his father's. He is a master of the perfectly opaque response. We now know that Ronald Reagan's famous line in the 1980 campaign—"There you go again!"—was carefully scripted in advance. This leads to visions of an entire team of W. Bush speech writers cogitating on how to achieve the perfect nonanswer. Examples:

"Whatever's fair."

"Whatever's right."

"I'm all right on that."

"Whatever is fair between the parties."

And, a recent gem of opacity:

"I will take a balanced approach on the environment."

That last one was Bush's death-defying leap to separate himself from all the candidates who have promised to take an unbalanced approach on the environment.

During an impassioned speech in support of free trade this month, Bush said, "If the terriers and bariffs are torn down, this economy will grow!"

Another great moment with Bush the Younger was his answer to the question, "Do you support affirmative action?"

Said the governor: "What I am against is quotas. I am against hard quotas,

quotas they basically delineate based upon whatever. However they delineate, quotas, I think vulcanize society. So I don't know how that fits into what everybody else is saying, their relative positions, but that's my position."

In South Carolina he told supporters: "This is still a dangerous world. It's a world of madmen and uncertainty and potential mential loss." OK, maybe it was "menshul."

the *Financial Times* of London noted that the Education Governor revealed the urgent need for higher standards in subject-verb agreement when he said, "Rarely is the question asked: Is our children learning?"

If you cast your mind back to the long-gone days of 1992, you may recall that after four years of Big George's pronounless prose, Bill Clinton was considered something of a wonder because he spoke in complete sentences. Indeed, in complete paragraphs. People actually wrote about it at the time: "He speaks in complete sentences."

Of course, that was compared to Big George, who once delivered this complete sentence: "It's no exaggeration to say the undecideds could go one way or the other." And a more typical bon mot: "To kind of suddenly try and get my hair colored, and dance up and down in a mini-skirt or something, you know, show that I've got a lot of jazz out there and drop a bunch of one-liners, I'm running for the president of the United States. I kind of think I'm a scintillating fellow."

And this happy thought on the recession: "Coming off a pinnacle, you might say, of low unemployment."

We were also accustomed to hearing from Dan Quayle in those days ("If we don't succeed, then we run the risk of failure"), so we're starting from a low threshold here—the rhetorical equivalent of having Dick Morris shape domestic policy.

*The Nation* recently described Al Gore as "an attack chihuahua" for a series of observations that cannot be described as in the positive vein. Gore accused Bill Bradley of being a quitter, a hypocrite, a disloyal Democrat, a "left-of-center insurgent," who would break the bank with his "throwback" healthcare proposal while addressing "only a small number of things at a time."

*The Nation* notes that Gore is a charter member of the Democratic Leadership Council, which campaigns for privatizing Social Security and voucherizing Medicare and school choice. This has not prevented Gore from assailing Bradley for proposing a debate on Social Security reforms and voucher experiments.

The only thing to be said for Gore's performance is that he can get through an entire debate without using the word *whatever*.

According to *The Dallas Morning News*, during the last debate in Iowa, when Alan Keyes accused Bush of doing nothing when the town of El Cenizo adopted Spanish as the language for all official business, Bush replied, "No es el verdad" (That's not the truth). That would, of course, be "la verdad" in Spanish.

Reminding us all of Jim Hightower's line when he was informed that Governor Bill Clements was studying Spanish: "Oh, good. Now he'll be bi-ignorant."

**January 2000**

# Blushing for Bush

■

WATCHING OUR HOMEBOY George Dubya as he wends his way—somewhat unsteadily—toward the presidency is a nerve-racking procedure. Face it, our reputation is on the line along with the governor's. All of us know that twenty million Texans can't be brought to agree on anything, including whether the guys who died at the Alamo were heroes or fools. Nevertheless, we are all being painted with the Bush brush, so whenever he makes a cake of himself, all of us get the blame ("Those Texans, so ignorant").

Relatively speaking, Bush is one of our better representatives on the national scene. In Washington, which seems to have been deeply scarred by LBJ's occasional lack of couth, we are still regarded as a tribe of Visigoths. ("And then, he lifted his shirt and showed us the scar!") Every time Governor Preston Smith, who had a terminal West Texas accent, went on television, I used to wince: "Our biggest problem after this hurricane is all the day-brees we got lyin' around." So, Dubya Bush doesn't seem like anyone we'd have to blush for.

But one national columnist, writing this week about how Bush favors the concealed-weapons law—and the amendment to the law that allows concealed weapons to be carried in church—wrote, "Apparently Texans feel so naked without their guns that they cannot even take time off to pray without the reassurance of their little metal friends nestled somewhere warmly on their persons." Another columnist decided not long ago to blame all twenty million of us for "bloodthirsty criminal justice officials. . . . Texas, where liberals are required to carry visas and compassion is virtually illegal . . . a state perfectly willing to execute the retarded and railroad the innocent . . . by far the most backward state in the nation when it comes to capital punishment . . ." etc.

So when Bush commits a gaffe, we all look bad, which brings us to the unfortunate matter of Jean Poutine, who is not the prime minister of Canada.

Some joker from a Canadian radio comedy show told Bush he had been endorsed by "Prime Minister Poutine of Canada." Whereupon Bush thanked the prime minister for his support and said how important our neighbors to the north are to us all. Unfortunately, *poutine* is a form of Canadian junk food made with potatoes, cheese, and brown gravy (sounds awful). Granted, you can't find a quorum of Texans who know who the prime minister of Canada is, so this sounds at first like another one of those stupid "gotcha" quizzes. But any Texan who's ever been involved in national politics does know that no foreign head of state would ever make an endorsement in either a primary or a general election.

Ever heard the phrase "that's an internal political matter"? If a head of state were to violate this long-standing diplomatic tradition, it would be a matter for stiff notes between state departments, apologies demanded—for all I know, breaks threatened in diplomatic relations and ambassadors recalled. It would be a whale of a flap. Why didn't Bush know that? True, the United States has been known to favor one side or the other in a foreign election. Among other memorable episodes, we worked to defeat Salvador Allende in Chile in the seventies, with the usual dubious results. But we do things like that *covertly;* we don't have the president instructing citizens of other countries on how he wants them to vote. Think of the ruckus.

**March 2000**

# The 2000 Vote

■

As GENERAL GEORGE PATTON said of war, "God help me, but I love it so." I realize that the only people in America having a good time right now are political reporters, but we haven't had this much fun since Grandpa fell in the fish pond. What could be more exciting than David Broder and Tom Oliphant trading thoughts on whether a heavy black voter turnout in north Florida will make all the difference?

OK, Nader voters. Let's talk.

I'm voting for Ralph. I'm voting for Nader because I believe in him, admire him, and would like to see his issues and policies triumph in our political life. I'm also voting for him because I live in Texas—where all thirty-two electoral votes will go to George W. Bush even if I stand on my head, turn blue, and vote for Gus Hall, the late communist.

I know that many of my fellow Nader voters are young people and probably don't want to hear from a geriatric progressive. (We had to walk three miles through the snow, barefoot, uphill both ways.) But I have learned some things just from hanging around this long, and with your permission, I will pass them on.

When I was your age, I was, I suspect, far angrier than most of you. Some people I loved died in Vietnam—it was an ugly, bad, nasty time. We'll not go into it again, but in 1968, I could not bring myself to vote for Hubert Humphrey. So I helped elect Richard Nixon president by writing in Gene McCarthy; and if you ask me, thirty years on, it's hard to think of a worse turn I could have done my country.

Nixon was a sorry, sick human being, with a gift for exploiting lower-middle-class resentment, envy, and bigotry for his own political purposes. This country remains a nastier place today because of Nixon.

None of that has any particular relevance to the election in 2000. Dan

Quayle was no Jack Kennedy, and George W. Bush is no Richard Nixon. What's more relevant here is my forty years' experience in Texas electoral politics.

Not to Texas-brag, but we are No. 1 in the art of Lesser Evilism. I have voted for candidates so putrid that it makes your teeth hurt to think about 'em. Why? Because they were better than the other guy.

So here you are, trying to spot that fine hairsbreadth of difference between the sanctimonious Gore and the clueless Bush, ready to damn both of them in favor of a straight shooter like Nader. Here's the problem: Government matters most to people on the margins. If I may be blunt about this, we live in a society where the effluent flows downhill. And the people on the bottom are drowning in it.

And it is precisely those citizens—whose lives sometimes literally depend on the difference between a politician who really does have a plan to help with the cost of prescription drugs and one who is only pretending that he does—whose lives can be harmed by your idealism.

The size of a tax cut doesn't matter to people in the richest 1 percent. They're in Fat City now; they don't need more money. But the size of a tax cut makes a real difference to Bush's oft-cited example of the single mom with two kids making $22,000 a year.

When you are barely making it in this society, hanging on by your fingernails, with every unexpected expense a crisis, it matters which is the lesser of two evils.

I know it's hard for young people to envision age or illness, or the sick feeling of frantic despair when your old wreck of a car finally dies (it always does this in traffic) and will not start again. People who work two and even three jobs to support their kids get so tired—you can't imagine how tired—and guilt and depression and anxiety all pile on, too. The difference between Gore and Bush matters to those folks.

This is an old argument between radicals and liberals; sometimes I'm on one side, and sometimes I'm on the other. In the primaries, I vote to change the world; in November, I vote for a sliver more for programs that help the needy.

I do not believe that things have to get worse before they can get better. I think you will find that most mothers object to the idea that you would deliberately do something to make a child's life worse in order to bring about some presumed greater good in the long run. I believe that the best can be the enemy of the better. I believe in taking half a loaf, or even a slice.

And how do we ever change the whole rotten system at that speed? Brick by brick, child by child, slowly, toward liberty and justice for all. The urgent, crucial need right now is to fix the money in politics. It can be done, it will be done, it is being done, and we will get better politics.

In Texas, we'll vote for Nader and a perfect world. You swing-state progressives need to make the hard choice—but you're not making it just for yourselves. Good luck to you all.

October 2000

# America 2000

IN THE LONG VIEW of history—always a consoling perspective at a time like this—the 2000 presidential campaign most likely will rank as a giant waste of time.

Our future depends on The Stuff They Wouldn't Talk About—economic globalization, global warming, the spread of AIDS, the need for some social control of new technologies, and the corruption of our political system. Al and Tipper Gore's big smooch got more ink.

Having set the proper tone of superiority here—it is now obligatory for journalists to drip disdain on the democratic process as we assist in deforming it—may I say that I'm mad as hell? Not only has this been a stupid campaign, but it has been a deceitful one.

Gore's reputation as a fibber and an exaggerator is apparently set in stone—despite the fact that he never claimed to have invented the Internet (although he assisted at its creation), that he was in fact a model for the lead character in *Love Story* (the stiff), that he never claimed he had discovered Love Canal, and that he did in fact have to work hard on his father's farm in Tennessee when he was a boy. That's the way it goes in Medialand.

Meanwhile, Texans have been enjoying the surreal experience of discovering that we live in Paradise and that we owe it all to George W. Bush, the fifth-most-important official in the state.

Now, the fact is that our state has a rotten record and always has had a rotten record, and that's a consequence of public policy here. We're a low-tax, low-service state, so we rank poorly on everything that government does.

Our public health care stinks; our criminal justice system is deeply racist (not to mention that it encourages lawyers to catch up on much-needed sleep); and we have a few other problems that would curl hair in someplace like Iowa.

Mostly, people here don't much notice any of this, being used to it. And besides, we're Texans, so we're actually proud of it.

Then along comes this campaign, and suddenly our governor is telling the rest of the country that we lead the nation in education and that he personally is responsible for this astonishing turn of events; that everyone in Texas has full access to health care; that each prisoner we fry has a competent lawyer; that the governor himself led the fight for a strong Patients' Bill of Rights; and that our air and water are crystal-clear under his environmentally friendly leadership.

(Actually, Bush never really made that last claim—he just says the other guy is lying when he says Texas is real polluted, even though it's real polluted.)

When all this started, I used to tell people calmly: "Well, I think you ought to look at his record, because it's pretty clear, and you can make up your mind from that." Now I feel like standing out by the highway in the rain with a sign that says: DON'T VOTE FOR GEORGE W. BUSH—HE'S NOT UP TO THE JOB.

I'm sorry—the man is inadequate. You cannot slide through life on your daddy's name, turning in a poor performance in school and the military, and a distinctly questionable performance in the business world, loaf through a few years in baseball trading Sammy Sosa, and then tell outrageous lies about your part-time performance in a powerless job. This is silly.

One of the few truly eerie things about W. is his inability to admit that he did it all on luck. Lots of people are born lucky in life, but they're not born blind to that fact. No one is asking him to feel guilty about it; awareness would suffice.

I've never found Bush ill-intentioned—just oblivious. In fact, I suspect that he's rather easily touched by people with sadder lives than his own.

What Bush does not get is the connection between policy and results in real people's lives. He really thinks we'd be better off if most of government was done by charities. He thinks that nice corporate polluters will volunteer to cut down on filth. I know he's good at politics, but he is not interested in governing. It bores him; he has no attention span for it.

If this were just an election that was going to put a lightweight in the White House, I wouldn't feel so bad. We can survive that. But I'm not sure that we can survive what comes with Bush, or more precisely, what's behind him.

On November 2, *The Wall Street Journal* ran a rather chilling article about the Business-Industry Political Action Committee, "an organization dedicated to keeping Congress in pro-business hands."

It was specifically about a congressional district in Kentucky where local and national business interests have organized to protect an incumbent who voted against the Patients' Bill of Rights. That's a simple fight: On one side you have the people, and on the other side you have the HMOs. So the HMOs are now buying that district.

Our political system is corrupted by money, and the only thing that George W. Bush wants to do about it is make it worse.

**November 2000**

# Lord Help Us

◼

GOOD GRIEF. HOLY COW. Wow. And Lord help us.

I don't know who wrote the script for this election, but it was so far over the top that the perp should be chucked out of the screenwriters' guild.

Naturally, we can think of reasons to be chipper about the outcome. George W. Bush is not a mean man, and he is not a nincompoop. This may strike you as faint praise, but media expectations about Bush have been so low that it sometimes seems necessary to report, "Look, he can jump over a match-box."

Besides, he has that same daffy inability to get a grip on the English language that his father has, thus providing glorious material for political humorists.

I happen to think that Bush is quite good at the political end of politics—at holding together a disparate coalition, at reaching out to unlikely suspects, and at making himself generally liked. There is much talk of a national-unity kind of government, rather like the one that Ehud Barak is trying to create in Israel. (Put a Democrat or two in the cabinet.)

The trouble is, when you win a close race, you owe all the members of your coalition big-time. You can't say to the National Rifle Association or the Confederation of Roof Manufacturers, "Go take a leap—we could have won without you." You pretty much have to say, "So what do you want?"

The only reason to be down about a Bush presidency is the money. We may well have just lost our last shot for a very long time at getting anything done about the money in politics. Unless John McCain makes fixing soft money the price of his participation—and the Bushies may not want him on the inside—we're not going to see campaign finance reform.

A House led by Tom DeLay and Dick Armey and a Senate led by Trent Lott and Mitch McConnell are not going to commit public campaign financing. Business just outspent labor in this election by more than 15 to 1, and the business folks ran the table, as they say in pool. They took it all.

And that means they're going to be even more difficult to dislodge next time, because it's harder to beat incumbents.

So it really will have to get worse before it gets better, as radicals often argue—and if the special interests lose their heads and go into a greed frenzy, as they did with tax cuts at the beginning of the Reagan years, that's what's going to happen. We already have a political system painfully close to legalized bribery, and it could get worse.

Because Bush is not interested in public policy—it notoriously bores him—what we've gotten in Texas is staff-driven policy. Texas doesn't have a cabinet form of executive; in Washington, Bush could theoretically put a team of Republican all-stars in the cabinet and govern that way, which might work out quite well.

There is still some question in my mind as to just how ideological Bush actually is. Some of Bush's early appointments as governor, especially the trio of pollution-loving watchdogs he put in at the state environmental protection agency, were quite eye-popping. But we've rarely seen hard-edged ideology from him in recent years, and he certainly ran well toward the center, and indeed ran away from the more right-wing parts of his own record.

All of which indicates that he's quite a fast learner. When you approve of a politician, this is known as flexibility; when you don't, it's called lack of principle—but in fact, politics requires accommodation. I'd be a lot more worried about Bush if he hadn't demonstrated flexibility.

If Bush has a mandate, it is to be a uniter and not a divider, to work with Democrats as well as Republicans and to restore civility in Washington. True story: In 1992, a governor named Bill Clinton told me that he thought the main reason he would be a good president was because he had been able to work well with Republicans in Arkansas.

May Bush have better luck.

**November 2000**

# Blushing for Bush II

■

FOR TERRIFIC ENTERTAINMENT, watch the Washington press corps swoon over George W. Bush. The famous charm offensive (he's calling congressmen by cute nicknames, like "Big George") has the chatting classes producing the most priceless gushing heard since Newt Gingrich bestrode the political world like a colossus.

The more alert among them have noticed that the policies don't seem to quite perfectly reflect the charm offensive. Welcome to Dubya's World's: Bush is a walking definition of cognitive dissonance—what you see is not what you get.

Frank Rich of *The New York Times* noted that in his relentless photo ops, Bush has "surely posed with more black Americans than voted for him." As Texans know, the eternal Bush photo op of the man posing yet again with small children of minority persuasion is always stepped up just before he does something awful. Like trying to knock 200,000 poor kids off a federal medical insurance program. This is compassionate conservatism.

Several of the swifter students in D.C. have questioned Bush's executive order reinstituting the Reagan gag rule on women's health clinics abroad, pointing out that the only consequence of this policy is to increase the number of abortions, as more women are unable to get contraceptives.

The question arises: Do we think Bush realizes this and did it anyway to pay off the religious right, or do we think he doesn't get it? And the answer, as always with Bush, is . . . it's hard to tell.

No one has ever been able to figure out if he understands the consequences of his policies. Or, as is frequently the case, if he knows his policies are having contradictory results.

One of the funniest weekend thumb-suckers was by Richard Berke in *The New York Times*, announcing to an astonished world that there are some Democrats who are still angry about the election. Imagine! Berke reports with a straight face, "This fury can be hard to detect in Washington, where, Mr. Ashcroft aside, every day brings more images of cheery Democrats embracing Mr. Bush."

The noncheery Democrats include Susan Albach of Dallas, who is in the ranks of those who are Not Handling This Well.

"Are you in anger or depression?" I inquired.

"I'm still in denial," she announced firmly.

The really smart folks in Washington are those keeping an eye on the numbers—how big is this tax cut, already at $2 trillion, going to get once the corporate lobbyists start porking out on it, and what's left for anything else? The profoundly dumb people in Washington are going around saying, "Recessions are good for you."

I love this line of argument, especially from pundits who make more than $1 million a year. Yes, they gravely opine, recessions are part of the business cycle (these are the same people who were saying until last month that we were in a New Economy and could look forward to perpetual growth), and furthermore, they are morally good for us. They cure irrational exuberance and hubris.

No one can deny that irrational exuberance and hubris have abounded in recent years, but that's not who gets punished by recessions. Last hired, first fired.

The working people who never got ahead at all in the nineties are the very ones who will be losing their jobs now, and the fatuous complacency with which the prospect is being greeted is another example of a disconnect so enormous that it's funny.

Sort of. But then, to quote Berke again, "This fury can be hard to detect in Washington."

**January 2001**

# Bush and Energy

■

GEORGE W. BUSH IS threatening to give us an energy policy that marches militantly in exactly the wrong direction.

Bush's views on energy are still those of a West Texas oilman. What oilmen want for energy policy is Drill More.

At one point during a debate with Al Gore, Bush suggested we encourage drilling in Mexico to lessen our dependence on "foreign" oil. Startled the Mexicans.

In addition to Bush, who took three oil companies into financial trouble, the new administration boasts Dick Cheney, CEO of Halliburton; Commerce Secretary Don Evans, chairman of Tom Brown oil; and Condoleezza Rice, a director of Chevron. Two of Bush's biggest donors are Ken Lay of Enron and energy player Sam Wyly, who put up the money for the phony ad praising Bush's environmental record.

The first fight is likely to be over the Arctic National Wildlife Refuge. Bush favors drilling in the ecologically fragile area, as does his choice for interior secretary, Gale Norton. The object of all the drilling is to bring prices down (not too far) so as to encourage consumption, thus causing us to use ever more fossil fuel. This is the totally backward way of going about an energy policy.

You can't get elected dog catcher in this country by advocating a sensible energy policy, which would certainly include slapping an additional tax on gasoline in order to discourage consumption. Even if that smart move is off the table because of politics, one can still push for more fuel-efficient cars.

There is a plan already in existence to ratchet up fuel efficiency, but it has been on hold for years as automobile lobbyists successfully fought its implementation by Congress.

Spencer Abraham, Bush's pick for energy secretary, was one of the leading players in the fight to put off higher fuel-efficiency standards. Abraham compiled a zero rating from the League of Conservation Voters.

Americans use five times as much fossil fuel as the other people on this planet on average, so of course we are contributing the lion's share of carbon dioxide, which is what causes global warming.

Bush would rather not think about that. Upton Sinclair once wrote, "It is difficult to get a man to understand something when his salary depends on his not understanding it." The income of those in oil depends on their not understanding global warming.

Understandably, the industry has put a significant amount of money into a public relations campaign trying to convince people that global warming is not happening, or not happening fast enough to worry about, or needs more study. I suspect that someday—before too long—that campaign will be seen as the wickedness it is.

The other part of the looming energy crisis was caused by the stupid deregulation of the utilities industry, and don't say I didn't warn you. Bush supported deregulation in Texas, and if his plan had been passed, Texas would be in as bad a shape as California, which deregulated only wholesale prices. We passed a more progressive version of deregulation, no thanks to Bush.

The dereg movement is not working—the new market-based system has not produced needed generating capacity, and those who own the power plants are ripping off everyone else.

Economist Paul Krugman points out that the problem is underinvestment, and "part of the reason for that underinvestment was the excessive enthusiasm of the financial markets for all things tech: When digital businesses are valued at hundreds of times earnings, while utilities have multiples more like ten, who's going to put money into boring things like generators and transmission grids?"

The usual "leave everything to the magic of the marketplace" crowd needs to take another look at the consequences of deregulation. The same power companies that failed to make the badly needed investments are now making money out the wazoo. Some marketplace. Some magic.

The reason that the utility industry was regulated in the first place is because it's a natural monopoly, and experience with monopolies indicates that you have to regulate the things. This is one of those deals, like the S&L mess, when you want to go back and check who pushed the ill-advised plan and what promises were made. (More energy! Cheaper rates! Pie in sky!) You would be well-advised not to listen to those same players again.

**January 2001**

# Bush and Energy II

■

**B**ACK-TO-BACK SPEECHES by the veeper and the only president we've got beggar the imagination. Let's have a new rule: If you pronounce the word *nukular,* you shouldn't go around nullifying nuclear treaties. Or building nuclear power plants.

When in the course of human events a treaty becomes outdated, the smart country does not announce it is breaking the treaty. This is unpleasantly reminiscent of numerous chapters involving Native Americans. Instead, the smart country calls upon its dear ally (provided they're still speaking) to renegotiate the treaty. This has a less threatening effect on the ally.

I don't know if a National Missile Defense system will work, and neither do you. Most experts not employed by the defense industry are dubious about it at best, but you never know how far we could get if we spend enough time and money on it. If we spend the first $60 billion, we'll probably be a lot further along than we are now, thus justifying the next $60 billion.

The problem is, it's massively stupid in terms of national security. What's a bigger threat to the United States: North Korea or global warming? Our children will live to see the answer to that. It's their future we're playing with.

Hearing Dick Cheney make a speech that was outdated by the standards of the oil industry in the 1960s was eerie. Reactionary Texas oilmen are thick on the ground here, but Cheney is a throwback. Not since the late H. L. Hunt was crawling around (which he did—crawl) have we heard such nonsense.

Cheney's National Energy Policy Development Group—two Texas oilmen, a CEO from the electricity-gobbling aluminum industry, and a tool of the energy companies, all members of the cabinet, meeting in secret—is pushing coal—hard. Unfortunately, it is the dirtiest source of electricity generation:

The administration not only has reneged on its promise to curb coal pollution, but now it proposes to ease the pollution controls already in place.

Naturally, the group is also pushing oil and gas—major contributors to global warming—and, incredibly enough, deemphasizing conservation. What kind of energy policy would abandon conservation, which is effective and costs nothing? OPEC is the only thing hurt by it. Under the Bush budget plan, renewable energy programs lose 36 percent of their piddly total funding of $373 million, according to *New Technology Week.*

Wind-generated electricity is already cheaper than nuclear-generated electricity. It's highly probable solar-powered photo-voltaic systems will also be cheaper before long: The city of San Francisco votes this fall on whether to back a $250 million bond issue for solar power. If we put $60 billion into researching and improving renewables, we'd not only save money, we could save the world. Quite literally.

One easy and simple way to bring down the price of gasoline is by letting fuel efficiency standards rise to where they already would be if the auto companies had not interfered via generous contributions to Congress. Some remarkable reporting by Jeff Plungis of the *Detroit News* reveals the auto companies have now wired the study being conducted by the National Academy of Sciences on fuel efficiency.

Nine of the thirteen panel members have ties either to the auto or oil industry; are free-market economists who do not believe in government regulation; or have criticized fuel efficiency standards in a very public way. My favorite guy on the panel is the "safety expert" who claims fuel efficiency standards have killed tens of thousands of people by forcing them into smaller cars.

Meanwhile, back in the world, fuel efficiency is at a twenty-year low, mainly due to the popularity of SUVs. Congress first passed fuel efficiency standards in 1975, when the average car got less than 14 miles per gallon. By 1985, under the required standards, that doubled to 27.5 mpg. It has since slipped to 24 mpg. Plungis reports that automakers have shifted virtually all their technological gains into bigger and more powerful engines, rather than improving fuel efficiency.

SUVs consume an additional 280,000 barrels of oil in this country every day. That is 15 percent of what OPEC cut in production in March 1999, according to news reports—the event that nearly doubled the price of gas. Half the new cars sold are now SUVs. It is neither difficult nor onerous to improve their mileage: It would cost about $700 additional per vehicle, but with a fuel saving of about $2,500 over the life of the behemoth.

Speaking of campaign contributions, *Time* magazine reports Cheney's aides consulted with the West Virginia coal baron Buck Harless, a Bush pioneer (at least $100,000); Stephen Addington of AEI Resources, whose executives gave more than $600,000 to Republicans last election; and of course, our old favorites, Peabody Energy—the biggest coal miner in the country—whose chairman gave over $250,000. Could this payoff possibly be more obvious?

**February 2001**

# Bush's Drug Problem

THAT WAS QUITE A remarkable moment that George W. Bush had in Mexico. You may have missed it or even assumed he was just pointing out the obvious again, but consider the implications of the president of the United States saying in Mexico, "One of the reasons why drugs are shipped, the main reason why drugs are shipped through Mexico to the United States, is because United States citizens use drugs." And that's not the first time that Bush has pointed out that our problem is not supply but demand.

Now, this does not necessarily mean that Bush has thought through the policy implications of his statement. Policy does not, actually, interest him much.

And it is also possible that he's suffering from cognitive dissonance on the subject, a disconnect common to politicians of all stripes. But the futility of the War on Drugs is apparent to everyone except politicians terrified of the dread accusation "Soft on Drugs."

The sad history of efforts to eradicate drug use in this country is pockmarked with recurring waves of hysteria, usually involving the association of some drug with some minority group. The Chinese and their opium dens, Mexicans and marijuana, blacks and crack—we literally scare ourselves silly, getting so scared of the menace of drugs that we react stupidly. That politicians feed our fears, milk them for electoral advantage, is another part of the sad pattern.

At the very least, I think we can expect Bush to support scrapping the annoying and presumptuous process of certification—our annual passing of judgment on Mexico's antidrug efforts. At best, Bush may see the real political opportunity here.

The cost of the War on Drugs, both in lives and dollars, is staggering. And people know it isn't working. The first party to stand up and say so will get a real windfall.

Bill Clinton, on his way out of office, told *Rolling Stone* magazine that he supports decriminalization of small amounts of marijuana and an end to the disparity of sentences for crack use vs. cocaine use. Of course, it wasn't terribly helpful of him to say this on his way out the door. NOW he questions mandatory sentences for nonviolent drug offenders.

But it is possible for practicing politicians to take these stands as well. The Republican governor of New Mexico, Gary Johnson, is famous for his crusade against draconian drug laws.

The terrific new film *Traffic* underscores the futility of the War on Drugs. We have a million people in prison on drug charges—more than the entire prison population of Western Europe. Federal spending has increased from $1 billion in 1980 to $20 billion on the drug war last year, and the states spend even more. Yet drugs are as available as ever. Both cocaine and heroin have gotten cheaper and purer during the past twenty years. This is not working.

The bad news is that Attorney General John Ashcroft has a terrible record in this area. He is a noted practitioner of the Git Tough school of political pandering. When he was in the Senate, Ashcroft denounced the idea of spending money on drug treatment as a trick to take money away from the War on Drugs.

According to *Drug War Facts*, compiled by Kendra Wright and Paul Lewin, 55 percent of all federal drug defendants are low-level offenders, such as mules or street dealers. Only 11 percent are classified as high-level dealers. Since the enactment of mandatory minimum sentencing for drug offenders, the Bureau of Prisons' budget has increased by 1,350 percent—from $220 million in 1986 to about $3.19 billion in 1997.

One of the most outrageous aspects of this is the seizure of property. During a ten-month national survey, it was discovered that 80 percent of the people who had property forfeited were never charged with a crime.

The U.S. Supreme Court has ruled that it is legal to take property from an owner who had no knowledge of its illegal use. There is no presumption of innocence, no right to an attorney, and no objection to hearsay. The burden of proof of innocence is on the property owner.

For all the money, time, and hysteria spent on the problem of illegal drugs, all illegal drugs combined kill about forty-five hundred Americans a year— 1 percent of the number killed by alcohol and tobacco. Rehabilitation is not only much cheaper than prison but also more effective in reducing drug use.

Powder cocaine and crack cocaine are two forms of the same drug with exactly the same active ingredient. The average sentence for low-level and first-time offenders for trafficking crack is ten years and six months; that's 59 percent longer than the average sentence for rapists.

So we are looking at a colossal, stupefying, incredibly expensive failure. Don't you think it's high time that we stopped pouring good money after bad?

**February 2001**

# Bush's Favorite Flavor

WHILE PRESIDENT G. W. BUSH keeps the populace amused with ludicrous policy proposals, the complete corporate takeover of government is well under way.

The pundit chorus was astounded by the diversity of Bush's cabinet appointees: blacks, Mexican Americans, a Chinese American woman, a Democrat. Wonder of wonders, a cabinet that looks like America. All hail Bush the Inclusive. This cabinet comes in exactly one flavor: corporate. Jim Hightower's newsletter, the *Hightower Lowdown*, lists the corporations now represented in the cabinet, either by former executives or by board members:

Bank of America, Dole Foods, Northwest Airlines, Columbia/HCA Health Care (Elaine Chao).

Lockheed Martin, plus major contributions from the American Trucking Association, Boeing, General Electric, Greyhound, Northwest Airlines, UPS, Union Pacific, and United Airlines (Norman Mineta).

Amoco, Chevron, Exxon, Ford, and Phillips 66, all funders of the Mountain States Legal Foundation, from whence sprang Gale Norton, plus the American Forest & Paper Association, Amoco, ARCO, the Chemical Manufacturers Association, and Ford, all funders of the Coalition of Republican Environmental Advocates, chaired by Ms. Norton.

Alcoa, International Paper Company, Eastman Kodak, and Lucent Technologies (Paul O'Neill).

QTC Medical Services, Lockheed Martin Integrated Systems, and Federal Network (Anthony Principi).

General Instrument Corporation, G. D. Searle & Co., Asea Brown Bavari, the Tribune Company, Gilead Sciences, Inc., RAND Corporation, and Salomon Smith Barney (Donald Rumsfeld).

America Online and General Dynamics (Colin Powell, who has an endless list of corporations that have paid him $100,000 to give a speech).

The oil industry is in a class by itself in this cabinet, boasting G. W. Bush himself, Veep Dick Cheney, and Commerce Secretary Donald Evans, all Texas oilmen.

John Ashcroft is particularly close to the Schering-Plough pharmaceutical company and was also heavily funded by BP Amoco, Exxon, Monsanto, Occidental Petroleum, Union Carbide, and Weyerhauser.

Spencer Abraham, the energy secretary, sponsored a bill to abolish the Energy Department and led the fight in the Senate to defeat greater fuel efficiency for SUVs, a cause dear to both auto and energy industries.

Ron Paige, the education secretary, is an enthusiastic corporatizer of the public schools. While he was superintendent in Houston, he privatized food services, payroll, and accounting, signed a contract with Coca-Cola to put Coke machines in the halls, and with Primedia Corporation to broadcast Channel One in the schools.

Ag Secretary Ann Veneman was on the board of Calgene, Inc., which produces genetically altered food, and was also connected with an agribusiness front group funded by Monsanto, Cargill, Archer Daniels Midland, Kraft, and Nestle.

Hightower once proposed that politicians be forced to wear the corporate logos of their biggest contributors on their clothes like NASCAR racers, so we'd know who they sold out to. These folks couldn't get them all on one outfit.

So you will not be amazed to learn that President Bush plans to solve the energy crisis in California by drilling for oil in the Arctic National Wildlife Refuge. Also among the prize policies announced so far: a $1.6 trillion tax cut, 42.5 percent of which goes to the wealthiest 1 percent of Americans and 60 percent to the richest 10 percent. National Missile Defense, a Rumsfeld project formerly known as Ronald Reagan's Star Wars, is being pushed along. Bush also proposed a school voucher program, now known as "opportunity scholarships," and "faith-based" social services (formerly known as "religious") by "faith-based" institutions (formerly known as "churches").

President Cognitive Dissonance is here: What you see is not what you get. What you hear is not what you get. What you get is what you get.

# W.'s Splendid Performance

■

So you had to figure George W. would skate through Europe on "the soft bigotry of low expectations" (the most memorable phrase his speechwriters have yet produced for him). He is not as bad as the Europeans thought he was—*quel triomphe!* And have our media not saluted "the spring in his step" and the hilarious moment when he greeted Prime Minister Tony Blair of Britain as "Mr. Landslide"?

What a regular guy! Plain-spoken. Straightforward.

Only Jesse Helms is grumpy.

I, too, would be enchanted by Dubya's splendid performance (only one mispronunciation of a world leader and the slight mishap concerning his assertion that Africa is a nation) if only he weren't so limited. W. Bush is not plain-spoken or straightforward. He is opaque, diaphanous, and so rarely says anything approaching actual meaning that it's headlines when he does: e.g., "Major league asshole." You can listen to an entire forty-five-minute speech by this man and still wonder, "Did he just say anything we should have noticed?" He is much given to reiteration of the obvious, as though it were news. This just in: "The cold war is over."

Having it both ways is something of a W. Bush signature. For example, when he was governor, he opposed the state's Patients' Bill of Rights, first vetoing the bill in '95 and later letting it become law only after it had been passed by a veto-proof majority, after he had fought it every step of the way, and even then he let the strongest part of the bill become law without his signature. He is apparently about to use the same ploy on the federal patients' bill: Oppose it every step of the way and then claim credit for it. He just pulled this stunt with the Federal Energy Regulatory Commission's long-awaited capitulation on price caps for Western energy.

Some progressives are taking comfort in the news that Bush is sinking in the polls, particularly the acute insight by the American people that he's more interested in helping large corporate donors than the public. Never did think the people were stupid. But the problem is not public recognition of what Bush is—most of us didn't vote for him to begin with. The problem is wasted time and money, years and billions being frittered away.

Time is especially a problem on three fronts—global warming, AIDS, and Russia, a seriously destabilized nuclear power. Putin promptly countered Bush's proposal for a National Missile Defense (NMD) shield with a promise to increase Russia's offensive weapons—duh. For those of you who remember your old arms control jargon, they're going to MIRV their MARVs, put multiple warheads on every missile. Though Putin, who seems to have a strong grip on reality, did remark he thought they had at least twenty years before they had to worry about the NMD.

The real concern with Russia is not that it is hostile but that it is falling apart. Their radar system is shot: They almost launched a nuclear strike against us in 1995 when they mistook a Norwegian research rocket for an incoming Trident missile. And they're less likely to lob a nuke at us than they are to sell some of what they've got to the usual suspects, or even have it stolen.

Meanwhile, W. continues his Alfred E. Neuman routine on global warming. The people sitting in the mess of Houston being eaten alive by mosquitoes in the wake of Tropical Storm Allison are not the only ones to notice that untoward weather events are coming more frequently. Even the insurance industry is rapidly passing nervous on the subject.

But this cheerful report should perk up your day no end: Treasury Secretary Paul O'Neill recently said, "If you set aside Three Mile Island and Chernobyl, the safety record of nuclear is really very good." This is the kind of positive thinking that makes our country great.

**August 2001**

# One Throws Up One's Hands

■

I WAS IN Paris for all of September. After 9/11, at the American Church on the Left Bank and the American Cathedral on the Right, the steps were covered with the most beautiful flowers and the most touching messages. They ranged from "God Bless America" to *"Nous Vous Aimons"* to *"Vive Les New Yorkers."* Many of the messages mentioned '44, Normandy, or the liberation of Paris. One, in a shaky, spidery hand, referred to the famous American declaration of World War I: "Lafayette, we are here," and added the assurance that the French would be with America once more.

All this was even more remarkable in that the French consider George W. Bush a hopeless fathead. The Europeans were much taken aback by W's language after the attack, but I must confess, I'm such a Texan I didn't even react. We'll "smoke 'em out and round 'em up"—sound plan. "Bring him in, dead or alive"—you bet your butt. I did, however, cringe at his use of the word *crusade*.

In the first few days, the French papers featured great deluges of prose on the awfulness and the horror of the attack, backed by tender portraits of the survivors. But there was from the beginning a slightly less sentimental tone in the coverage than in the American press, an immediate practicality about the consequences, and a severe avoidance of the bathetic.

By the weekend of September 15, the French press was pointing out, in the most tactful fashion, that this administration has notably preferred unilateralism to multilateralism but now the great need for fullest cooperation with the allies was revealed. The second point made by the French press was that G. W. Bush must now, surely, recognize the folly of the missile defense shield, it having just been so painfully demonstrated to be not at all what is needed. So when the news came from Washington that actually the missile defense shield was more likely to pass now since no one in Washington was in a mood to deny Bush anything he says he needs, the French press grew impatient.

In the French language, *one* is the preferred pronoun for the opinionated individual. The French avoid the egotistical *I* and the presumptuous *everybody.* So when the illogical decision on missile defense came down, it forced one to throw up one's hands and shake one's head and sigh. One was not happy.

One was also gravely concerned by the call-up of fifty thousand reservists and bellicose quotes from Bush and Cheney. The problem, one agreed with one along the *quai,* was the use of the word *war.* For war, the military forces of one country must attack the military forces of another. Therefore, this was not a war. It was a crime of the most horrible variety. One must find the perpetrators. One must bring them to justice. One is inclined to think an international tribunal, such as for Slobodan Milošević, would be a proper forum.

BACK HOME IN Texas, and the sign outside our neighborhood strip joint says, HOT BABES, COLD BEER, NUKE 'EM, GW.

My worry is that Bush is painting himself into a corner with his rhetoric. This is not a war; it's a gigantic police operation in the face of a crime beyond all understanding.

Fear is at the root of most evil. As Boots Cooper, age eight, said after a close encounter with a chicken snake: "Some things'll scare you so bad, you'll hurt yourself." These dotty proposals to breach the Constitution fall into that category. We cannot make ourselves more secure by making ourselves less free. According to reporting in the *Los Angeles Times* and *The New York Times,* the terrorists got in and stayed through loopholes in the visa system, not some fundamental constitutional flaw.

When I returned from Paris, I was hoping we'd start thinking outside the box. Now I'm hoping we'll just start thinking.

One more Texas sign, in front of a pharmacy: GENERIC PROZAC NOW IN, GOD BLESS AMERICA.

**November 2001**

# Civil Liberties Matter

WHOA! THE PROBLEM IS the premise. We are having one of those circular arguments about how many civil liberties we can trade away in order to make ourselves safe from terrorism, without even looking at the assumption—*can* we can make ourselves safer by making ourselves less free? There is no inverse relationship between freedom and security. Less of one does not lead to more of the other. People with no rights are not safe from terrorist attack.

Exactly what do we want to strike out of the U.S. Constitution that we think would prevent terrorist attacks? Let's see, if civil liberties had been suspended before September 11, would law enforcement have noticed Mohammed Atta? Would the FBI have opened an investigation of Zacarias Moussaoui, as Minneapolis agents wanted to do? The CIA had several of the 9/11 actors on their lists of suspected terrorists. Exactly what civil liberty prevented them from doing anything about it?

In the case of a suspected terrorist, the government already had the right to search, wiretap, intercept, detain, examine computer and financial records, and do anything else it needed to do. There's a special court they go to for subpoenas and warrants. As it happens, they didn't do it.

Changing the law retroactively is not going to change that. Certainly, we had a visa system that had more holes than Swiss cheese. What does that have to do with civil liberties? When we don't give an agency enough money to do its job, it doesn't get done.

As you may have heard, Immigration and Naturalization has been a bit overwhelmed in recent years. In fairness to law enforcement, it's hard to imagine how anyone could have seen this one coming. It's always easy to point the finger after the fact. It was just a damnable act.

Absolutely nothing in the Constitution would have prevented us from stopping 9/11, so why would we want to change it? I also think we're arguing from the wrong historical analogies. Yes, during past wars civil liberties have been abrogated and the courts have even upheld this. We regret it later, but we don't seem to learn from that.

But the Bush administration's rhetoric aside, we are not at war. War is when the armed forces of one country attack the armed forces of another. What we're looking at is more akin to the nineteenth-century problem with anarchists, the terrorists of their day. And we made some memorable errors by giving in to hysteria over anarchists.

In the infamous 1886 Haymarket Square affair in Chicago, after a bomb killed seven policemen, eight labor leaders were rounded up and "tried," even though there was no evidence against them—four hanged, one suicide, three sentenced. Historians agree they were all innocent.

Nicola Sacco and Bartolomeo Vanzetti, executed in 1927, were finally exonerated by the state of Massachusetts in 1977. That outbreak of hysteria over "foreign anarchists" led to, among other abuses, a wave of arrests for DWI: "Driving While Italian." And no one was ever made safer from an anarchist bomb by the execution of innocent people. We all know that other groups, from the Irish to the blacks to the Chinese, have been targeted for legal abuse over the years—all betrayals of our laws, values, and the sacrifices of genera- tions. Let's not do it again.

The counter-case was neatly put by David Blunkett, the British Home Secretary: "We can live in a world with airy-fairy civil liberties and believe the best in everybody—and they will destroy us." Unless, of course, we destroy ourselves first.

*Fascism* is not a word I throw around lightly, but what do you think *happened* in Germany in the 1930s? The U.S. Constitution was written by men who had just been through a long, incredibly nasty war. They did not consider the Bill of Rights a frivolous luxury, to be in force only in times of peace and prosperity, put aside when the going gets tough. The Founders knew from tough going. They weren't airy-fairy guys.

We put away Tim McVeigh and the terrorists who did the 1993 World Trade Center bombing without damaging the Constitution. If the laws break into some apartment full of al-Qaeda literature and plans of airports, absolutely nothing prevents them from hauling in the suspects and having a nice, cozy, coplike chat with them. Because there's evidence. That's what they call "due process."

When there is no evidence, no grounds for suspicion, we do not hold citizens indefinitely and without legal representation. Very airy-fairy of us, to be sure. Foreign citizens have only limited rights in this country, depending on their means of entry—different for refugees, permanent residents, etc. So what's the problem?

Attorney General John Ashcroft has been so busy busting dying marijuana smokers in California and doctors in Oregon who carry out their terminal patients' wishes to die in peace, he obviously has no time to consider the Constitution. But he did swear to uphold it.

**November 2001**

# The False War

■

THE STATE OF the Union was fairly surreal Tuesday night. We won the war against Afghanistan, but we're still at war with al-Qaeda, so we have to go attack North Korea.

The big paper-shredders at Enron are finally coming to a halt, so we should go ahead and pass huge corporate tax cuts to help all the other companies that use aggressive accounting practices and need the dough. They especially need the rebates on the taxes they didn't pay. We're a better people than we were on September 10, so let's all donate four thousand hours to the country, except for those who are too busy stashing their loot in offshore banks so they won't have to pay taxes.

To further this noble scheme, the taxpayers will pony up to fund volunteers with religious groups. Does this mean Mormon missionaries will get paid to knock on our doors and persuade us that Joseph Smith and Brigham Young are the light and the way?

I'm clearly confused, but I think some of my colleagues are, too. During the run-up to the State of the Union speech, I heard apparently sane commentators state that since George W. Bush is reading a biography of Teddy Roosevelt, he would speak out against "the malefactors of great wealth" and possibly even endorse campaign finance reform.

I may be confused by Bush, but these folks have absolutely no idea who he is. Let's try this again, team. George W. Bush sides with the malefactors of great wealth not because he is a tool of the rich or because Enron bought him with campaign contributions—that's who he is, that's what he really believes, that's his life experience.

Here's one example from his oilfield career. When Bush was in the oil business, his failing company Spectrum 7 was bought by Harken Energy. Bush and his two partners got $2 million in stock in exchange for a company that had lost $400,000 in the six months prior to the sale. Bush himself got stock worth about $500,000 and an annual consulting fee of $120,000, later reduced to $50,000.

In June 1990, Bush sold two thirds of the Harken stock he had acquired in the Spectrum 7 deal at $4 a share—$318,430 more than it was worth when he got it. A month before Bush sold his stock, the Harken board appointed Bush and another company director, E. Stuart Watson, to a "fairness committee" to determine how restructuring would affect ordinary stockholders.

Smith, Barney, Harris, Upham & Co., the financial consultants hired by Harken, told Bush and Watson only drastic action could save the company. So Bush sold his stock before the news became public. According to *U.S. News & World Report*, there was "substantial evidence to suggest that Bush knew Harken was in dire straits." Insiders liquidating large blocks of stock are required to notify the Securities and Exchange Commission immediately. Bush reported the sale eight months after the federal deadline. Although the SEC does prosecute flagrant violators of insider-reporting rules, according to *The Wall Street Journal*, first-time violators usually get only a warning letter.

This not-so-ancient history may not strike you as relevant, so let's move on to a current policy conflict. The Bush administration's policy on international money-laundering changed after September 11. Bill Clinton, you may recall, was leading the charge by developed countries to go after offshore banks used by terrorists, drug dealers, tax dodgers, and other trash. Bush had called off that effort, but it gained new urgency after the attacks, and part of last fall's anti-terrorism law contained new provisions against international money-laundering.

The Senate Banking Committee held a hearing Tuesday on how the new law is working. Senator Paul Sarbanes of Maryland, the committee chair, criticized two new regulations concerning "shell banks"—front operations used by people hiding their wealth. Under the anti-terrorism law, American financial institutions are not permitted to have correspondent accounts—that is, deposit accounts that banks have in other banks, with shell banks. According to *The New York Times*, Sarbanes said the new regulation lets American institutions off the hook if their foreign customers certified they were not fronting for shell banks. Another provision permits correspondent accounts from shell banks if a real bank owns 25 percent of the shell bank's shares. Sarbanes said it was "a broad loophole," inviting trouble.

Another way to launder money is International Business Companies, or IBCs—shell companies not required to file any public notice of who their officers and directors are. There's no need to reveal the identity of its shareholders; no need to file any financial statements or keep any accounts. No income, capital gains, or inheritance taxes. One pamphlet touting a Bahamian IBC closes with: " 'Pinch me! I'm dreaming,' you may be saying."

Indeed you may.

January 2002

# I ❤ Enron

■

ADMIT IT, YOU'RE wallowing in Enron. Aside from the fact that it wrecked a bunch of people's lives, it is a beautiful scandal. Naturally, there is a special Texas element of looniness. Our governor, Rick (Goodhair) Perry, appointed an Enron executive to the state's Public Utilities Commission last summer, the better to regulate energy companies. The very next day, Perry got a $25,000 contribution from Ken Lay, which would have raised questions except Governor Perry cleared up the whole matter by explaining the contribution was "totally coincidental." This news relieved everybody and gave the governor a new nickname, Old Coincidence.

But then it turned out there had been a cover-up, literally, involving Perry's appointee. When Democrats asked for the public records on the new commissioner, they found a curious blank under the part about brushes with the law: It had been whited out. It was a sophisticated cover-up, but it came unraveled, and we learned the new commissioner had once shot a whooping crane under the impression that it was a goose and had to pay a $15,000 fine under the Endangered Species Act. Kind of thing that could happen to anyone. George W. Bush himself once shot a protected killdeer on the theory that it was a dove. Of course, the whooper is five feet tall, so there was a general sentiment that anyone who can't tell a whooper from a goose shouldn't be trying to regulate energy anyway, and the fellow resigned. Totally coincidentally, of course.

Like all historic events, the Enron scandal has already started to affect the language. The stick-up artist goes into the Jiffy Mart to pull a heist. He whips out his rod and says, "Put 'em up, this is an aggressive accounting practice."

I love the Enron scandal. Did you know that Enron's board of directors twice voted to suspend its own ethics code in order to create private partnerships? Wasn't that thoughtful of them? If they hadn't voted to suspend the ethics code, they would have been in violation of it. Why didn't we think of that?

The funniest line so far about Enron is, "This is not a political scandal." It was totally coincidental that they made all those political contributions. Disinterested public service was their only motive, putting high-quality people in public office. And they never got a thing for it. Not natural gas deregulation, or deregulation of the energy futures market when Wendy Gramm was chair of the Commodities Futures Trading Commission, or a new chairman of the Federal Energy Commission, or calling off the pressure on offshore banks, or exemption from oversight on derivatives, or government contracts, or having the governor of Texas (George W.) call the governor of Pennsylvania to report what a fine company Enron is during the fight over energy de-reg in that state, or pressure from Dick Cheney on India to ease up on the disastrous Enron investment there, or input into Bush's national energy policy, or hundreds of millions in tax rebates under the economic stimulus plan despite not having paid any taxes in four of the last five years. Enron hired James Baker, the former secretary of state, to go to Kuwait to help drum up business there shortly after the Gulf War ended because it didn't want to have any political influence. It hired Ralph Reed and Bill Kristol and Lawrence Lindsey and lots of other people for the exact same reason. It was all totally coincidental.

Further comedy is to be found in the interviews with Enron's fired workers, who solemnly report they have been to the unemployment office to apply for the compensation to which they are entitled and the experience was "demeaning" or "humiliating." Some were even *put on hold!* As we say in Texas, no shit? What we have here is a case of professionals being treated exactly like workers. Gee, do you think that has any political implications? Enron is the gift that keeps on giving. Yes, there is joy in Mudville. Wallow away.

**March 2002**

# Doctor! Doctor!

■

**H**AVE YOU NOTICED that the health-care system is not working? In fact, it's falling apart. And the most curious thing about that is how few of the people for whom the system still works—and they're the ones who make the decisions—are aware of it.

It's like the old story about frogs and hot water. If you drop a frog into boiling water, it will leap to get out, but if you drop a frog in cool water and then gradually heat it up, the beast doesn't notice. Or so they say. Another factor is the now-constant cognitive dissonance we have in this country as a result of the ever-widening gap between most people and the people who run things. If you have health insurance, the system is a pain in the behind but it works. If you don't have health insurance, you are flat out of luck. And in case you hadn't noticed, more and more employers are deciding not to offer health insurance, or using "temporary" workers or outsourcing various tasks so they won't have to cover the workers.

If you don't have health insurance, the system is an insane nightmare. A new book by Dr. Rudolph Mueller, *As Sick as It Gets: The Shocking Reality of America's Healthcare*, lays out the problems as well as any I've read. But the book is just one more grain of sand in the beaches of evidence we already have that the system is breaking up.

At South by Southwest, the Austin music festival, a panel on health care for musicians—who are largely uninsured—produced this nugget: Did you know there are more than one thousand concerts given every week by musicians for other musicians to raise enough money for an operation or medical treatment of some kind? It's a beautiful tradition, but it doesn't work. All the generosity of all the musicians in the country—and so many of them are endlessly generous with their time and talent—doesn't begin to cover the cost of medical treatment for even a few.

As they say in bridge circles, let's review the play. Ten years ago, we knew the system was a mess and Bill Clinton got elected in large part by promising to do something about it. Hillary Clinton got the assignment and conventional wisdom in the political world is that she blew it. She did make political mistakes in her approach, but the far more important reason the attempt at reform failed is that the insurance industry spent $10 million to defeat the bill. Remember Harry and Louise?

Since then, the politicians have been afraid to try reform. The smartest of them, including Bill Clinton and Senator Ted Kennedy, have been trying to move the ball incrementally—tinkering with Medicare and Medicaid, starting a program to insure poor children. But the system is falling apart faster than they can move to fix it. A Patients' Bill of Rights is not the answer. It won't provide health insurance for a single additional individual.

The most maddening thing about the sheer stupidity of America's health-care system is that the far better alternative is perfectly clear. Every other industrialized nation manages to do this better than we do. The answer is universal health insurance, a single-payer system. Every time we start to get serious about reform, the right wing starts screaming, "Socialized medicine, socialized medicine." And then we're all supposed to run, screaming with horror. But if you want to see horror in action, try the emergency room of any large public hospital in this country. And for a truly hilarious experience, try to get emergency medical help on Christmas Eve.

Look, this should not be a for-profit system. We need to phase out all for-profit or investor-owned provider and insurance organizations. Mueller suggests a onetime fair buyout of all such organizations. The good news is that doctors are no longer impeding serious reform—in fact, doctors are having such a hard time under the current system, they've been radicalized on the subject and can now be counted on to help with reform.

Conservatives reflexively start moaning about the cost of a "big, new government program." Actually, what's costly is the system we have now. Americans already spend 58 percent more than the weighted average of similar nations for health care.

"It is a system wasteful beyond belief and manipulated by a lobby focused on providing the highest profits for the their self-interest and their investors, and mammoth cash flows to companies that should not exist or not be involved in health care. The system is also paying for an extremely large number of sick people who would not be sick under any decent universal health care system," writes Mueller.

Sitting around deploring the current system will not fix it—there are citizen action groups all over the country working on this problem. It is easy to find them and get involved. You don't have to be on the Internet; the phone book works fine. We can't wait for the political system to get round to doing something about this: We need to help ourselves now.

**March 2002**

# The IQ of Bush's Gut

WELL, THINGS DO seem to be going to hell, don't they? The beauty of having fled to Mexico for a week to escape the endless blat of television news is that it leaves you with enough energy to tackle the subject of the Middle East—if not with cheer, at least with hope.

And that does appear to be the missing ingredient here—the expectation that anything at all can be done about the situation. Of course it can. The Israelis and the Palestinians are not condemned to some eternal hell where they have to kill each other forever. There is no military solution, but there is a political solution—and they will get there. The United States is obliged to broker the deal because there's no one else to do it.

The situation could certainly use a couple of good funerals, but failing that luck, we have to deal with what's there. It is possible to deal with people who are beyond persuasion by either fact or logic, which to an outsider is certainly how both the Israelis and the Palestinians now seem to be behaving. Political solutions to apparently intractable situations can be manufactured. While the world has been paying very little attention, the Irish Republican Army has actually been destroying its own weapons dumps. Who thought there was a solution in Northern Ireland five years ago? Or on Cyprus, where the Greeks and the Turks enjoyed a history of hostility of far superior antiquity to that in the Middle East? This can be done.

The second important point is that the situation demands respect for its moral complexity. That's where we are slightly handicapped by our president, the moral simplifier. From the beginning, the trouble with "war against terrorism" has been the definition of terrorism and the immutable fact that one man's terrorist is another man's freedom fighter. After he got us involved in this war on a noun, Bush then upped the ante and announced it was a war between good and evil, and we would continue until we had eradicated evil. Oh man, this is going to be a long sucker.

It is precisely because of this rigid good-versus-evil oversimplification that Bush has been sort of snookered by Ariel Sharon into blindly supporting his actions because they are supposed to be "anti-terrorist."

The worst news I've read lately is several reports quoting people close to Bush saying, "He feels in his gut . . ." He feels in his gut it is his mission in life to fight terrorism. He has a bad gut reaction to Arafat. Trust me on this when Bush starts thinking with his gut, we're in big trouble.

Let me say for the umpteenth time, George W. is not a stupid man. The IQ of his gut, however, is open to debate. In Texas, his gut led him to believe the death penalty has a deterrent effect, even though he acknowledged there was no evidence to support his gut's feeling. When his gut, or something, causes him to announce that he does not believe in global warming—as though it were a theological proposition—we once again find his gut ruling that evidence is irrelevant. In my opinion, Bush's gut should not be entrusted with making peace in the Middle East.

Bush's gut does not like complexity. When you're in the middle of a moral crusade against evil, it's damned annoying to have to stop and grapple with unpleasant complications, such as that we have to keep letting Afghani farmers grow opium poppies, or that our allies the Saudi Arabians foment terrorism, or that our allies the Pakistanis seem to have quite a few "freedom fighters" of their own. Moral complexity is a condition of life, and we will serve neither our own interests nor those of the Middle East if we keep pretending this is good versus evil.

There are many Palestinian terrorists. The Palestinians also have legitimate grievances that must be addressed. Sharon himself started this second intifada with his cruelly reckless and deliberately inflammatory visit to the Temple Mount. Took no genius to see what that was going to touch off. If you want to blame this intifada on someone in particular, Sharon is the leading candidate.

It is, however, more useful to concentrate on what can be done now. Any settlement will have to include getting the Israeli settlers off the West Bank—another instance where Sharon has ill-served Israel. Removing the settlers is not a job anyone would envy—that's where one sees the fanaticism on the Israeli side.

There has been much discussion of the suicide bombers as though this were some huge new spanner in the works. Everyone from shrinks to political scientists has had a go at explaining them, but it is at base a political phenomenon, a function of anarchy and powerlessness. I believe Sharon has reacted in a criminally stupid way, guaranteed to do no good at all. He is so focused on his old enemy Arafat that he is destroying Al Fatah, which will leave, of course, only Hamas.

Actually, as a conflict, the Israeli-Palestinian mess is a known quantity similar to other conflicts over territory. It is the United States that is facing the truly bizarre situation: terrorists without territory.

I am in no particular position to preach to American Jews (or anyone else, come to think of it), but as a deeply worried Christian supporter of Israel, I think American Jews have an important role to play in this delicate and dangerous situation. The impulse of all Jews to support Israel totally—especially when Israelis are being blown up—is entirely understandable. But it's not necessarily helpful to Israel in this situation.

I do not think this is a time that calls for uncritical support. Despite the occasional full-page ad from some group pledging blind fidelity to Israel and blaming everyone but Sharon, I am impressed with the level of real debate and even agonizing going on among American Jews. Anyone who tells you criticizing Israel at this parlous time is somehow helping the Palestinians must be as dumb as, well, John Ashcroft, who maintains that to question the president is to help terrorists.

It is troubling that the Bush administration approaches this new attempt at negotiation so tepidly—indeed, as though it has been dragged into it kicking and screaming. It has always been a worry that Bush has so little expertise on the Middle East around him—Condi Rice, who may be his best, is notoriously weak in this area.

It truly doesn't help to play the blame game, but this administration was warned again and again that the escalating violence would finally break into catastrophe. And still they did nothing, apparently out of blind anti-Clintonism: Clinton pushed for a Middle East peace, therefore Bush wouldn't. Hell of a policy. Onward.

Last week, I began a sentence by saying, "If Bush had any imagination . . ." and then I hit myself. Silly me. But if he did, he could put together an extraordinary peace commission involving any combination of Jimmy Carter, Colin Powell, Bill Clinton, George Mitchell, James Baker, Kofi Annan, Nelson Mandela . . . you get the idea. You can name your own players. Meantime, all we can do is wish Godspeed to Powell.

# Halliburton

◼

THE SECURITIES AND EXCHANGE Commission is now investigating Halliburton—the company formerly run by Vice President Dick Cheney—for accounting irregularities. What took so long?

Dick Cheney's record at Halliburton is one of the most undercovered stories of the past three years. When you consider all the time and ink spent on Whitewater, the neglect of the Cheney-Halliburton story is unfathomable.

The proximate cause of the SEC investigation is an "aggressive accounting practice" at Halliburton approved by the accounting firm Arthur Andersen—a little matter of counting revenue that had not yet been received, $100 million worth. *The New York Times* reports two former executives of Dresser Industries, which merged with Halliburton in 1998, say Halliburton used the accounting sham to cover up its losses. Dresser may have thought it got a bad deal in that merger because of that $100 million "anticipation" on the credit line, but the deal turned out to be much more sour for Halliburton.

Cheney bought himself a former Dresser subsidiary facing 292,000 claims for asbestos-caused health problems. He said at the time the merger was "one of the most exciting things I've ever been involved in" and predicted it would benefit Halliburton's customers, employees, and shareholders. The first thing that happened was Halliburton eliminated ten thousand jobs. (It was always amusing to hear Cheney on the campaign trail in 2000 claiming he had been out in the private sector "creating jobs.")

According to executives at Halliburton, Cheney knew about the asbestos liability before the merger and considered the risk. Because of the liability, Halliburton's stock has fallen from over $60 to under $20. In January, the company had to deny rumors it was going into bankruptcy. In other words, Cheney pretty well ruined the business. Of course, what the company wants to do now is have Congress pass a new law limiting asbestos liability.

Even more interesting is Halliburton's governmental record under Cheney. In an August 2000 report, the Center for Public Integrity noted that Cheney had said publicly the United States should lift restrictions on American corporations in countries listed by the government as sponsoring terrorism. Hey, that was then, this is now.

Despite repeatedly claiming his company would not do business with Iraq—he was defense secretary during the Persian Gulf War—Halliburton racked up $23.8 million in sales to Iraq in '98 and '99. It did so by using two European subsidiaries, so Halliburton was not directly violating the sanctions against Iraq. Hey, it was business.

And striking another blow for freedom from government interference, Cheney led Halliburton into the top ranks of corporate welfare hogs, benefiting from almost $2 billion in taxpayer-insured loans from the U.S. Export-Import Bank and the Overseas Private Investment Corp. In the five years before Cheney joined the company, it got a measly $100 million in government loans. Cheney also specialized in getting government contracts for the firm. During his five years as CEO, Halliburton got $2.3 billion in contracts, compared to only $1.2 billion in the five years before he took over.

Most of the government work was done by Halliburton subsidiary Brown & Root, the construction firm, thus reinstating a fine old Texas tradition. Brown & Root was Lyndon Johnson's major money source: It was to LBJ what Enron was to George W.

This brings to mind a famous story from the Kennedy-Johnson campaign in 1960 relished by Texans. It's after the election, and the Democrats win. Kennedy and Johnson are sittin' in the Oval Office the first day, and the phone rings. It's the pope of Rome (Texans used to specify "of Rome," lest you should confuse him with some other pope) on the phone. He says, "John, my boy, the Vatican roof is leaking something fierce, we were hopin' y'all might fix it for us."

"Of course, Mr. Pope, sir. Just let me check with my vice president. Lyndon, the pope's on the phone and wants to know if we can fix the Vatican roof for him."

"That's fine with me," says Johnson. "Just make sure Brown & Root gets the contract."

Nice to see tradition reassert itself.

# Hypocrisies

**It's the little things, the itty-bitty things.
It's the little things that really piss me off.**

SONG BY ROBERT EARL KEEN

GOSH, SILLY US, getting in a swivet over war and peace. The president is on vacation! He's giving interviews to *Runner's World*, not *Meet the Press*. He and Defense Secretary Rumsfeld didn't even *talk* about Iraq during their meeting at Crawford. It was all the media's fault. We were "churning," we were in "a frenzy." Heck, Bush himself has never even mentioned war with Iraq, much less going it alone.

We don't have to worry, so party hearty, and try not to make a big deal out of the fact that Bush's lawyers are now claiming he can launch an attack on Iraq without congressional approval *because the permission given by Congress to his father in 1991 to wage war in the Persian Gulf is still in effect.*

Since that's all cleared up, here are a few little nuggets you might like to chew on:

- Bush went to Pennsylvania to meet with the nine coal miners rescued earlier this summer to congratulate them. He also cut the budget for the Mine Safety and Health Administration by $4.7 million out of $118 million total: enforcement was cut, as were mine inspections for coal dust (which causes black lung disease), and the chest X-ray program was cut entirely. Bush filled five of the top positions at MSHA with coal industry executives.
- Earlier this month, the Associated Press used a computer analysis to dig up some interesting news about congressional spending pat-

terns. Since the Republicans took over Congress in 1994, tens of billions of dollars in federal spending have moved from Democratic to GOP districts. Last year, there was an average of $612 million more spending for congressional districts represented by Republicans than by Democrats. AP also reports that when Democrats last controlled the House and wrote the budget, the average Democratic district got $35 million more than the average Republican district.

That's quite a shift, and the AP says the change was "driven mostly by Republican policies that moved spending from poor rural and urban areas to the more affluent suburbs and "GOP-leaning farm country. . . . In terms of services, that translates into more business loans and farm subsidies, and fewer public housing grants and food stamps."

Now one could take the attitude of Majority Leader Dick Armey, who was quoted by the AP on this subject as saying, "To the victor goes the spoils." On the other hand, that means more government subsidies are going to people who need them less. The recently passed farm bill, a subject on which I find myself in complete harmony with the *National Review,* weighed in at $190 billion, a grossly disproportionate share going to corporate farmers: Ten percent of farmers will get 69 percent of the subsidies, according to *The New York Times.* President Bush signed the $190 billion horror and then made a great show, at his public relations event in Waco, of vetoing $5 billion in what he deemed was unnecessary spending in the homeland security bill.

• The media have achieved such a perfect he said–she said knot of confusion on the story of Bush and Harken energy, it would be a wonder if the public ever gets any of it straight. Even though the Center for Public Integrity has posted the relevant documents from Harken on its website (www.publici.org), the news has been buried under a scrum of pundits shouting, "It's old news" or "Is not, it's new news." All I can say is, if Slick Willie Clinton had ever eeled out from under information like this, Rush Limbaugh would've had a heart attack.

Just for the record, George W. Bush had not just one but four Harken stock transactions worth more than $1 million during the time he was on the board. And in each case he was months over deadline in reporting the matter to the Securities and Exchange

Commission. Second, newly posted documents show that Bush, who claims he had no idea Harken was in trouble when he dumped his stock in late June 1990, was in fact warned twice: Harken's CEO sent him a memo on June 7 predicting that Harken would run out of money before the end of the month and that it would then be in violation of numerous debt agreements.

Even more egregious, Bush was clearly involved in the phony Aloha Petroleum deal. Aloha was a Harken subsidiary that was sold to a partnership of Harken insiders at an inflated price, a perfect little gem of an example of the kind of fake, pump-the-bottom-line transaction later perfected by Enron. Bush's business career is a small-scale model of exactly the corrupt corporate practices now under fire.

In case you missed the theme here, it's hypocrisy.

August 2002

# More Hypocrisy

■

Excuse me: I don't want to be tacky or anything, but hasn't it occurred to anyone in Washington that sending Vice President Dick Cheney out to champion an invasion of Iraq on the grounds that Saddam Hussein is a "murderous dictator" is somewhere between bad taste and flaming hypocrisy?

When Dick Cheney was CEO of the oil-field supply firm Halliburton, the company did $23.8 million in business with Saddam Hussein, the evildoer "prepared to share his weapons of mass destruction with terrorists."

So if Saddam is "the world's worst leader," how come Cheney sold him the equipment to get his dilapidated oil fields up and running so he to could afford to build weapons of mass destruction?

In 1998, the United Nations passed a resolution allowing Iraq to buy spare parts for its oil fields, but other sanctions remained in place, and the United States has consistently pressured the U.N. to stop exports of medicine and other needed supplies on the grounds they could have "dual use." As the former secretary of defense under Bush the Elder, Cheney was in a particularly vulnerable position on the hypocrisy of doing business with Iraq.

Using two subsidiaries, Dresser-Rand and Ingersoll-Dresser, Halliburton helped rebuild Saddam's war-damaged oil fields. The combined value of these contracts for parts and equipment was greater than that of any other American company doing business with Iraq—companies including Schlumberger, Flowserve, Fisher-Rosemount, General Electric. They acted through foreign subsidiaries or associated companies in France, Belgium, Germany, India, Switzerland, Bahrain, Egypt, and the Netherlands.

In several cases, it is clear the European companies did no more than loan their names to American firms for the purpose of dealing with Hussein. Iraq then became America's second-largest Middle Eastern oil supplier.

This story was initially reported by the *Financial Times* of London more than two years ago and has since been more extensively reported in the European press. But as we have seen with the case of Harken Energy and many other stories, there is a difference between a story having been reported and having attention being paid to it (a distinction many journalists have trouble with). Thus the administration was able to dismiss the new information on shady dealings at Harken as "old news" because not much attention was ever paid when the old news was new.

When Cheney left Halliburton, he received a $34 million severance package despite the fact that the single biggest deal of his five-year career there, the acquisition of Dresser Industries, turned out to be a huge blunder since the company came saddled with asbestos liability.

Halliburton, America's No. 1 oil-services company, is the nation's fifth-largest military contractor and the biggest nonunion employer in the United States. It employs more than 100,000 workers worldwide and does over $15 billion a year. Halliburton under Cheney dealt with several brutal dictatorships, including the despicable government of Burma (Myanmar). The company also played questionable roles in Algeria, Angola, Bosnia, Croatia, Haiti, Somalia, and Indonesia.

Halliburton also had dealings with Iran and Libya, both on the State Department's list of terrorist states. Halliburton's subsidiary Brown & Root, the old Texas construction firm that does much business with the U.S. military, was fined $3.8 million for reexporting goods to Libya in violation of U.S. sanctions.

If you want to know why the Democrats didn't jump all over this story and make a big deal out of it, it's because—as usual—Democrats are involved in similar dealings. Former CIA director John Deutsch is on the board of Schlumberger, the second-largest oil services firm after Halliburton, which is also doing business with Iraq through subsidiaries.

Americans have long been aware that corporate money has consistently corrupted domestic policy in favor of corporate interests, and that both parties are in thrall to huge corporate campaign donors. We are less accustomed to connecting the dots when it comes to foreign policy. But there is no more evidence that corporations pay attention to anything other than profits in their foreign dealings than they do in their domestic deals.

Enron, as usual, provides some textbook examples of just how indifferent to human rights American companies can be. Halliburton's dealings in

Nigeria, in partnership with Shell and Chevron, provide another such example, including gross violations of human rights and environmental abuses.

No one is ever going to argue that Saddam Hussein is a good guy, but Dick Cheney is not the right man to make the case against him. I have never understood why the Washington press corps cannot remember anything for longer than ten minutes, but hearing Cheney denounce Saddam is truly "Give us a break" time.

**September 2002**

# The Clinton Wars Continue

WATCHING SOME DIPSTICK the other day on Fox News carry on with great certainty about Hillary Clinton and her evil motives—and I don't think this guy actually spends a lot of time tête-à-tête with Mrs. Clinton while she reveals her deepest thoughts to him—I wondered, "Lord, when are these people going to get over it?"

I think the answer is never, because most people have a very hard time forgiving those whom they have deeply wronged. I know that's sort of counterintuitive, but think about some of the bad divorces you have known. When we have done something terrible to someone, we often need to twist it around so it's their fault, not ours.

So we continue to suffer this deformity in our public life because of what Sid Blumenthal calls "this perverse episode," the scoundrel time.

Just last week, *The Wall Street Journal*, reminded of the Vince Foster suicide by Mrs. Clinton's new memoir, *Living History*, wrote a nasty, callous, defensive editorial. It's a classic of the genre of exculpating yourself by blaming others. Since Foster named *The Wall Street Journal* in his suicide note, you might think the paper would, if not acknowledge responsibility, at least have the common decency to express some regret.

I had to force myself to start Blumenthal's book, *The Clinton Wars*, because I'm still exhausted from the whole megillah, but then I couldn't stop reading it. It's perversely fascinating. The year this country wasted on the impeachment was the most tawdry, the nastiest, the ugliest, the sorriest chapter I've ever seen in politics.

I watched it from my vantage point in Texas and naturally concluded—as did everyone else in the country with a lick of common sense—that everyone in Washington, D.C., had completely lost their minds.

I'm still ambivalent about it. The late, great Billie Carr of Houston—a woman who had taught the baby Bill Clinton how to do politics when he came over to Texas in 1972—was invited to the White House in the middle of the Monica Lewinsky mess. Billie got all gussied up, sashayed up to Clinton in the receiving line, and said to him, "You dumb son of a bitch." Thank heavens, I always thought, somebody said to him exactly what every American wanted to say. (Clinton started laughing as Billie proceeded to tear him a new one, and said, "I knew you were gonna do this, Billie.")

On the other hand, Clinton is one of the most brilliant natural politicians I have ever observed—I put him in a category with Lyndon Johnson and the late Texas Lieutenant Governor Bob Bullock. That his presidency could have been so seriously damaged by what was, in fact, a vast right-wing conspiracy is a horrible indictment of politics in our time.

The most depressing thing about Blumenthal's book is that it keeps reminding you that these nasty little ideological zealots set out from Day One to commit the Politics of Personal Destruction. They had no honor, and they had no shame. They were just out to get him any way they could, and when sex proved a convenient route, they used it—hypocrisy, be damned.

Blumenthal, who was in the center of that cyclone, has accomplished something remarkable—he has actually written a rather detached account of it all. If I had been that close to it—and received that much personal abuse—I doubt I could write without anger, even now.

A couple of times Blumenthal cites some advice Hillary Clinton gave him: "Remember, it's never about you. Whatever you think, it's not about you."

This is not to say there is not some score-settling in this book: The number of reporters who allowed themselves to be used by Kenneth Starr and his ideological wrecking crew is a depressing tally in itself. Blumenthal shames the press corps simply by being meticulous himself. "Here is what he would have found if he had bothered to check . . ." is his general method. I found only one error in the book—it was George W. Bush who repeatedly failed in the oil business, not his father, who made $6 million back when that was real money.

*The Clinton Wars* has been criticized for not being more balanced about the flawed presidency—the Clintons themselves are almost entirely blameless in this account. But if that's what Blumenthal had set out to do, he would have written some other book.

I've heard many people say, "But they made it so easy for people to attack them." That may be true, but it's still blaming the victim, isn't it?

The Clinton wars reflect no credit on anyone, but I still think it was journalism, or what passes for journalism these days, that most disgraced itself. We should all be required to read this book.

**June 2003**

# The Failures of 9/11

■

THE CONGRESSIONAL REPORT by the committees on intelligence about 9/11 partially made public last week reminds me of the recent investigation into the crash of the *Columbia* shuttle—months of effort to reconfirm the obvious.

In the case of the *Columbia*, we knew from the beginning a piece of insulation had come loose and struck the underside of one wing. So, after much study, it was determined the crash was caused by the piece of insulation that came loose and struck the underside of the wing.

Likewise in the case of 9/11, all the stuff that has been blindingly obvious for months is now blamed for the fiasco.

The joint inquiry focused on the intelligence services, concluding that the FBI especially had been asleep at the wheel. And that, in turn, can be blamed at least partly on the fact that the FBI, before 9/11, had only old green-screen computers with no Internet access. Agents wrote out their reports in longhand, in triplicate. Although the process is not complete, the agency is now upgrading its system: many agents finally got e-mail this year.

My particular bête noire in all this is the INS (Immigration and Naturalization Service), which distinguished itself by granting visas to fifteen of the nineteen hijackers, who never should have been given visas in the first place. Their applications were incomplete and incorrect. They were all young, single, unemployed males, with no apparent means of support—the kind considered classic overstay candidates. Had the INS followed its own procedures, fifteen of the nineteen never would have been admitted.

The incompetence of the INS was underlined when it issued a visa to Mohamed Atta, the lead hijacker, six months after 9/11. In the wake of the attacks, the Bush administration promised to increase funding for the INS, to get the agency fully computerized with modern computers and generally up to speed. All that has happened since is that INS funding has been cut.

Much attention is being paid to the selective editing of the report, apparently to protect the Saudis. I think an equally important piece of the report is on the bureaucratic tangle that prevents anyone from being accountable for much of anything.

The CIA controls only 15 percent to 20 percent of the annual intelligence budget. The rest is handled by the Pentagon, despite widespread agreement that it needs to be centralized. The Bush administration has ignored these calls, mostly because Defense Secretary Donald Rumsfeld doesn't want to give up any power.

*Time* magazine reports, "It was striking that the Pentagon came under such heavy fire in last week's bipartisan report for resisting requests made by CIA director Tenet before 9/11, when the agency wanted to use satellites and other military hardware to spot and target terrorists in Afghanistan."

But the most striking thing about this report is that none of its conclusions and none of its recommendations have anything to do with the contents of the PATRIOT Act, which was supposedly our government's response to 9/11. All the could-haves, would-haves, and should-haves in the report are so far afield from the PATRIOT Act it might as well be on another subject entirely.

Once again, as has often happened in our history, under the pressure of threat and fear, we have harmed our own liberties without any benefit for our safety. Insufficient powers of law enforcement or surveillance are nowhere mentioned in the joint inquiry report as a problem before 9/11. Yet Attorney General John Ashcroft now proposes to expand surveillance powers even further with the PATRIOT II Act. All over the country, local governments have passed resolutions opposing the PATRIOT Act and three states have done so, including the very Republican Alaska.

The House of Representatives last week voted to prohibit the use of "sneak and peek" warrants authorized by the PATRIOT Act. The conservative House also voted against a measure to withhold federal funds from state and local law-enforcement agencies that refuse to comply with federal inquirers on citizenship or immigration status. All kinds of Americans are now waking up to the fact that the PATRIOT Act gives the government the right to put American citizens in prison indefinitely, without knowing the charges against them, without access to an attorney, without the right to confront their accusers, without trial. Indefinitely.

The report was completed late last year, but its publication was delayed by endless wrangles with the administration over what could be declassified. Former Georgia senator Max Cleland, who served on the committee, said the report's release was deliberately delayed by the White House until after the war in Iraq was over because it undercuts the rationale for the war. The report confirms there was no connection between Saddam Hussein and al-Qaeda.

"The administration sold the connection to scare the pants off the American people and justify the war," Cleland said. "What you've seen here is the manipulation of intelligence for political ends."

**July 2003**

# The Wrong Way

■

THERE ARE MESSY-DESK people and there are clean-desk people. I'm a major messy. About every six months, I am seized by a desire to Get Organized, so I start doing archaeological excavations into the midden heap on my desk. The result this time was a sort of time-lapse photography of where the country is headed.

Going through stacks of old newspaper articles, speeches, reports, studies, and press releases at a high rate of speed left one overwhelming impression: deception ... government by deception. I'd like pass along some of what I found without the usual journalistic standards of sourcing because I want to re-create the impression it all left—rather like leafing through a book rapidly, catching a sentence here and there. Leaving aside the missing weapons of mass destruction (hey, we found the oil), I found so many little things that fit the same pattern.

- Administration announces with great fanfare new regs to control listeria, a deadly bacteria that can contaminate certain foods. Great, they put in new regs, but first they eviscerated them so they have no real impact.
- U.S. Agency for International Development chief Andrew Natsios blasts NGOs (that's the jargon for nongovernmental organizations—private groups engaged in humanitarian assistance) for not doing enough PR for the United States. They're supposed to be helping starving and sick people, not flacking for America. Either talk up the United States, Natsios threatened, or he would personally tear up their contracts. (Great, some little Ethiopian kid on the edge of starvation, eyes dull, belly swollen, has to listen to a lecture on U.S. beneficence before he gets some oatmeal.)

- New study shows eight million mostly low-income taxpayers will get no benefit from the latest round of tax cuts, despite repeated assurances that it would help everybody who pays income taxes.
- Cost of photo-op with the president at a June fund-raiser: $20,000. Cost of a "leadership luncheon" with Karl Rove: must raise $50,000 for reelection.
- "American officials are considering a plan to use Iraq's future oil and gas revenues as collateral to raise cash to rebuild the country. Several U.S. companies, including Halliburton and Bechtel, which are jostling for the lucrative reconstruction contracts, are reportedly pushing the scheme to expedite the commissioning process." That means there's no Marshall Plan, we're not going to rebuild Iraq, we're going to take their oil to pay our corporations to fix what we messed up.
- President nominates Daniel Pipes to the board of the United States Institute of Peace. This is one of a series of cruel-joke appointments: Pipes is a Middle East expert whose vision of ending the Israeli-Palestinian conflict is no negotiation, no hope for compromise, and no use for diplomacy. He wants the Palestinians defeated, period. Just the man for the Institute of Peace.
- On Friday, April 11, three days after "coalition" forces entered Baghdad, the Interior Department announced a settlement with the state of Utah that effectively destroys the executive branch's key powers to protect the wilderness, reversing three decades of environmental policy. Starting immediately, oil, gas, and mineral companies are granted access to more than two hundred million acres of public lands. Bet you saw a lot of headlines about that one.
- Innumerable articles documenting the collapse of our dysfunctional health-care "system."
- "And I said on my program, if, if the Americans go in and overthrow Saddam Hussein and it's clean, he has nothing, I will apologize to the nation, and I will not trust the Bush administration again."—Fox News commentator Bill O'Reilly on *Good Morning America*, March 18.
- "The White House today defended the decision of congressional negotiators to deny millions of minimum-wage families the increased child tax credit, saying the new tax law was intended to help people who pay taxes, not those who are too poor to pay." The

poorest people in this country pay exactly the same percentage of their income in payroll taxes as wealthy people do in total taxes.

"Ain't gonna happen," said House Republican Majority Leader Tom DeLay. The only way DeLay would support tax cuts for the working poor would be if for every $1 in tax cuts to the working poor, rich people got another $22 in tax cuts. Lends new meaning to phrase "without DeLay."

• Two and half million jobs have disappeared since Bush took office. Real wages have stagnated or declined. Retirement savings have shrunk. People are losing health insurance, retirement benefits, and overtime.

• The "death tax," as the Republicans so cleverly misnamed the estate tax, which affects 2 percent of all Americans, has now been replaced by the Bush birth tax—if you're born in this country, you're in debt—you have to help pay back the money the Bushies took out of Social Security, plus the interest on the debts they're running up.

My thanks to all the people and publications whose research I have used without credit today. You have all contributed to this brief portrait of a country headed in the wrong direction.

**August 2003**

# Where's the Accountability?

AT THE BEGINNING of the summer, several of us who are not exactly upbeat about our prospects in Iraq urged the administration to Do Something before it was too late—like, by the end of the summer.

Now what? Our people are over there like staked goats in the desert, the administration won't ask other countries or the United Nations for help, they won't send more troops, and the NGOs are pulling out. There was no apparent connection between Iraq and al-Qaeda before this war, but there sure as hell is now. We have already lost more soldiers in the "peace" than we did during the war.

And still no weapons of mass destruction. I realize all the good little boys and girls are supposed to "get over" the missing weapons of mass destruction, but I cannot brush this aside with the careless élan of the neo-con hawks ("doesn't matter," "makes no difference," "who cares?"). Public officials need to be held to some standard of accountability for what they say.

In a separate column, I will try to Be Constructive about our current plight, but I think it is important to remember how we got here. May I remind you of what we were repeatedly told?

> "Simply stated, there is no doubt that Saddam Hussein now has weapons of mass destruction."—*Dick Cheney, August 26, 2002*

> "Right now, Iraq is expanding and improving facilities that were used for the production of biological weapons."—*George W. Bush, September 12, 2002*

> "The Iraqi regime possesses and produces chemical and biological weapons. It is seeking nuclear weapons."—*Bush, October 7, 2002*

"We've also discovered through intelligence that Iraq has a growing fleet of manned and unmanned aerial vehicles that would be used to disperse chemical or biological weapons across broad areas. We're concerned that Iraq is exploring ways of using the UAVs for missions targeting the United States."—*Bush, October 7, 2002*

"The evidence indicates that Iraq is reconstituting its nuclear weapons program. Saddam Hussein has held numerous meetings with Iraqi nuclear scientists, a group he calls his 'nuclear mujahideen'—his nuclear holy warriors. Satellite photographs reveal that Iraq is rebuilding facilities at sites that have been part of its nuclear program in the past."—*Bush, October 7, 2002*

"We know for a fact there are weapons there."—*Ari Fleischer, January 9, 2003*

"Our intelligence officials estimate that Saddam Hussein had the materials to produce as much as five hundred tons of sarin, mustard, and VX nerve agent."—*Bush, January 28, 2003*

"We know that Saddam Hussein is determined to keep his weapons of mass destruction, is determined to make more."—*Colin Powell, February 5, 2003*

"We have sources that tell us that Saddam Hussein recently authorized Iraqi field commanders to use chemical weapons—the very weapons the dictator tells us he does not have."—*Bush, February 8, 2003*

"Intelligence gathered by this and other governments leaves no doubt that the Iraq regime continues to possess and conceal some of the most lethal weapons ever devised."—*Bush, March 17, 2003*

"Well, there is no question that we have evidence and information that Iraq has weapons of mass destruction, biological and chemical, particularly."—*Fleischer, March 21, 2003*

"There is no doubt that the regime of Saddam Hussein possesses weapons of mass destruction. As this operation continues, those weapons will be identified, found, along with the people who have produced them and who guard them."—*General Tommy Franks, March 22, 2003*

"I have no doubt we're going to find big stores of weapons of mass destruction."—*Kenneth Adelman, Defense Policy Board, March 23, 2003*

"We know where they are. They are in the area around Tikrit and Baghdad."—*Donald Rumsfeld, March 30, 2003*

"We'll find them. It'll be a matter of time to do so."—*Bush, May 3, 2003*

"I never believed that we'd just tumble over weapons of mass destruction in that country."—*Rumsfeld, May 4, 2003*

"U.S. officials never expected that we were going to open garages and find weapons of mass destruction."—*Condoleezza Rice, May 12, 2003*

"They may have had time to destroy them, and I don't know the answer."—*Rumsfeld, May 27, 2003*

"We based our decisions on good, sound intelligence, and the—our people are going to find out the truth. And the truth will say that this intelligence was good intelligence. There's no doubt in my mind."—*Bush, July 17, 2003*

To quote Bill O'Reilly of Fox News, "And I said on my program, if, if the Americans go in and overthrow Saddam Hussein and it's clean, he had nothing, I will apologize to the nation, and I will not trust the Bush administration again."—March 18, 2003

*September 2003*

# Call Me a Bush-Hater

◼

AMONG THE MORE amusing cluckings from the right lately is their appalled discovery that quite a few Americans actually think George W. Bush is a terrible president.

Robert Novak is quoted as saying in all his forty-four years of covering politics, he has never seen anything like the detestation of Bush. Charles Krauthammer managed to write an entire essay on the topic of "Bush-haters" in *Time* magazine as though he had never before come across a similiar phenomenon.

Oh, I stretch memory way back, so far back, all the way back to—our last president. Almost lost in the mists of time though it is, I not only remember eight years of relentless attacks from Clinton-haters, I also notice they haven't let up yet. Clinton-haters accused the man of murder, rape, drug-running, sexual harassment, financial chicanery, and official misconduct. And they accuse his wife of even worse. For eight long years, this country was a zoo of Clinton-haters. Any idiot with a big mouth and a conspiracy theory could get a hearing on radio talk shows and "Christian" broadcasts and nutty Internet sites. People with transparent motives, people paid by tabloid magazines, people with known mental problems, ancient Clinton enemies with notoriously racist pasts—all were given hearings, credence, and air time. Sliming Clinton was a sure road to fame and fortune on the right, and many an ambitious young right-wing hit man like David Brock, who has since made full confession, took that golden opportunity.

And these folks didn't stop with verbal and printed attacks. From the day Clinton was elected to office, he was the subject of the politics of personal destruction. They went after him with a multimillion-dollar smear campaign funded by Richard Mellon Scaife, the right-wing billionaire. They went after him with lawsuits funded by right-wing legal foundations (Paula Jones), they got special counsels appointed to investigate every nitpicking nothing that ever happened (Filegate, Travelgate), and they never let go of that hardy perennial Whitewater. After all this time and all those millions of dollars wasted, no one has ever proved that the Clintons did a single thing wrong. Bill Clinton lied about a pathetic, squalid affair that was none of anyone else's business anyway, and for that they impeached the man and dragged this country through more than a year of the most tawdry, ridiculous, unnecessary pain. The day President Clinton tried to take out Osama bin Laden with a missile strike, every right-winger in America said it was a case of "wag the dog." He was supposedly trying to divert our attention from the much more breathtakingly important and serious matter of Monica Lewinsky, and who did he think he was to make us focus on some piffle like bin Laden?

"The puzzle is where this depth of feeling comes from," mused the ineffable Mr. Krauthammer. Gosh, what a puzzle that is. How could anyone not be just crazy about George W. Bush? "Whence the anger?" asks Krauthammer. "It begins of course with the 'stolen' election of 2000 and the perception of Bush's illegitimacy." I'd say so myself, yes, I would. I was in Florida during that chilling postelection fight, and am fully persuaded to this good day that Al Gore actually won Florida, not to mention getting 550,000 more votes than Bush overall. But I also remember thinking, as the scene became eerier and eerier, "Jeez, maybe we should just let them have this one, because Republican wingnuts are so crazy, their bitterness would poison Gore's whole Presidency." The night Gore conceded the race in one of the most graceful and honorable speeches I have ever heard, I was in a ballroom full of Republican Party flacks who booed and jeered through every word of it.

One thing I acknowledge about the right is that they're much better haters than liberals are. Your basic liberal—milk of human kindness flowing through every vein, and heart bleeding over everyone from the milk-shy Hottentot to the glandular obese—is pretty much a strikeout on the hatred front. Maybe further out on the left you can hit some good righteous anger, but liberals, and I am one, are generally real wusses. Guys like Rush Limbaugh figured that out a long time ago—attack a liberal and the first thing he says is, "You may have a point there."

To tell the truth, I'm kind of proud of us for holding the grudge this long. Normally, we'd remind ourselves that we have to be good sports, it's for the good of the country, we must unite behind the only president we've got, as Lyndon used to remind us. If there are still some of us out here sulking, "Yeah, but they *stole* that election," well, good. I don't think we should forget that.

But, onward. So George Dubya becomes president, having run as a "compassionate conservative," and what do we get? Hell's own conservative and dick for compassion.

His entire first eight months was tax cuts for the rich, tax cuts for the rich, tax cuts for the rich, and he lied and said the tax cuts would help average Americans. Again and again, the "average" tax cut would be $1,000. That means you get $100, and the millionaire gets $92,000, and that's how they "averaged" it out. Then came 9/11, and we all rallied. Ready to give blood, get out of our cars and ride bicycles, whatever. Shop, said the president. And more tax cuts for the rich.

By now, we're starting to notice Bush's bait-and-switch. Make a deal with Ted Kennedy to improve education and then fail to put money into it. Promise $15 billion in new money to combat AIDS in Africa (wow!) but it turns out to be a cheap con, almost no new money. Bush comes to praise a job-training effort, then cuts the money. Bush says AmeriCorps is great, then cuts the money. Gee, what could we possibly have against this guy? We go along with the war in Afghanistan, and we still don't have bin Laden.

Then suddenly, in the greatest bait-and-switch of all time, Osama bin doesn't matter at all, and we have to go after Saddam Hussein, who had nothing to do with 9/11. But he does have horrible weapons of mass destruction, and our president "without doubt," without question, knows all about them, even unto the amounts—tons of sarin, pounds of anthrax. So we take out Saddam Hussein, and there are no weapons of mass destruction. Furthermore, the Iraqis are not overjoyed to see us.

By now, quite a few people who aren't even liberal are starting to say, "Wha the hey?" We got no Osama, we got no Saddam, we got no weapons of mass destruction, the road map to peace in the Middle East is blown to hell, we're stuck in this country for $87 billion just for one year and no one knows how long we'll be there. And still poor Mr. Krauthammer is hard-put to conceive how anyone could conclude that George W. Bush is a poor excuse for a president.

Chuck, honey, it ain't just the 2.6 million jobs we've lost: People are losing their pensions, their health insurance, the cost of health insurance is doubling, tripling in price, the administration wants to cut off their overtime, and Bush was so too little, too late with extending unemployment compensation that one million Americans were left high and dry. And you wonder why we think he's a lousy president?

Sure, all that is just what's happening in people's lives, but what we need is the Big Picture. Well, the Big Picture is that after September 11, we had the sympathy of every nation on Earth. They all signed up, all our old allies volunteered, everybody was with us, and Bush just booted all of that away. Sneering, jeering, bad manners, hideous diplomacy, threats, demands, arrogance, bluster.

"In Afghanistan, Bush rode a popular tide; Iraq, however, was a singular act of presidential will," says Krauthammer.

You bet your ass it was. We attacked a country that had done nothing to us, had nothing to do with al-Qaeda, and turns out not to have weapons of mass destruction.

It is not necessary to hate George W. Bush to think he's a bad president. Grown-ups can do that, you know. You can decide someone's policies are a miserable failure without lying awake at night consumed with hatred.

Poor Bush is in way over his head, and the country is in bad shape because of his stupid economic policies.

If that makes me a Bush-hater, then sign me up.

**November/December 2003**

# The Uncompassionate
# Conservative

◼

IN ORDER TO UNDERSTAND why George W. Bush doesn't get it, you have to take several strands of common Texas attitude, then add an impressive degree of class-based obliviousness. What you end up with is a guy who sees himself as a perfectly nice fellow—and who is genuinely disconnected from the impact of his decisions on people.

On the few occasions when Bush does directly encounter the down-and-out, he seems to empathize. But then, in what is becoming a recurring, almost nightmare-type scenario, the minute he visits some constructive program and praises it (AmeriCorps, the Boys and Girls Club, job training), he turns around and cuts the budget for it. It's the kiss of death if the president comes to praise your program. During the presidential debate in Boston in 2000, Bush said, "First and foremost, we've got to make sure we fully fund LIHEAP [the Low Income Home Energy Assistance Program], which is a way to help low-income folks, particularly here in the East, pay their high fuel bills." He then sliced $300 million out of that sucker, even as people were dying of hypothermia, or, to put it bluntly, freezing to death.

Sometimes he even cuts your program before he comes to praise it. In August 2002, Bush held a photo op with the Quecreek coal miners, the nine men whose rescue had thrilled the country. By then he had already cut the coal-safety budget at the Mine Safety and Health Administration, which engineered the rescue, by 6 percent, and had named a coal-industry executive to run the agency.

The Reverend Jim Wallis, leader of Call to Renewal, a network of churches that fight poverty, told *The New York Times* that shortly after his election, Bush had said to him, "I don't understand how poor people think," and had described himself as a "white Republican guy who doesn't get it, but I'd like to." What's annoying about Bush is when this obtuseness, the blinkeredness of his life, weighs so heavily on others, as it has increasingly as he has acquired more power.

There was a telling episode in 1999 when the Department of Agriculture came out with its annual statistics on hunger, showing that once again Texas was near the top. Texas is a perennial leader in hunger because we have forty-three counties in South Texas (and some in East Texas) that are like Third World countries. If our border region were a state, it would be first in poverty, first in the percentage of schoolchildren living in poverty, first in the percentage of adults without a high school diploma, fifty-first in income per capita, and so on.

When the 1999 hunger stats were announced, Bush threw a tantrum. He thought it was some malign Clinton plot to make his state look bad because he was running for president. "I saw the report that children in Texas are going hungry. Where?" he demanded. "No children are going to go hungry in this state. You'd think the governor would have heard if there are pockets of hunger in Texas." You would, wouldn't you? That is the point at which ignorance becomes inexcusable. In five years, Bush had never spent time with people in the colonias, South Texas' shantytowns; he had never been to a session with Valley Interfaith, a consortium of border churches and schools and the best community organization in the state. There is no excuse for a governor to be unaware of this huge reality of Texas.

Take any area—environment, labor, education, taxes, health—and go to the websites of public-interest groups in that field. You will find page after page of minor adjustments, quiet repeals, no-big-deal new policies, all of them cruel, destructive, and harmful. A silent change in regulations, an executive order, a funding cutoff. No headlines. Below the radar. Again and again and again. Head Start, everybody's favorite government program, is being targeted for "improvement" by leaving it to the tender mercies of Mississippi and Alabama. An AIDS program that helps refugees in Africa and Asia gets its funding cut because one of the seven groups involved once worked with the United Nations, which once worked with the Chinese government, which once supported forced abortions.

So what manner of monster is behind these outrages? I have known George W. Bush slightly since we were both in high school, and I studied him closely as governor. He is neither mean nor stupid. What we have here is a man shaped by three intertwining strands of Texas culture, combined with huge blinkers of class. The three Texas themes are religiosity, anti-intellectualism, and machismo. They all play well politically with certain constituencies.

Let's assume the religiosity is genuine; no one is in a position to know otherwise. I leave it to more learned commentators to address what "Christian" might actually mean in terms of public policy.

The anti-intellectualism is also authentic. This is a grudge Bush has carried at least since his college days when he felt looked down on as a frat rat by more cerebral types. Despite his pedigree and prep schools, he ran into Eastern stereotypes of Texans at Yale, a common experience at Ivy schools in that time. John F. Kennedy, the consummate, effortlessly graceful, classy Harvard man, had just been assassinated in ugly old Dallas, and Lyndon Johnson's public piety gave many people the creeps. Texans were more or less thought of as yahoo barbarians somewhere between *The Beverly Hillbillies* and *Deliverance*. I do not exaggerate by much. To have a Texas accent in the East in those days was to have twenty points automatically deducted from your estimated IQ. And Texans have this habit of playing to the stereotype—it's irresistible. One proud Texan I know had never owned a pair of cowboy boots in his life until he got a Nieman Fellowship to Harvard. Just didn't want to let anyone down.

. For most of us who grow up in the "boonies" and go to school in the East, it's like speaking two languages—Bill Clinton, for example, is perfectly bilingual. But it's not unusual for a spell in the East to reinforce one's Texanness rather than erode it, and that's what happened to Bush. Bush had always had trouble reading—we assume it is dyslexia (although *Slate*'s Jacob Weisberg attributes it to aphasia); his mom was still doing flash cards with him when he was in junior high. Feeling intellectually inferior apparently fed into his resentment of Easterners and other known forms of snob.

Bush once said, "There's a West Texas populist streak in me, and it irritates me when these people come out to Midland and look at my friends with just the utmost disdain." In his mind, Midland is the true-blue heartland of the old vox pop. The irony is that Midland along with its twin city, Odessa, is one of the most stratified and narrow places in the country. Both are oil towns with amazingly strict class segregation. Midland is the white-collar, Republican town; Odessa is the blue-collar, Democratic town. The class conflict plays out in an annual football rivalry so intense that H. G. Bissinger featured it in his bestselling book, *Friday Night Lights*. To mistake Midland for the *volk* heartland is the West Texas equivalent of assuming that Greenwich, Connecticut, is Levittown.

In fact, people in Midland are real nice folks: I can't prove that with statistics, but I know West Texas and it's just a fact. Open, friendly, no side to 'em. The problem is, they're way isolated out there and way limited too. You can have dinner at the Petroleum Club anytime with a bunch of them and you'll come away saying, "Damn, those are nice people. Sure glad they don't run the world." It is still such a closed, narrow place, where everybody is white, Protestant, and agrees with everybody else.

The machismo is what I suspect is fake. The minute he is questioned, he becomes testy and defensive. That's one reason they won't let him hold many press conferences. When he tells stories about his dealings with two of the toughest men who ever worked in politics—the late Lee Atwater and the late Bob Bullock—Bush, improbably, comes off as the toughest mother in the face-down. I wouldn't put money on it being true. Bullock, the late lieutenant governor and W's political mentor in Texas, could be and often was meaner than a skilletful of rattlesnakes. Bush's story is that one time, Bullock cordially informed him that he was about to fuck him. Bush stood up and kissed Bullock, saying, "If I'm gonna get fucked, at least I should be kissed." It probably happened, but I guarantee you Bullock won the fight. Bush never got what made Bullock more than just a supermacho pol—the old son of a bitch was on the side of the people. Mostly.

The perfect absurdity of all this, of course, is that Bush's identification with the sturdy yeomen of Midland (actually, oil-company executives almost to a man) is so wildly at variance with his real background. Bush likes to claim the difference between him and his father is that, "He went to Greenwich Country Day and I went to San Jacinto Junior High." He did. For one year. Then his family moved to a posh neighborhood in Houston, and he went to the second-best prep school in town (couldn't get into the best one) before going off to Andover as a legacy.

Jim Hightower's great line about Bush, "Born on third and thinks he hit a triple," is still painfully true. Bush has simply never acknowledged that not only was he born with a silver spoon in his mouth—he's been eating off it ever since. The reason there is no noblesse oblige about Dubya is because he doesn't admit to himself or anyone else that he owes his entire life to being named George W. Bush. He didn't just get a head start by being his father's son—it remained the single most salient fact about him for most of his life. He got into Andover as a legacy. He got into Yale as a legacy. He got into Harvard Business School as a courtesy (he was turned down by the University of Texas Law School). He got into the Texas Air National Guard—and sat out Vietnam—

through Daddy's influence. (I would like to point out that that particular unit of FANGers, as regular air force referred to the "Fucking Air National Guard," included not only the sons of Governor John Connally and Senator Lloyd Bentsen, but some actual black members as well—they just happened to play football for the Dallas Cowboys.) Bush was set up in the oil business by friends of his father. He went broke and was bailed out by friends of his father. He went broke again and was bailed out again by friends of his father; he went broke yet again and was bailed out by some fellow Yalies.

That Bush's administration is salted with the sons of somebody-or-other should come as no surprise. I doubt it has ever even occurred to Bush that there is anything wrong with a class-driven good-ol'-boy system. That would explain why he surrounds himself with people like Eugene Scalia (son of Justice Antonin Scalia), whom he named solicitor of the Department of Labor—apparently as a cruel joke. Before taking that job, the younger Scalia was a handsomely paid lobbyist working against ergonomic regulations designed to prevent repetitive stress injuries. His favorite technique was sarcastic invective against workers who supposedly faked injuries when the biggest hazard they faced was "dissatisfaction with co-workers and supervisors." More than five million Americans are injured on the job every year, and more die annually from work-related causes than were killed on September 11. Neither Scalia nor Bush has ever held a job requiring physical labor.

What is the disconnect? One can see it from the other side—people's lives are being horribly affected by the Bush administration's policies, but they make no connection between what happens to them and the decisions made in Washington. I think I understand why so many people who are getting screwed do not know who is screwing them. What I don't get is the disconnect at the top. Is it that Bush doesn't want to see? No one brought it to his attention? He doesn't care?

Okay, we cut taxes for the rich and so we have to cut services for the poor. Presumably there is some right-wing justification along the lines that helping poor people just makes them more dependent or something. If there were a rationale Bush could express, it would be one thing, but to watch him not see, not make the connection, is another thing entirely. Welfare, Medicare, Social Security, food stamps—horrors, they breed dependency. Whereas inheriting millions of dollars and having your whole life handed to you on a platter is good for the grit in your immortal soul? What we're dealing with here is a man in such serious denial it would be pathetic if it weren't damaging so many lives.

Bush's lies now fill volumes. He lied us into two hideously unfair tax cuts; he lied us into an unnecessary war with disastrous consequences; he lied us into the PATRIOT Act, eviscerating our freedoms. But when it comes to dealing with those less privileged, Bush's real problem is not deception, but self-deception.

**November/December 2003**

# Heroes and Heels

## (and Madonna)

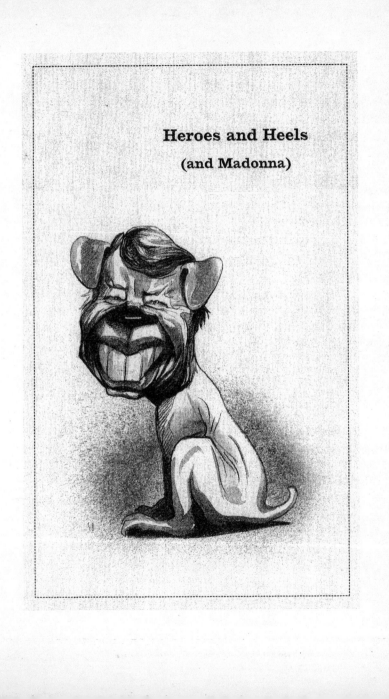

# Jessica Mitford

◾

J ESSICA MITFORD ROMILLY Treuhaft, known as Decca, who died last month, was among the handful of great muckraking journalists of our time. Peter Sussman of the Society of Professional Journalists puts her in a class with Upton Sinclair, Rachel Carson, and Ralph Nader. "Only funny."

Always funny. Lord knows, she could bring 'em down. She drove the entire funeral industry into collective apoplexy with *The American Way of Death* (1963), eventually leading the Federal Trade Commission to issue regulations for the industry; drove the Famous Writers School into richly deserved bankruptcy; and, in general, had quite a string of notches on her gun. She was also a wit, a charmer, a rebel, an ex-Communist, a lifelong radical, a beauty, and a lady. She led the most extraordinary life, with honor and with humor throughout.

Think of the leftist women writers of her generation and ask yourself whom you would have wanted to be friends with. Lillian Hellman, with all that Sturm und Drang? Mary McCarthy, with that backstabbing streak? Nonsense. You would have wanted to know Decca, of course, because she was such fun.

Toward the end of her life she was working on an update of *The American Way of Death*, for which reason she arrived in Houston last summer to visit the American Funeral Museum, of which it must be said, it's there. In fact, it's a multimedia museum. We toddled through the exhibits until we reached Embalming, where we perched on a bench to view a short documentary. Pyramids appeared on-screen and the narrator announced portentously, "The art of embalming was first discovered by the ancient Egyptians."

Decca said quietly, "Now *there* was a culture where the funeral directors got *completely* out of control."

She was hot on the trail of the story of the astonishing new concentration of ownership in the funeral industry. Except it's now called "the death-services industry," with that penchant for ghastly euphemism Decca pilloried so memorably. Something called Service Corporation International is swallowing its competition at such a clip that before long we'll all have to pay them to get planted. Decca went off incognito to price crypts at a local SCI crematorium. The "grief counselor" started by showing her the el cheapo model. "Wouldn't be caught dead in it," she snorted.

The news magazines invariably used to start profiles of Decca, "Born the daughter of an eccentric British peer . . ." as though she had done nothing else in her life. But it was a lulu of a life. To take it at a gallop, her eldest sister was the splendid comic novelist Nancy Mitford; her sister Diana married Sir Oswald Mosley, a leading British Fascist, and spent World War II in prison; her sister Unity fell in love with Hitler and shot herself at the outbreak of the war; her brother, Tom, was killed in Burma; her sister Pamela raised horses; and her sister Debo became the Duchess of Devonshire.

Decca Mitford sensibly decided to get out of the nest at an early age: She eloped with her cousin Esmond Romilly when she was nineteen and went off to fight for the Communists in the Spanish Civil War. Since both were scions of great families, a British destroyer was dispatched to bring them back. They married in France, but not until later: *quel scandale.*

The Romillys immigrated to America in 1939, tended bar, sold stockings, what have you. All fodder for great stories later told by Decca. Romilly enlisted in the Royal Canadian Air Force ("I'll probably find myself being commanded by one of your ghastly relations," he observed) and was killed in action in 1941, leaving Decca with their baby daughter, Dinky. (So strong is the Mitford mania for nicknames that I never knew Dinky's real name was Constancia until I read it in Decca's obituary.) She went to work for the Office of Price Administration in Washington and moved in with those generous progressive Southern souls Clifford and Virginia Durr. Since Decca and Virginia both had the gift of making hardship into marvelous stories, tales of that household have become almost legendary.

In 1943, Decca married Robert Treuhaft, a calm, witty, radical, Harvard-trained lawyer. They were married for fifty-three years, and for fifty-three years she was in love with him. Thought he hung the moon, and all that other 1930s love-ballad stuff. Her dear friend Maya Angelou recalled, "My God, they had been married for two hundred years and every time she heard his car pull up in the driveway she'd say, 'Bob's here; it's Bob!' "

Decca once said that she felt she had never really known her sister Nancy because she lived within an "armor of drollery." Decca herself would make almost anything into a joke: When summoned to appear before the House Un-American Activities Committee in San Francisco, she took the per diem expense check she got from the government and donated it to the Communist Party. She and her husband remained party members in Oakland, California, until 1958; their adventures are described in her political memoir, *A Fine Old Conflict.*

A Decca story from the C.P. days: She had long since realized that fund-raisers and parties were part of "the struggle." Some humorless party appa-ratchik had entrusted her with organizing a chicken dinner for the faithful, and was giving her instructions. When it came to procuring the main course, he wanted to direct Decca to politically correct poultry farmers. He looked left and looked right, apparently suspicious of FBI wiretaps. "There are certain comrades in—" he broke off. He scribbled a note and pushed it across his desk. "Petaluma," it read. After further instruction, Decca said she had just one ques-tion. "Do you think the chickens should be—" she began. She looked left, looked right, checking for bugs, and scribbled, "broiled or fried?"

A not-so-funny Decca story: At the height of the McCarthy era, that great liberal Hubert H. Humphrey proposed that membership in the Communist Party be made a crime. Decca was trying to explain to Dinky, then eight, that all of them might be sent away to detention camp. "Camp?!" cried Dinky in delight, envisioning tennis and canoeing. Decca told it as a good story. Armored with drollery.

Decca Mitford was not fearless: She was brave. Much as she ridiculed those English public-school virtues, like spunk and pluck, she was herself guilty of one of them: She was gallant. Her gallantry was beyond simple courage. It sometimes takes courage to see injustice and then stand up and denounce it. Gallantry requires doing so without ever becoming bitter; gal-lantry requires humor and honor.

Decca and her friend Marge Frantz invented the "roar-o-meter" to mea-sure how absurd the world could be. Much as she relished the world's silliness, there is a true north in all her work—a passion for social justice and concern for those who are being beaten and battered.

I think some people who knew her only slightly assumed Decca Mitford glided through this world with the complete self-assurance that comes from an aristocratic background. She was not much given to regrets—I don't think anyone ever heard her whine about anything, even though she lost two chil-dren and her first love—but she remained deeply aggrieved that she had never been allowed to have a formal education. Her mother, Lady Redesdale, reactionary even for her day, believed girls did not need school. To the end of her life, Decca earnestly made lists of books she thought she should have read and quizzed friends about what they were reading: Dinky says that when she was a child, her mother used to sail in to confront teachers and school administrators but later confessed she was terrified of them. The only time she remembers her mother being seriously angry with her was when she dropped out of Sarah Lawrence. Took Decca three days to get over it.

One of the best stories is about the time Decca was invited to become a distinguished professor at San Jose State University. She was deeply thrilled, but the position required her to take a loyalty oath. She refused to give the school her fingerprints, providing toe prints instead. A great and glorious uproar ensued, and, alas, it ended with her becoming, as she put it, "an extinguished professor." She learned recently that plans were afoot at the University of California, Berkeley, to raise money for a chair in her name in investigative journalism. "I'm to be a chair, Bobby," she marveled. "A chair."

In her long life as a journalist-activist—interviewing prisoners, scouring the fringes of Oakland for her husband's labor and civil rights cases, going to Mississippi, confronting police chiefs, taking on the medical profession—she never lost the sense that it was all a grand adventure. Shortly before her death, she said, "Well, I had a good run, didn't I?"

**August 1996**

# Erwin Knoll

◾

THEY CALLED FROM Madison November 2 to tell me Erwin Knoll had died. That afternoon, when I went out to collect the mail, I found the familiar *Progressive* envelope with its familiar copy of the magazine and the familiar note from Erwin. As Johnny Faulk used to say, that jerked the stopper.

Such an un-farewell note: just one of Erwin's kind, funny little verbal doodles and, for the first time ever, not a mention of my next deadline.

Knoll and I had a running joke: Ever since I've written a column for this magazine, I have been abysmal about deadlines. The first notice, the second notice, the telephoned plea from Madison, the this-time-we-really-mean-it call.

"Okay, okay, by four o'clock this afternoon, I promise." But by four, the day is over, and the next morning is just as good, so what-the-hey! It's always there by noon. Or so.

I told Erwin years ago, the most liberal thing about me is that I'm good at guilt and—except for newspaper columns, which I do on some kind of automatic pilot—the only way editors ever get pieces out of me is to guilt-trip me. Victor Navasky is a master at this. Erwin refused to play the game. Being an even better liberal than I, he was convinced he could get me to work by positive reinforcement alone. So every month came the wry note about how great the last column was, and by the way, here's the next official deadline.

My boss, Liz Faulk, tapes Erwin's notes to my computer screen when *The Progressive*'s deadline draws near. "What shall we do with this?" she asked about Erwin's last note. "We don't want to just put it in the files."

"Save it," say I, "and tape it to my computer screen with every new deadline date so Erwin can non-guilt-trip me from the grave. 'Still useful, though dead.' He'd love that."

———

WHILE WE were having a beer at the Cafe Montmartre in Madison in late October, I got stuck trying to explain my politics to some younger members of *The Progressive* staff.

"I don't have an agenda, I don't have a program," I said. "I'm not a communist or a socialist. I guess I'm a left-libertarian and a populist, and I believe in the Bill of Rights the way some folks believe in the Bible. Hell. Erwin, do you have a political identity, I mean, can you describe yourself in programmatic terms?"

"Of course not," said Erwin promptly. Erwin, the perfect anti-ideologue. What free mind would ever abandon its intelligence to someone else's creed? "I have only two irreducible principles. One is nonviolence: I am a pacifist. I believe violence is never a solution. And the other is freedom of speech, the First Amendment."

Sign me up for Erwin's Party.

Adjectives never do as much as stories, I think. I can tell you Erwin Knoll was kind, gentle, thoughtful, and had an exceptionally large mind. It doesn't mean near as much as telling real stories about him. Which he knew, too. The last evening we spent together, talking to young staffers on his magazine, was inspired by something Ben Sidran, the great jazz pianist from Madison, said about his tradition: that jazz is an art that has to be passed down by hand, for young musicians to just listen to the great recordings is not enough. They have to actually play with jazz musicians to get the sense of fun and improvisation.

Independent journalism in this country is likewise a rather endangered craft, or even art form, if you want to be pretentious. And it, too, has to be passed down from hand to hand. And so we sat there, the two of us, regaling the youngsters with tales of Izzy Stone and Andrew Kopkind, Bob Sherrill and Ronnie Dugger, Frosty Troy and William Brann.

If you are a younger journalist and no one ever tells you these stories, how are you to know that there's another way to do it? A whole different tradition? That success is not becoming a talking-head celebrity, saying what everyone else says?

My own peculiar role at *The Progressive* is to provide regular instruction in the science of how to keep laughing, even though you've considered all the facts. And there never was such a magazine for making you consider all the facts as Erwin Knoll's *Progressive*. And there was never anyone easier to make laugh than Erwin Knoll.

# Madonna

∎

I AM WORRIED about Madonna. Okay, actually I'm worried about Madonna and me. Because of this woman, I'm in danger of being consigned to premature Old Poophood.

On the subject of Madonna, I resemble the Senate Judiciary Committee—I just don't get it. I achieve positively Bushian levels of not getting it.

I went along fine for quite a while with Madonna, feeling vaguely fond of her on the slender grounds that I understand her Fashion Statement. Although a lifelong fashion dropout, I have absorbed enough by reading *Harper's Bazaar* while waiting at the dentist's to have grasped that the purpose of fashion is to make A Statement. (My own modest Statement, discerned by true cognoscenti, is, WOMAN WHO WEARS CLOTHES SO SHE WON'T BE NAKED.) And Madonna's Statement is as clear as a Hill Country spring. It is: I'M A SLUT! What's more, it seems to be made with a great deal of energy and good cheer. I rather liked it.

But then Madonna took up *la vie littéraire,* invading my turf as it were, and I felt constrained to develop an opinion of her literary talents. Without, of course, reading her book, since no sane person is going to fork out fifty-seven bucks for her oeuvre. Even if she does have a comprehensible Fashion Statement. Careful study of the publicity about Madonna's book left me with a strong desire to say to her, "Young woman, stop making an exhibition of yourself." Since Madonna makes a living by making an exhibition of herself, it seemed a singularly bootless impulse.

C. R. Ebersole of Houston, who happens to be my former Sunday-school teacher, passed along his opinion that Madonna has done more for dogs than anyone since Albert Payson Terhune. I did not inquire why my former Sunday-school teacher paid $57 for a book called *Sex.*

Thinking I might be of the wrong gender to appreciate Madonna, I called my friend Aregood in Philadelphia, whose taste in women is notoriously ecumenical. Aregood says you can tell you're out of touch with your fellow Americans when the reigning sex goddess is someone you wouldn't take home with you if she were the last woman left in the bar. He also says Sophia Loren is still his idea of a sex goddess.

I struggled with the concept of impending Old Poophood. I was, in my day, fairly with it, verging on hip. When I was in college, I carefully suppressed the fact that I knew all the words to every song Bob Wills ever wrote, and listened assiduously to Dave Brubeck and Edith Piaf. Later, I was among the first on my block to discover Bob Dylan, Janice Joplin, and The Band. You see, we're talking no mean record on the Cutting Edge Front.

I admit to recent slippage—both punk rock and rap slipped right by me. But with the large tolerance that comes from being a nonparent, I have been given to loftily assuring my offspring-impaired friends that every generation is entitled to some form of music that will drive anyone over twenty out of the room. I believe this is meet, just, and probably part of God's plan.

Several of my advisers on contemporary culture have tried to persuade me that Madonna's redeeming social value lies in her apparently premeditated pattern of pushing all known taboos to the limit and beyond, in order to force her fans to think seriously about their own choices. Her fans seem to consist largely of thirteen-year-old girls. I believe this is a reflection of how difficult it is to be a thirteen-year-old female in our society.

When I was thirteen, I yearned to be an arthur. As I understood it, arthurs got to live in New York or Paris and hang out in sophisticated places like the Algonquin or Harry's Bar with terribly witty people, all of them exchanging bon mots that would later be collected by literary historians. Sounded like a good deal to me.

Then I became an arthur. All that happened was my publisher sent me to a lot of radio stations in places like Garden City, Kansas, where deejays kept asking me, "So, Miss Ivv-ins, what *is it* about Texas?" No bon mots occurred.

Then I got sent to a literary tea in New York at the Waldorf Astoria, so my hopes were high. My fellow *littérateurs* on that occasion turned out to be Elmore Leonard, who writes those great tough-guy murder mysteries; Professor Henry Gates of Harvard, who is big on the multicultural circuit; and Ivana Trump, who paid somebody to write a book for her. My publisher says it is better than Marilyn Quayle's book.

We all addressed 350 blue-haired ladies at the literary tea, and I held up well until Ivana (she asked me to call her that) explained to the ladies that in addition to *la vie littéraire,* she is quite busy. She hass ze shildren, she hass ze sharities, and also she iss bringing out a new line of toiletries. I at once became enchanted with the marketing possibilities for arthurs. Elmore Leonard can sell "Eau de Detroit Funk, A Cologne for Men." Gates can retail a line of soul food, sort of like Paul Newman's Popcorn: Skip Gates' Pickled Pigs' Feet. I shall endeavor to sell Molly Ivins' BBQ-Flavored Vaginal Gel.

I dunno. You grow up, you finally get to be an arthur, and there you are with Ivana Trump and Madonna. What the hell would Albert Payson Terhune say?

**January 1993**

# Rush Limbaugh

∎

ONE OF THE things that concerns a lot of Americans lately is the increase in plain old nastiness in our political discussion. It comes from a number of sources, but Rush Limbaugh is a major carrier.

I should explain that I am not without bias in this matter. I have been attacked by Rush Limbaugh on the air, an experience somewhat akin to being gummed by a newt. It doesn't actually hurt, but it leaves you with slimy stuff on your ankle.

I have a correspondent named Irwin Wingo in Weatherford, Texas. Irwin and some of the leading men of the town are in the habit of meeting about ten every morning at the Chat'n'Chew Café to drink coffee and discuss the state of the world. One of their number is a dittohead, a Limbaugh listener. He came in one day, plopped himself down, and said, "I think Rush is right: Racism in this country is dead. I don't know what the niggers will find to gripe about now."

I wouldn't say that dittoheads, as a group, lack the ability to reason. It's just that whenever I run across one, he seems to be at a low ebb in reasoning skills. Poor ol' Bill Sarpalius, one of our dimmer Panhandle congressmen, was once trying to explain to a town hall meeting of his constituents that Limbaugh was wrong when he convinced his listeners that Bill Clinton's tax package contained a tax increase on the middle class. (It increased taxes only on the wealthiest 2 percent of Americans.) A dittohead in the crowd rose to protest: "We don't send you to Washington to make responsible decisions. We send you there to represent us."

The kind of humor Limbaugh uses troubles me deeply, because I have spent much of my professional life making fun of politicians. I believe it is a great American tradition and should be encouraged. We should all laugh more at our elected officials—it's good for us and good for them. So what right do I have to object because Limbaugh makes fun of different pols than I do?

I object because he consistently targets dead people, little girls, and the homeless—none of whom are in a particularly good position to answer back. Satire is a weapon, and it can be quite cruel. It has historically been the weapon of powerless people aimed at the powerful. When you use satire against powerless people, as Limbaugh does, it is not only cruel, it's profoundly vulgar. It is like kicking a cripple.

On his TV show, early in the Clinton administration, Limbaugh put up a picture of Socks, the White House cat, and asked, "Did you know there's a White House dog?" Then he put up a picture of Chelsea Clinton, who was thirteen years old at the time and as far as I know had never done any harm to anyone.

When viewers objected, he claimed, in typical Limbaugh fashion, that the gag was an accident and that without his permission some technician had put up the picture of Chelsea—which I found as disgusting as his original attempt at humor.

On another occasion, Limbaugh put up a picture of Labor Secretary Robert Reich that showed him from the forehead up, as though that were all the camera could get. Reich is indeed a very short man as a result of a bone disease he had as a child. Somehow the effect of bone disease in children has never struck me as an appropriate topic for humor.

The reason I take Rush Limbaugh seriously is not because he's offensive or right-wing, but because he is one of the few people addressing a large group of disaffected people in this country. And despite his frequent denials, Limbaugh does indeed have a somewhat cultlike effect on his dittoheads. They can listen to him for three and a half hours a day, five days a week, on radio and television. I can assure you that David Koresh did not harangue the Branch Davidians so long nor so often. But that is precisely what most cult leaders do—talk to their followers hour after hour after hour.

A large segment of Limbaugh's audience consists of white males, eighteen to thirty-four years old, without college education. Basically, a guy I know and grew up with named Bubba.

Bubba listens to Limbaugh because Limbaugh gives him someone to blame for the fact that Bubba is getting screwed. He's working harder, getting paid less in constant dollars, and falling further and further behind. Not only is Bubba never gonna be able to buy a house, he can barely afford a trailer. Hell, he can barely afford the payments on the pickup.

And because Bubba understands he's being shafted, even if he doesn't know why or how or by whom, he listens to Limbaugh. Limbaugh offers him scapegoats. It's the "feminazis." It's the minorities. It's the limousine liberals. It's all these people with all these wacky social programs to help some silly, self-proclaimed bunch of victims. Bubba feels like a victim himself—and he is—but he never got any sympathy from liberals.

Psychologists often tell us there is a great deal of displaced anger in our emotional lives—your dad wallops you, but he's too big to hit back, so you go clobber your little brother. Displaced anger is also common in our political life. We see it in this generation of young white men without much education and very little future. This economy no longer has a place for them. The corporations have moved their jobs to Singapore. Unfortunately, it is Limbaugh and the Republicans who are addressing the resentments of these folks, and aiming their anger in the wrong direction.

In my state, I have not seen so much hatred in politics since the heyday of the John Birch Society in the early 1960s. In those days, you couldn't talk politics with a conservative without his getting all red in the face, arteries standing out in his neck, wattles aquiver with indignation—just like a pissed-off turkey gobbler. And now we're seeing the same kind of anger again.

Fairness & Accuracy in Reporting has a sweet, gentle faith that truth will triumph in the end, and thinks it is sufficient to point out that Limbaugh is wrong. I say it's important to point out that he's not just wrong but that he's ridiculous, one of the silliest people in America. Sure, it takes your breath away when he spreads some false and vicious rumor, such as the story that Vincent Foster's body was actually discovered in an apartment owned by Hillary Clinton. Or when he destroys an important lobby-control bill by falsely claiming that it would make the average citizen subject to lobbying laws. Yes, that's sick and perverse.

But it's important to show people that there is much more wrong with Limbaugh's thinking than just his facts. Limbaugh specializes in ad hominem arguments, which are themselves ridiculously easy to expose. Ted Kennedy says, "America needs health-care reform." Limbaugh replies, "Ted Kennedy is fat."

Rush Limbaugh's pathetic abuse of logic, his absurd pomposity, his relentless self-promotion, his ridiculous ego—now those, friends, are appropriate targets for satire.

# Phil Gramm I

■

$\mathbf{M}$IAMI, FLA. — the most curious part of the story about Phil Gramm and the savings and loan owner is not the cupidity but the stupidity. Whatever one may have thought of Senator Gramm previously, *dumb* was not a word that sprang to mind. But to be helping an S&L owner to whom one was indebted in 1989—after Jim Wright's fall, after the Keating Five, after the whole damn thing had blown wide open—leads us to suspect that our Phil is, well, no rocket scientist.

Gramm, of course, maintains that the aid he provided Jerry Stiles, who did $53,000 worth of free work on Gramm's vacation home, was "routine," and, one would gather, perfunctory. And the freebie itself was motivated only by Senator Gramm's noble desire to provide work for unemployed Texans.

Generosity of interpretation is in the eye of the beholder. Can't wait to hear what Jim Wright has to say about it. Dickie Flatt, too.

My quarrel with Gramm stems not from anything he may have done that was illegal, or at best unethical, but rather from his Business As Usual MO Gramm, spouting his right-wing populism, went to the Senate and promptly fell into the most advanced patterns of legal extortion—to wit, collecting political action committee money like a panhandling fool.

I grant you the fault is not Gramm's, but the system's. On the other hand, he has consistently voted against every effort to reform the despicable system of legalized bribery masquerading as campaign contributions that has corrupted the entire political process.

For at least one year, he was the Senate cham-peen PAC money collector, and he's always right near the top. Lately, as chairman of the Senate Republican Campaign Committee, he's become even more aggressive at scooping up lobby money for his party.

As a member of the Senate Banking Committee, Gramm earned a perfect goose egg—a big, fat zero rating—from the Campaign for Financial Democracy, the S&L watchdog organization.

Gramm's other, less loveable tricks are well known to his colleagues. "Grammstanding" is what his colleagues in the Texas congressional delegation call it when Gramm, having fought some nice goodie for a Texas town—say a new post office for East Boot—then rushes out when the thing is finally approved, despite his vote, to announce it and claim credit for it.

Another favorite Gramm trick is to vote for projects that will help Texas and then to vote against appropriating money for them, so he can retain his reputation as a fiscal watchdog and deficit buster. This ancient and dishonorable legislative practice is usually described by a word beginning with *chicken*.

All in all, I've no quarrel with Phil Gramm's performance as a standard-issue, right-wing Republican carrying water for big-money special interests. That, one should expect. But his pose as a friend of the "little man" has always annoyed me.

An ancillary matter reflecting no particular discredit on Gramm, but again on the system as a whole, is the nonperformance of the Senate Ethics Committee. Under what bizarre stretch of logic did they conclude that $53,000 of free work on a vacation home was *not* a gift under the Senate rules. Clearly, the Senate rules police need their heads examined.

While on the subject of idiotic Senate rules, or lack thereof, note the current flap over alleged sexual harassment by Senator Bob Packwood. The new women senators have vowed to strengthen Senate rules against sexual harassment. I have a better idea. Why doesn't the Senate put itself under the same laws against sexual harassment they passed for everyone else in the country? Eh?

**December 1992**

# Phil Gramm II

∎

I THINK IT PROVES there is a God," said one Texas liberal of Senator Phil Gramm's presidential campaign, which is going nowhere fast. Gloating is in violation of the liberal creed, which calls for compassion at all times, especially for those who are getting kicked around. On the other hand, we are talking about Phil Gramm.

*The New Republic* pronounced him "profoundly amoral, committed only to his own political advancement, ruthless in getting his way and untrustworthy in accounting for his actions." That pretty much sums up the press reaction to our boy Phil so far. And we are not talking about "the liberal media" here. *Mean, heartless, amoral, ruthless,* and *calculating* are words that have appeared in profiles of Gramm across the board.

Public reaction, as measured in various polls, hovers around 9 percent support from Republicans nationally. His presidential campaign is already a standard joke; there are several variations on "the candidate for those who think Bob Dole is not mean enough."

Of course, I would no more write off Phil Gramm at this point than I would get near a wounded rattler. At one of his many extremely profitable money-raising soirees earlier this year, Gramm quoted Ben Franklin's line that a man can have but three reliable friends: an old wife, an old dog, and ready money. Gramm went on to say that he has a young wife, an old dog, and "Thanks to you and your support tonight, I have the most reliable friend that you can have in American politics, and that is ready money."

The dread words *John Connally* do occur, do they not? (For those who have forgotten, Connally, always a boardroom favorite, ran for president in 1980, spent $6 million, and got one delegate.)

Nevertheless, Gramm is sitting on one of the biggest campaign kitties in history, off to a flying start with $5 million "left over" from his Senate campaign and augmented by more millions collected since ($4.1 million at one event in February—a world record). Gramm, twice the chair of the National Republican Senatorial Committee, is familiar with almost every big giver in politics. He received more money from medical and insurance interests opposed to President Clinton's health-care reforms than any other member of Congress. With his characteristic kindness, he said of health-care reform: "We have to blow up this train and the rails and trestle and kill everyone on board."

But Gramm's single largest special-interest donor group continues to be oil and gas. During a discussion of pending legislation, a reporter recently suggested to Gramm that the bill under discussion would help natural gas companies but hurt homeowners. Gramm replied, "Any policy has winners and losers."

One of the most telling things about Phil Gramm is that those who know him best like him least. One of the safest bets in Washington for years now has been who would win a secret Senate poll for Most Disliked Member. Gramm's inevitable response is: "I didn't come to Washington to be loved, and I haven't been disappointed." One member of Congress who has dealt with him describes him as "pond slime," which is pretty much the general reaction.

The word *grammstanding* comes from the man's notorious habit of claiming credit for work he didn't do; some lowly Texas lawmaker will toil away for months to get a post office or a factory or some modest piece of pork for his district, only to find that Gramm, who never helped and often hurt the effort, has sprung forth with a news release claiming credit for same.

So far, Gramm's presidential campaign has netted him (a) publicity about an ill-fated 1974 investment in a dirty movie with his then brother-in-law (Gramm has denied knowledge of the nature of the film, although the ex-brother-in-law insists that he knew); (b) publicity about his own "Willie Horton," an ex-drug dealer whom Gramm's office helped spring from prison with unhappy results (again, Gramm says he knew nothing of the episode, despite some evidence that he did); and (c) renewed publicity about the Jerry Stiles case.

Stiles was a savings and loan rip-off artist who cost the taxpayers $200 million. He was convicted last year on eleven counts of conspiracy, bank bribery, and misapplication of funds. In 1987, Stiles advanced Gramm $117,000, interest-free, for renovation of Gramm's vacation home on the Eastern Shore. Three months after the work was finished, Stiles billed Gramm $63,433. Gramm had been pushing legislation that would have helped Stiles' failing S&Ls. By 1989, when Stiles was in big trouble with federal regulators, Gramm urged the regulators to go gently on Stiles and to consider his pleas for help and waivers from federal rules.

Rather than gloating about Gramm's foundering campaign, I think we should consider some of the troubling questions that this raises about Texas politics and Texas voters. Why is it that we have elected and reelected a man so unpleasant that his own colleagues can't stand him and whose record in politics disqualifies him for higher office? The question is not what's wrong with Phil Gramm, but what's wrong with us.

**July 1995**

# Phil Gramm III

WOULD A BLEEDING-HEART liberal kick a guy while he's down? Should a girl like I, in whom the milk of human kindness flows copiously for everyone, from protein-shy Hottentots to the glandular obese, actually aim a few swift boots at the prone form of Senator Phil Gramm? Nah. But it's tempting.

We liberals do sometimes forsake our vows of compassion for all mankind. I recall publicly gloating about the defeat of some of the noxious fat-heads Texas used to send to Congress. But hell, I even felt sorry for Richard Nixon when he left. There's nothing you can do about being born liberal—fish gotta swim, and hearts gotta bleed.

From the Texas Democratic point of view, it's a shame that Gramm didn't stay in at least through New Hampshire and spend himself broke. Now, he'll just come home and clobber whoever the Democrat is with his leftover millions.

It's hard to write about Gramm without sounding mean; the national reporters' favorite line was, "Even his friends don't like him." The most touching story I ever heard about Gramm was from a fellow senator who used to tell Gramm: "You'll never be president, Phil, because you've got no heart."

For some reason, Gramm, who has more than amply demonstrated his indifference to what his colleagues think of him, took this guy seriously. For years afterward, whenever he'd done anything that remotely smacked of compassion, he'd come up to this senator and say: "Whatta ya think, whatta ya think—am I showing heart yet?"

Well, it is sort of touching.

From the point of view of the rest of the country, Texas and Phil Gramm must look like Enid and Joe Waldholtz. Most people keep asking, "But what did she ever see in him?" while the kinder ones reply, "She *must* have married him for money. Give her a little credit—it *couldn't* have been love."

What can we say? We keep electing the guy by two-digit percentage margins, and in the rest of the country, he can't buy his way out of single digits with $20 million. And that's just Republicans.

He may be a schmuck, but at least he's our schmuck? (I always think of him as a schmuck from Georgia, but then, I don't like him.)

I suppose we could just blame him on the Aggies, but I think that's some kind of "ist"—universityist? While Austin snores along in its false sense of superiority, Texas A&M has in fact become a great university. I'm not suggesting that we ban Aggie jokes as politically incorrect, but let's at least recognize reality.

My real problem with Phil Gramm is ill-timed; it's the wrong season to make this case, but I'll try anyway. Set aside that I don't agree with him about anything. I don't agree with Representative Charlie Stenholm, a Blue Dog Democrat, about anything either. But you notice that Stenholm and the rest of the Blue Dogs have been sweating like farm workers to find a compromise on the budget impasse in Washington. They understand that compromise is necessary.

In this, the era of ideologues, that is a most unfashionable position. There are seventy-three Republican freshmen and one Speaker in the House who consider compromise treachery. And Phil Gramm considered compromise treachery before compromise-as-treachery was cool. I suppose we should give him credit for being ahead of his time; Texans always have liked a hard-ass.

Now that *politician* is a dirty word (not that it was ever reminiscent of roses), it seems awfully dated to bring up names like Sam Rayburn, Lyndon B. Johnson, Ralph Yarborough, and Barbara Jordan. But they were politicians. They fought hard and they compromised because they thought it was for something quaintly called the greater good. Or maybe they just wanted to move the ball. In any case, in the phrase of the kindergarten report card, they worked and played well with others. And no one ever considered them sissies because of it.

Phil Gramm does not work or play well with others. Never has. And I don't think that works well for Texas. "Go along to get along" is not an inspirational philosophy, and only God knows how much moral cowardice it has covered up over the years. Serve your time, collect your chits, and cash 'em in for your home state? No, I'd say we could ask for more than that from our senators. But I've never seen Phil Gramm collect or cash a chit for anyone except Phil Gramm. And that is one in the ribs to a man who's down. God forgive me.

**February 1996**

# Morris Udall

■

TUCSON, ARIZ. — damn, life's a funny ol' female-dog, idn't she? Here I am, back in Tucson, one of my favorite places in the U.S. of A. and also the place of one of my most bitter professional regrets.

I did a man wrong here one time. I didn't mean to, and it didn't make much difference, but there it is. The man's name is Morris Udall, representative from Tucson, and the year was 1976.

Six, I think it was, Democrats were scrapping for the presidential nomination that year. Ol' Jerry Ford looked beatable. Among the less likely contenders were Jimmy Carter, a former governor of Georgia with the charisma of a day-old pizza, and Mo Udall, an ace guy with the misfortune to be from Arizona (three electoral votes).

*The New York Times Sunday Magazine* was fixing to run profiles on each of these six candidates, and they called me to profile Udall—I think because I, in Texas, was the farthest-West journalist they'd ever heard of. Texas, Arizona—it all looks the same from New York.

In those days, I was what is known in our trade as "hungry," which is supposed to mean "fiesty, ambitious, willin' to go after a story like a starvin' dog." Actually, I was plain hungry: Six years at *The Texas Observer* left me below the poverty line, and I jumped at that assignment.

So I came over to Arizona and investigated Mo Udall's life, times, finances, family life, psychological health, and public record back to Year Aught. I'll tell you now what I should have told you then: Morris Udall is a man of exceptional decency, integrity, courage, honesty, and intelligence. On top of that, he's funny. If you could have forced Congress to take a vote at that time just on the question of who was the finest human being then serving—secret ballot, no consequences, just vote your conscience—I swear to you that Udall would have won hands down.

And did I report this? Hell, no. I was looking for warts; I wanted dirt. Besides, I was afraid of being conned, of looking like a naïve hick. I dug through his campaign contributions. (I found union money! Do you know how brave you have to be to support unions in Arizona?) I dug through his psychohistory. (The Udalls are a famous Mormon family. Mo split from the church and became a Jack Mormon after commanding an all-black troop in the army). I wrote about his being one-eyed. (At one point, he was a one-eyed professional basketball player—some handicap.)

Faced with the disgusting reality of a truly decent politician, I did my dead-level best to be nasty. I didn't cut him an inch of slack; I thought that was my job, the way they did it in the big leagues.

My grudging report that I hadn't been able to find anything actually wrong with Udall duly appeared in print. Imagine my surprise when *The New York Times'* famed political correspondent R. W. Apple followed my reserved appraisal of Udall with a puff piece about Jimmy Carter. (Johnny Apple, you know perfectly well that was a puff piece.) Every venial sin of Udall's that I had held up to the merciless light of day, Apple glossed over gaily in the case of Carter. The profiles appeared from one Sunday to the next, but the politicians described in them were not judged by a single standard. To put it mildly.

Well, Jimmy Carter turned out to be a man of character and decency, too—he just wasn't much of a politician, and Mo Udall was a good one.

My continuing regret is that what I wrote was accurate, but it wasn't *true.* I was trying so hard to prove I could be a major-league, hard-hitting journalist that I let the real story go hang itself.

The real story is the sheer decency of Morris Udall. When I am asked if there are any heroes left in politics, I always think of Udall. He's retired now, victim of a sad, slow, wasting disease. I suppose you could say that Udall is to Arizona liberals what Barry Goldwater is to Arizona conservatives: an incurably honest man of principle. Or you could say that Morris Udall is to Arizona liberals what Ev Mecham is to Arizona kooks. I think he'd like to have it end with a joke.

Speaking of remarkable figures from the past, those of us in the small but select circle that follows South Dakota politics were delighted to see Bill Janklow with the nomination for governor again. Last time Janklow was governor, he contributed greatly to the public entertainment. Among the more colorful charges leveled against him were that he wore a rabbit suit and carried a machine gun in his car trunk. (I can't remember if any of that is true or not, I just recall the offbeat charm of it all.) The thing to remember about Dakota politics is that the Dakotas only *look* normal—underneath is a wide streak of Dakota weirdness. For normal, you have to go to Nebraska.

**June 1994**

# Richard Nixon

◼

**Q**UEL TRIOMPH for the old Trickster. One last time we got a new Nixon. The Dead Nixon was, according to all those glowing tributes on television, a man of vision, courage, and leadership. For those of you thinking you must have lost your marbles lately to have forgotten what a great American Richard Nixon was, here's a little pop quiz to refresh your memories.

*How did Bob Haldeman, who was Nixon's closest aide in the White House, describe Nixon in writing from prison?*

"Dirty, mean, coldly calculating, devious, craftily manipulative, the weirdest man ever to live in the White House."

*What did Nixon think of the Supreme Court?*

He nominated two men, Clement Haynsworth and G. Harrold Carswell, to the Court, both of whom were found unfit to serve there by the United States Senate. According to Haldeman, if Nixon had gotten a single vote on the Court, he would have defied its order to turn over the Watergate tapes. "When the Court ruled 8-to-0 against Nixon, it unknowingly averted what might have been a supremely critical confrontation between the executive and judiciary powers."

*How did Nixon see the executive branch?*

According to John Ehrlichman, shortly before the 1972 election Nixon called a "landmark meeting" at Camp David to plan the "capture" of the executive branch. "It was Nixon's intent to repopulate the bureaucracy with our people. We would seek new laws to permit the dead and disloyal wood to be cast out." Nixon admired John Dean because "he had the kind of steel and really mean instinct we needed to clean house after the election in various departments and to put the IRS and Justice Department on the kind of basis it should be on." The IRS was to be used to get those on the enemies list.

In his diary Nixon wrote, "There simply has to be a line drawn at times with those who are against us, and then we have to take action to deal with them effectively." Of a bureaucrat who had failed to knuckle under to the White House, Nixon said, "We're going to get him . . . there are many unpleasant places a bureaucrat can be sent." At other times, Nixon ranted about the "Jewish cabal" in the bureaucracy he was convinced was trying to make him look bad, and ordered a head count of Jews in certain sections of the government.

"The Democrats have the Jews and the Negroes, and let them have them. In fact, tie them around their necks," Nixon said. He hated the "Jewish press" (i.e., the major newspapers) and warned an aide to "stay away from the arts— the arts are full of Jews." He used the word *nigger* and believed blacks were genetically inferior.

*What did Nixon think of reformers?*
Hated them. Those who harped on honesty in government were "hypocrites, little bastards, sanctimonious frauds, people who couldn't butter a piece of bread."

*And what did Nixon think of the American people?*
He told Theodore White about campaigning, "All the while you're smiling, you want to kick them in the shins."

*How many Americans died in Vietnam after Richard Nixon ran on a platform of having a "secret plan" to end the war and promised to get us out within six months of his inauguration?*
Twenty-one thousand.

*What was the Huston Plan and who felt it threatened civil liberties?*
The Huston Plan was intended to control Nixon's enemies by wiretapping their phones, opening their mail, burglarizing their homes and offices. J. Edgar Hoover was horrified by it. It was the official policy of the administration and suspended the Fourth Amendment.

*How did historian Barbara Tuchman describe Nixon's legacy?*
"An accumulated tale of cover-up, blackmail, suborned testimony, hush money, espionage, sabotage, use of federal powers for the harassment of 'ene-

mies,' and a program by some fifty hired operators to pervert and subvert the campaigns of Democratic candidates by 'dirty tricks,' or what in the choice language of the White House crew was referred to as 'ratfucking.' The final list of indictable crimes would include burglary, bribery, forgery, perjury, theft, conspiracy, and obstructing justice."

*How did Charles Colson describe George McGovern's 1972 campaign?*
"Just about the dirtiest, meanest presidential campaign in this nation's history."

*Richard Nixon has been described by his biographer as "a humorless man"; did he ever say anything funny?*
Yes. Upon being shown the Great Wall of China, Nixon said, "This is, indeed, a great wall."

**June 1994**

# Barbara Jordan

■

THE PUBLIC BARBARA JORDAN from the directory of distinguished Americans is easy. She was always a First and an Only.

First woman, only black; in the Texas Senate, in the Texas congressional delegation, from the entire South. She served on the judiciary committee during the decision on Richard Nixon's impeachment. Her great bass voice rolled forth, "My faith in the Con-sti-tu-tion is whole, it is com-plete, it is to-tal." She sounded like the Lord God Almighty and her implacable legal logic caught the attention of the entire nation.

The degree of prejudice she had to overcome by intelligence and sheer force of personality is impossible to overestimate. She wasn't just black and female: she was homely, she was heavy, and she was dark black. When she first came to the Texas Senate, some of her colleagues referred to her as "that nigger-mammy washerwoman." It was considered a great joke in those years to bring one's racist friends into the Senate gallery when B.J. was due to speak: they would no sooner spot her and gasp, "Who is that nigger?" than she would open her mouth and out would roll language Lincoln would have envied. Her personal dignity was so massive, even those who admired her hesitated to approach her. No one will ever know how lonely she was at the beginning.

Her friend Congresswoman Eleanor Holmes Norton justly reminds us that Barbara Jordan was not effective solely because she sounded like God. Among educated Southern blacks—Jordan's Baptist preacher daddy was one—speaking with perfect enunciation was one way of fighting the everlasting stereotype. Jordan was born and raised in the Fifth Ward of Houston, the biggest black ghetto in the biggest state in the Lower Forty-eight. She went to Texas Southern University and Boston University law school. It was neither her exceptional voice nor her extraordinary diction that got her ahead in life, but the force of her intellect.

One of those quaint Texas sayings is: "If you don't know the difference, it don't make any difference." Barbara Jordan knew the difference: which is to say she was so smart it almost hurt. Lord, she was a good legislator; but never wasted a minute on a hopeless cause, no matter how righteous. Don't ask any of the Senate liberals of that era about Jordan; ask those cornered-cottonmouth, mean-as-hell-with-the-hide-off conservatives what they thought of Jordan. Fought her on the floor in head-up debate, fought her in the back room over article 53, subsection C, part II: Jordan always knew what she was talking about, and almost always won. She traded some public suck-up with the Texas Democratic Establishment of that day—Lyndon Johnson, Ben Barnes—and got the first black congressional district ever drawn in Texas. Smart trade.

As it happened, the night B.J. spoke in favor of the impeachment of Richard Nixon, it was also *sine die* (the last night) of the Texas legislative session. Dozens of bills were still in the balance, every member was bargaining, finagling, and sweating through the final hours: came B.J.'s turn to speak on national television and the entire Texas capital came to a halt. Legislators, aides, janitors, maids, everyone gathered around scattered television sets to hear this black woman speak about the meaning of the Con-sti-tu-tion. And they cheered for her as though they were watching the University of Texas pound hell out of Notre Dame in the Cotton Bowl.

She cut her own congressional career short. She said later she didn't have the patience to deal with the legislative process anymore. But it seems likely she already knew she had this weird variant of multiple sclerosis and that it would kill her before long (took almost fifteen years as it turned out). Of course she wanted a seat on the Supreme Court and Jimmy Carter could have given it to her. If there is one thing I would ask you to accept on faith, it is that Barbara Jordan had Judicial Temperament. Her faith in the Con-sti-tu-tion was whole, it was complete, it was total. I consulted her about appointments from Robert Bork to Clarence Thomas, and never found her less than fair. George Bush the Elder will tell you the same.

In the last years of her life, B.J. was a magnificent teacher, at the LBJ School of Public Affairs. For many more students she was quite simply the stonewall inspiration for a life in public service. No perks, no frills, no self-righteousness, no money, no glory: just a solid commitment to using government to help achieve liberty and justice for all—within the realm of the practical: She was always practical.

Her role as a role model may well have been her most important. One little black girl who grew up in the Fifth Ward used to walk by Jordan's house every day on her way to Wheatley High School and think, "Barbara Jordan lived right here in my neighborhood. Barbara Jordan grew up right here, too." Today Ruth Simmons is the president of Smith College.

Jordan was a helluva poker player, used to play regularly with a group of women friends. And before the disease twisted her poor hands so badly, she loved to play guitar. Sing, my God, with a voice like that do you doubt she could sing? It was like God singing the blues. "St. James Infirmary"—Let her go, let her go, Looord, let her go.

But let's not let her go without remembering that the Woman Who Sounded Like God had a very dry, very wry sense of humor.

Former Senator Don Kennard of Fort Worth once took the ghetto-bred Jordan deer-hunting in South Texas. As dawn broke, the two of them were talking quietly in a clearing, leaning comfortably against an old, tumped-over table. Suddenly Kennard glanced over the table and there stood a beautiful buck. "There's your buck, Barbara, take the shot," he urged. But she got buck fever and just couldn't do it. So Kennard took the shot and that buck dropped straight down like a rock. The two of them strolled over to inspect their prize, whereupon the buck shot straight up again and took off like a bat out of hell, without a scratch on it. Jordan said, "Good thing you're a better senator than you are a deer slayer."

One time, Barbara Jordan invited Ann Richards, who later became governor of Texas, but was then a mere county commissioner, out to Jordan's house in the country for dinner. Jordan lived down a dirt road and had a troublesome, indeed totally batty neighbor. This neighbor had taken it into her head that she owned all the land along the dirt road, and consequently kept locking the gates on it. Jordan, never one to miss an opportunity to Make Government Work, asked Commissioner Richards to do something about the locked gates. Richards dutifully made some phone calls, but was never able to get the dingbat to see reason.

Time went by and Professor Jordan invited Governor Richards to another dinner at her house. As they meandered down the dirt road, Ann inquired idly, "Barbara, whatever happened to that dreadful neighbor of yours? Did she ever quit lockin' the gates on you?"

Jordan, the great voice still strong, said, "Well, Ann. I am pleased to report that the woman in question has since died. And gone to hell."

Today Barbara Jordan is the first and only black woman resting in the Texas State Cemetery.

# Ralph Yarborough

T HE IRONY OF RALPH Yarborough's death coming so quickly after Barbara Jordan's escaped no one. There went 60 percent of the courage, 50 percent of the compassion, and 50 percent of the intellect in Texas politics in just a few days. My God, we are bereaved.

Yarborough the Lion-Hearted, dead at ninety-two, at least had his full measure of years. And to what splendid use he put them. If you look back through "Raff" Yarborough's years with the full benefit of historical perspective, his integrity and courage are astounding. He was simply right, so early, so often, and with such courage.

Politically, he was a very lonely man. From his early days in the attorney general's office in the 1930s (when he fought for the dedication of the oil royalties on our public lands for the public schools) to the 1960s (when he was the only Southern senator to vote for the Civil Rights Act in 1964 and one of the very first to oppose the war in Vietnam), Yarborough often fought alone.

Since I cannot begin to encompass his entire political career, I will only try to give you a sense of him, of how he worked and spoke and was, and of his passion for justice. He was pure East Texas populist but with a populism informed by vast learning. His 1927 grade-point average at the University of Texas at Austin's law school is the stuff of legend. He was a judge at thirty-three. He read so widely that he knew whole civilizations the way most of us know the neighborhoods in our town. He had not an ounce of arrogance to him; he dedicated his life to "plain folks."

Picture a campaign summer in the 1950s, say, in East Texas, Raff Yarborough on the back of a flatbed truck with a C&W band in tow. Yarborough on a tear, explaining to plain folks in plain words the right and the wrong of Jim Crow, of McCarthyism, of communism, of Hispanic field workers, of the oil companies ripping off Texas, of the gutless politicians who let it happen.

Any politician who gets off an applause line today will stop and enjoy the clapping. Not Yarborough. Folks would start clapping, and he'd get off an even better line over the applause. And then another. And then another. And then another, until the people were on their feet cheering, and then, he'd top them all.

We had retail politics in those days, and going out to hear Raff Yarborough talk was high entertainment; everybody would bring Granny and the kids and a blanket and a picnic and settle down to hear him. It was better than the Chautauqua. No one makes speeches that long nowadays; Yarborough never did learn to shorten them for the television age. The Bible and Homer, Sam Houston and Marcus Aurelius, James Madison and Bob Wills, all in one speech. And always with that drumbeat for justice, simple justice, because he believed so passionately that's what this country is about.

In those days, children, there were no Republicans in Texas. Young people used to call home from college to report to their parents that they'd actually met one. We had only two flavors of Democrats. The Democratic Establishment was Lyndon B. Johnson, who whored for the oil companies back then; Allan Shivers, who was a dreadful man; and John Connally, who served them both. Yarborough fought them all, and against a stacked deck to boot. The party had the unit rule and all other manner of rules that could be used to suppress dissident opinion. This lead to famous walkouts and shutouts at state conventions. The liberals' greatest exit line was to march out singing, to the tune of "The Battle Hymn of the Republic," "John Bowden Connally lies a-moldering in the grass: John Bowden Connally is a goddamn horse's ass."

The means used to defeat and suppress Yarborough, who was anathema to the Establishment, were legion. One of the most famous was *The Port Arthur Story*, a "documentary" film used to defeat Yarborough in his 1954 gubernatorial race. It was the first half-hour political ad ever run on statewide television, and it began with a camera panning the deserted streets of downtown Port Arthur.

"This," said the announcer, "is what happens when organized labor comes to your city." The retail clerks in Port Arthur were attempting to unionize at the time, but the deserted streets were not the consequence of fearsome organized labor; they were deserted because they were filmed at 5:30 A.M.

Raff used to claim that the Establishment had spent "meel-yons and meel-yons of dollars" to defeat him, and so they did. Lloyd Bentsen finally beat him in the 1970 primary by spending the then-unimaginable sum of $6 million. In a Yarborough campaign, it was always the people against the money, and as money came to weigh more and more in our politics, voices like Raff's were squeezed out of office. But never silenced. That great trumpet sounded again and again, calling to the best in us, for freedom, for justice, for peace.

**January 1996**

# Jesse Helms I

∎

CONGRESS IS MARCHING steadily from dumb to dumber on foreign aid under the leadership, as it were, of Senator Jesse Helms and Representative Ben Gilman.

Foreign aid is the easy hands-down winner for the title of Least Understood Government Program. Public-opinion polls show that most Americans believe we spend about 20 percent of our money trying to help other countries; actually, just 1 percent of our budget goes to foreign aid, and less than 0.5 percent goes to economic and humanitarian assistance, which makes all the difference in the world to poor nations. Ireland spends more of its gross national product helping people in other countries than we do, not to mention every other nation with a claim to decency and wealth; Denmark spends more than six times what we do, and last time I checked, no one was calling Denmark the world's last remaining superpower.

In some ways, foreign aid deserves its generally lousy reputation among Americans because for a long time we did it mostly wrong. Our foreign aid establishment was sort of like the U.S. Army Corps of Engineers used to be— just couldn't stop itself from building huge projects in defiance of common, economic, and environmental sense. We were always funding enormous dam projects, from which corrupt local politicians got very rich, and building highways in countries where no one had bicycles. The concept of "appropriate technology" took a long time to take root in the collective mind of our foreign aid people.

But that fight has been won long since, and perhaps the most misunderstood fact about foreign aid is that the really critical part of it is not run by the government at all. What the government does is provide funding to "NGOs," which is bureaucratese for "non-government organizations." There are thirty-five thousand of these private groups, an astonishing range from Catholic

Relief Services to CARE to the Adventist Development and Relief Agency International. In Africa, Asia, and Latin America, they are at work building schools and sewer systems, training health-care workers, teaching new agricultural techniques, and making tiny loans to start cottage industries, also known as micro-businesses.

The Helms-Gilman plan to gut foreign aid takes aim at the very heart of these people-to-people efforts: They are advocating cuts of about 11 percent, supposedly "across the board"—but because military aid and aid to Israel and Egypt are politically sacrosanct, the cuts will disproportionately affect the very people-care programs that do the most good and make the most difference. Many of those agencies expect cuts of 30 to 50 percent.

Through the 1950s and '60s, the United States provided about half of all aid money spent worldwide; by 1993, that had gone down to 17 percent. From 1985 to 1995, our foreign aid spending went down by 47 percent, so the new cuts are coming on top of cutbacks whose horrific effects can already be seen. We're not talking about hydroelectric dams in places where no one can afford electricity; we're talking about an estimated one million babies a year whose lives are saved by oral rehydration therapy, the simple remedy for severe diarrhea that costs about $1 per baby. A 30 percent cut in family planning would result in an estimated 600,000 more unintended pregnancies each year, not to mention 180,000 more unsafe abortions and 4,000 more maternal deaths.

As they say in the military, that's a lot of bang for the buck.

Helms, who has been conducting a jihad against foreign aid for years, wants to dismember the U.S. Agency for International Development and put the remaining pieces into the State Department. The trouble with that idea is that the State Department, by its nature, deals with those who are in power. Foreign aid will inevitably become more politicized, so that instead of supporting the Sisters of Mercy who go into the slums to save children, we'll be funneling money through corrupt dictators, who are highly unlikely to use it to help their people.

We could, of course, wash our hands like Pontius Pilate and let the rest of the world go to hell in a handbasket on the grounds that it's not our problem. That's quite a popular stand these days. "Hey, we have our own problems; we have hungry and homeless people right here." But you'll notice that the new isolationists who want to cut off foreign aid aren't big on helping the homeless and hungry here, either.

One of the political oddities of our time is that Republicans keep declaring themselves to be the great experts on foreign relations, saying that President

Clinton doesn't know what he's doing. Clinton could waffle on international crises like Bosnia from now 'til eternity and still not do as much damage as Helms wants to do in one bill.

**July 1995**

# Jesse Helms II

∎

I AM INDEBTED TO Jon Stewart of the Comedy Channel and to *The Daily Show*, the last real news program on cable television, for the idea of a collection of quotes from Senator Jesse Helms:

- On the subject of President Clinton visiting North Carolina: "Mr. Clinton better watch out if he comes down here. He'd better have a bodyguard."
- "I'm going to sing 'Dixie' to her until she cries," of Senator Carol Moseley-Braun after debating her on the merits of the Confederate flag.
- "*The New York Times* and *The Washington Post* are both infested with homosexuals themselves."
- "The destruction of this country can be pinpointed in terms of its beginnings to the time that our political leadership turned to socialism. They didn't call it socialism, of course. It was given deceptive names and adorned with fancy slogans. We heard about New Deals, and Fair Deals, and New Frontiers, and Great Society."

Years ago, Larry L. King, the Texas writer, observed in the wake of the political defeat of a couple of unusually unpleasant Texas congressmen, Birchers both, that, "It is not enough that we rejoice over their electorally recumbent forms, but we need to add a few swift kicks while they are down."

Of course I was appalled—the most unliberal sentiment I ever heard. As King himself observed, we liberals weep copiously over everyone from milk-shy Hottentots to the glandular obese. An old and ailing Jesse Helms is not one to crow over. But nor is it necessary to forget—in the wake of all this folderol about how he was "a man of principle"—what those principles actually were.

Helms has been anti-black, anti-gay, anti-woman, and anti-progress. He was perfectly willing to use his power for partisan nastiness and for petty provincial politics. His main claim to fame is that he protected Big Tobacco and his home-state textile industry. I have liked a lot of outspoken conservatives over the years. Helms is not one. I give him this, he never had good hair. A fine example of the sixteenth-century thinker. Onward.

I don't know how the political world looks to you, but it seems to me in my lifetime liberals have been right about three important things. We were right about race. We were right about Vietnam. And, by 1980, when our deficit was $50 billion dollars (!) under Jimmy Carter, I thought: "Gosh, maybe we should let the conservatives run things for a while. At least they understand the bottom line."

Two trillion dollars of debt later, I was not quite so persuaded. That was the last time I ever thought the conservatives should be in charge.

*Plus ça change:* Bush has now blown the entire budget surplus on this huge tax cut for the rich. The silliest line of commentary is this phony wringing of hands and wailing, "If only we had known three months ago what we know today!"

Of course we knew three months ago there was going to be no surplus. We were quite regularly told so by an enormous array of experts. Bush went from saying we needed a tax cut because times were so good to saying we needed a tax cut because times were so bad.

I am a great admirer of John Maynard Keynes, who first pointed out that government needs to spend more money during recessions, but there is a difference between frittering money away on tax cuts for the rich and using the public's money for public purposes of lasting benefit to all.

If Congress wants a public works program, here's one suggestion. Somewhere between one third and one half of all the public schools in America are between dilapidated and falling apart (many of them in rural areas as well as inner cities). This is not a problem addressed by mass testing. To put money into schools is a sound investment of public money, it pays off in the future, and you don't have to do it again for quite some time. That would in turn give the ever-pressed school districts more leeway to hire more and better teachers.

The three things we know work to improve the schools are smaller classes, longer school days or school years, and well-equipped classrooms. The physical plant of schools is not, of course, as important as good teachers. But until we figure out a way to clone good teachers, we know fixing the windows, walls, roofs, floors, wiring, and plumbing will do much good.

**August 2001**

# Jacobo Timerman

■

ONE OF THE GREAT heroes is gone. Jacobo Timerman, the Argentine journalist and great warrior for human rights, has died.

With awe and reverence, I report that Timerman at one time or another ticked off practically everybody. He was of the Saul Alinsky school when it came to popularity—Alinsky, the great Chicago radical, was once given some award and afterward said to his organizers, "Don't worry, boys, we'll weather this storm of approval and come out as hated as ever."

I would call Timerman a fearless man, but he wasn't fearless. He was brave.

His book *Prisoner Without a Name, Cell Without a Number*—the account of his thirty-month imprisonment and torture by the Argentine military in the late 1970s—is one of the most poignant testimonies ever written by a political prisoner and will remain a classic of world literature. In it, he never poses as a hero but instead writes frankly about the terror and loneliness he experienced, weeping silently in his cell as his captors passed and spat the word *Jew!* at him.

His memoirs, on which he was working at the end of his life, reportedly deal extensively with his fears. But courage is not the absence of fear—it is the ability to fight despite fear. And Timerman always did.

Jacobo Timerman was born in 1923 in Bar, Ukraine, in a Jewish family that fled the pogroms when he was five and settled in the Jewish quarter of Buenos Aires. He grew up in poverty and all his life fought for powerless people. He was a radical in the tradition of Upton Sinclair, John Dos Passos, Jack London, Erich Maria Remarque, and Henri Barbusse.

As a teenager, he became a passionate Zionist, but he was never a man of party. He had studied engineering, but in 1950 he joined a Buenos Aires newspaper and soon became a respected political reporter.

He and some other young journalists started a weekly newsmagazine in the manner of *Time*. He later sold it and started the newspaper *La Opinion*, another successful progressive publication.

In 1976, a military junta overthrew President Isabel Perón and began the infamous "dirty war" against the leftist terrorists called Montoneros and anyone else who opposed the junta. Timerman often received death threats from both the right and the left; he sometimes published defiant responses on his front page. The Montoneros bombed his home; the junta finally had him arrested.

The military charged Timerman with being part of an alleged conspiracy to set up a Jewish state in southern Argentina; Jews make up 1 percent of the population of Argentina but accounted for 10 percent of the victims of the "dirty war." Officially Argentina now claims that more than nine thousand people "disappeared" during that war, but most human-rights groups place the figure closer to thirty thousand.

After two and a half years of torture, during which three judicial proceedings found no evidence against Timerman, the Argentine Supreme Court ordered his release. An international human-rights campaign helped to free him; Jimmy Carter, Cyrus Vance, Henry Kissinger, Alexander Solzhenitsyn, the Vatican, and many human rights organizations all helped. The junta finally illegally stripped Timerman of his citizenship, took all his property, and deported him to Israel.

Timerman arrived shortly before Israel's war against Lebanon, which culminated in the hideous massacres of civilians at Sabra and Shatila. Of course, Timerman spoke out against the atrocities and wrote a scathing book, *The Longest War*. He also wrote, with his usual piercing vigor, against the Israeli torture of Palestinians.

Naturally, this made Timerman, the lifelong Zionist, highly unpopular in Israel. He left the country.

Timerman also had a cameo role in American politics. The pro-Israeli magazine *The New Republic* attacked him for *The Longest War*, and even before he went to Israel, the neoconservative intellectuals, in a most despicable episode, tried to destroy his reputation.

Christopher Hitchens of *The Nation* once heard Irving Kristol, editor of the right-wing *Commentary*, say that Timerman had made up the entire story of his imprisonment and torture—that it had never happened. This was after Timerman's testimony had destroyed the nomination of Ernest Lefever to be President Reagan's point man on human rights. Lefever so patently did not care about human rights that the nomination was offensive to the point of being obscene.

At the time, the Reaganites, who disliked Carter's policy of emphasizing human rights, were advancing a peculiar theory that torture and oppression by left-wing or "totalitarian" regimes were evil but that torture and oppression by right-wing or "authoritarian" regimes were somehow forgivable. It was not known at the time, but the Argentine junta had a contract to train the Nicaraguan contras being supported by the Reagan administration. In a memorable appearance before the Senate Foreign Relations Committee, Timerman quietly noted that when you are being tortured, it really doesn't make much difference to you what the politics of your torturers are.

Timerman's devotion to human rights, unlike that of some Americans, was never swayed by his political perspective. He often attacked the Soviet Union and Fidel Castro. His book *Cuba: A Journey* contains, among other things, a brilliant attack on Gabriel García Márquez, the respected left-wing writer who has been notably uncritical of Castro.

What a record, what a life. Go with God, brave fighter.

**November 1999**

# Tom DeLay I

■

AFTER KENNETH STARR, the man most responsible for the impeach-ment of President Clinton was House Majority Whip Tom DeLay, a Texan best known for campaign fund-raising techniques that smack of extortion and political judgments based exclusively on radical right-wing passions.

Were it not for DeLay, Clinton almost surely would have been censured late last year and the case would have been closed. But DeLay wanted nothing less than Clinton's expulsion, to say nothing of prolonging Washington's tawdry morality play. After all, in terms of political advancement and consoli-dation of personal power, the former bug exterminator is probably the biggest winner in Washington.

No matter what the fallout from the impeachment process, most observers think there is little chance that the power DeLay had before it started will be diminished, at least in the immediate future. And chances are he will never stop trying to triumph over the president.

He knew how to win during the impeachment debate last fall. In public, DeLay said GOP congressmen were free to vote their consciences. But his col-leagues had no doubt about how he wanted them to behave, nor of the pun-ishment that awaited them if they did otherwise. They knew that the man who wants to restore DDT to the American landscape, and who treats the Constitution like a bug, has the power to cut off their political funding.

For his part, DeLay talked about "secret evidence," which turned out to be a rumor that Clinton had made unwelcome sexual advances to a woman twenty years ago. The woman in question has told conflicting versions of the episode. In mid-February she recanted her earlier denials that Clinton had misbehaved.

After the impeachment vote, DeLay issued a statement saying a censure vote could never have succeeded because "the White House will never negotiate in good faith." Then he went back to his discredited secret evidence and urged senators to examine what he called the "reams of evidence that have not been publicly aired and are available only to members."

DeLay, fifty-two, is a somewhat beefy-faced fellow with a helmet of perfectly groomed dark hair. He's normally genial, with the air of a small-town car dealer experienced at being professionally affable. He and his wife of thirty-one years, Christine, have a daughter, Danielle, and two foster children. When DeLay is not angry, he comes across not as a nut but as a man given to ill-advised enthusiasms—such as bringing back DDT. Nothing, however, in his manner or conversation would lead you to think he is a natural leader.

The son of an oil field–drilling contractor, he grew up in Texas and spent part of his childhood in Venezuela. He graduated from the University of Houston in 1970 and went to work for a pesticide company. Several years later DeLay bought his own outfit, Albo Pest Control, which he boasts was the "Cadillac of exterminators" in Houston.

He ran for the Texas Legislature in 1978 because he was upset about government regulation of pesticides and how much it was costing him. "Dereg" has been his slogan ever since. One colleague has said DeLay wasn't "a player" in the Legislature and was neither a Goody Two-shoes nor a raving ideologue.

In 1984 he ran for Congress from a district on the Gulf Coast, part of a region that boasts more than half of the nation's petrochemical production and one fourth its oil-refining capacity.

In his early years in Congress, DeLay tended to keep his bizarre views out of the headlines. But in 1988 one of his barmier moments occurred in public. According to the *Houston Press*, DeLay gave an impassioned defense of Dan Quayle, who was then under fire for using family ties to get into a National Guard unit and out of serving in Vietnam. DeLay explained to reporters a theretofore little-noted phenomenon. DeLay claimed there was no room in the army for people like himself and Quayle because so many minority youths had gone into uniform to escape poverty and the ghetto. This remarkable explanation left his audience dumbfounded. After DeLay left the microphone, a television reporter asked, "Who was that idiot?"

In 1994 DeLay started his own political action committee, called Americans for a Republican Majority, and a "corporate alliance" called Project Relief, composed mostly of lobbyists who wanted relief from government regulations. According to the Federal Election Commission, DeLay received more contributions from PACs than any Republican other than Newt Gingrich in the 1996 campaign. The money lobbyists give to Armpac is in turn distributed to Republican candidates, who then owe DeLay both votes and loyalty. His contributions to the famous class of Republican freshmen in 1994 enabled him to win his race for majority whip by three votes.

During the 1995 budget crisis, DeLay was instrumental in getting Gingrich to close the government. "Screw the Senate. It's time for all-out war," he said. Then, when Gingrich decided to cut a deal with Clinton, DeLay led an unsuccessful rebellion against Gingrich. Republicans, including DeLay, contended that Clinton had blindsided them by going on television to attack the party minutes after they thought they had a deal. DeLay never trusted him again: "I don't believe a word he says." Despite the hideous drubbing that Republicans took in the polls, DeLay still says, "Our biggest mistake was backing off from the government shutdown. We should have stuck it out."

In 1996 DeLay reacted to Clinton's State of the Union address with rage. Asked by a reporter if he had liked any part of the speech, DeLay bellowed, "Are you kidding! I was so shocked I couldn't even boo. I've never seen such a performance. I got knots in my stomach watching the president of the United States look straight into the eyes of the American people and lie. I have already counted twenty-one lies, and I didn't even have an advance copy of the speech." Eventually, DeLay claimed to have found forty-seven lies but the State of the Union address faded from the news.


TOM DELAY'S power may continue to grow, but there is no question that his ludicrous political judgments have made him vulnerable. He is, after all, seen as the man largely responsible for giving the Republican revolution its image as mean, radically extreme, and in bed with corporate special interests. He not only favored the folly of shutting down the federal government in 1995 but is almost solely responsible for the widespread impression that Republicans are out to gut every environmental protection law ever passed.

On the House floor DeLay described the Environmental Protection Agency as "the Gestapo of government, purely and simply . . . one of the major claw hooks that the government maintains on the backs of our constituents." He introduced bills to destroy both the Clean Air and the Clean Water acts, and let lobbyists help him draft legislation calling for a moratorium on federal regulations. According to their own pollsters, this anti-environmental image has cost the party dearly.

DeLay's anti-environmental passions go back to his days as a bug exterminator in Houston, when he came to admire DDT. He believes the forbidden poison is a benign substance that should be in use today, and also believes the pesticides mirex and chlordane should be brought back. The EPA says mirex and chlordane are both dangerous to human health: Mirex is cited as a possible carcinogen and was found in breast milk all over the South in the seventies. DeLay claims that the EPA's ban on mirex caused fire ants to spread throughout the South.

DeLay also dismisses evidence linking chlorofluorocarbons to destruction of the ozone layer. When the three scientists who discovered the link were awarded the Nobel Prize in chemistry in 1995, DeLay sneeringly called it "the Nobel appeasement prize." DeLay does not believe in acid rain: He holds that the acid ruining Northeastern lakes is in the soil, and he suggests adding lime. He does not believe in global warming either: "It's the arrogance of man to think that man can change the climate of the world. Only nature can change the climate. A volcano, for instance."

DeLay's normal fare is hyperbole. He once described the Democrats' constituents as "Greenpeace, Queer Nation and the National Education Association." But then he also told *The New Republic* that he was proud of his own coalition, "all kinds of people, from the Christian Coalition to the Eagle Forum, from Arco to Exxon."

His real constituency is the lobbying corps, and the sleazy smell that rises from their vigorous cooperation is another reason for DeLay's vulnerability. His motto is blunt: "If you want to play in our revolution, you have to live by our rules." DeLay's rules are upfront, apparent to anyone who cares to look. On his desk he keeps a list of the four hundred largest political action committees and the amounts and percentages they've contributed to Republicans and Democrats. Those committees that have given heavily to the GOP are labeled "friendly," the others "unfriendly." He also pressures corporations and trade groups to fire Democrats and hire Republicans as their lobbyists. Says DeLay, "We're just following the adage of punish your enemies and reward your friends. We don't like to deal with people who are trying to kill the revolution. We know who they are. The word is out." His fund-raising letters to lobbyists are blunt enough to help earn him the nickname the Hammer.

In late 1995 *The Washington Post* reported on DeLay's "friendly" and "unfriendly" lists, and soon after, Ralph Nader's Congressional Accountability Project began an investigation. In September 1996 CAP director Gary Ruskin asked the House Committee on Standards of Official Conduct to investigate possible violations of standards of congressional conduct by DeLay. Citing the lists, Ruskin suggested DeLay may have directly linked campaign contributions to official action, in violation of the House rule barring "considerations such as political support, party affiliation or campaign contributions" from affecting "either the decision of a member to provide assistance, or the quality of the help that is given."

Ruskin also raised questions about DeLay's brother Randy, who practiced law by himself in Houston until Tom got elected majority whip. Randy promptly became a registered foreign lobbyist and in one year (according to federal records) banked more than $550,000. Along the way, Randy appears to have lobbied his brother on behalf of his clients—and gotten results.

The "vigorous assistance by Representative DeLay in support of the efforts of his lobbyist brother produces the clear impression," said Gary Ruskin, "that Representative DeLay has provided special and inappropriate political favors to his brother and to Cemex," a Mexican cement manufacturer. Citing other cases in which the DeLay brothers had worked for the same goal, Ruskin suggested that the whip's actions may have violated the Code of Ethics for Government Service that says no one in government should "discriminate unfairly by the dispensing of special favors or privileges to anyone."

DeLay was undeterred, and eventually the House Ethics Committee dismissed the complaint. The Committee did advise him it was "particularly important" for a person in his position to avoid any hint that a "request for access or for official action" was linked to campaign contributions.

Then, during the Senate trial, there were headlines concerning allegations that DeLay had not told the truth five years ago in a deposition regarding a business dispute with a former associate in the pest-control business. DeLay testified under oath that he had not been involved with the company for two or three years, even though he filed congressional financial disclosure forms saying otherwise. An aide tried to squelch the stories, blaming "political enemies" and asserting that "eventually the truth will come out."

For all his bluster, DeLay appears to have used "legalese and lawyerese to do two-steps around the questions." Those words, ironically, are his own: He uttered them in denouncing President Clinton for allegedly trying to evade the truth. No matter how the various cases play out, DeLay has certainly made himself vulnerable to charges of hypocrisy.

WHEN DELAY sees an opponent, his instinct is to get rid of him. In 1997 he attacked federal judges who had made rulings that annoyed him and declared his intention to impeach them. "As part of our conservative efforts against judicial activism, we are going after judges," he said. "We intend to . . . go after them in a big way." DeLay never mentioned criminal conduct as grounds for impeachment, except insofar as he regarded political views other than his own as criminal. His efforts were so outrageous that even fellow right-wingers opposed his plans.

DeLay may be more sensitive about his vulnerability than his "acid tongue" and "penchant for rhetorical excess," to cite two euphemisms from the press about him, suggest. In April 1997 Wisconsin Representative David Obey brandished what was by then a two-year-old *Washington Post* article describing how lobbyists wrote drafts of legislation with DeLay's help. DeLay denied "categorically that it ever happened" and challenged Obey to identify the participants. When Obey waved the article under DeLay's nose, DeLay shoved him and called him a "gutless chickenshit."

After the shoving incident, DeLay's spokesman said, "The reason Mr. DeLay was upset was that Obey . . . had questioned his integrity." DeLay ought to be used to that by now.

Last summer, during the House's struggle over campaign finance reform, DeLay was the point man for anti-reformers. Day after day he stood in the well, using every parliamentary advantage leadership gives to kill the reform. A majority of House members ultimately voted for it anyway.

"Most Americans deplore what Larry Flynt is doing and at the same time hope he comes up with something truly dreadful on Tom DeLay," satirist Calvin Trillin observed. Probably true. DeLay may turn out to have been the wrong man at the wrong time for his own cause. He was, after all, an adequate number two when Newt Gingrich's departure left a vacuum in GOP leadership. DeLay had no hesitation about stepping into the vacuum—and recklessly taking the party over a cliff by identifying the unpopular impeachment process with the Republican Party. Will voters get even in 2000? DeLay seems heedless of the risks and ever more consumed by his desire to punish Bill Clinton. He's laughing now, but maybe not last.

**May 1999**

# Tom DeLay II

▪

Toronto — oh, no, how embarrassing. Here I am, visiting the neighbors, who inquire—in their calm, polite, rational, Canadian way—if I could possibly explain for them . . .

Being Canadian is like living next door to the Simpsons. Here are all these patient, sensible, kind people (I swear, their real national motto is "Now, let's not get excited") living right next to "the States," where some hideously noisy psychodrama is always going on.

Although I have yet to encounter a Canadian who will say so in as many words—they are well-mannered folk—they clearly think we have gone completely around the twist this time.

"Could you explain," asked a gentleman from the Canadian Broadcasting Corp., "this congressman—is it DeHay?"

"DeLay," I replied with morbid presentiment.

"Yes, Congressman DeLay of your state of Texas."

Sometimes it's hard to know what to say. Really, really hard. Our Man DeLay, the former bug exterminator from Sugar Land, Texas, has recently distinguished himself by attacking President Clinton for having expressed regret about America's role in the slave trade and for having apologized for sitting by while genocide occurred in Rwanda, the latter event having occurred on Clinton's watch.

Said DeLay of Clinton, according to *The New York Times:* "Here's a flower child with gray hairs doing exactly what he did back in the sixties: He is apologizing for the actions of the United States wherever he went. It just offends me that the president of the United States is directly or indirectly attacking his own country in a foreign land. It just amazes me."

DeLay, the Republican majority whip, also said: "He didn't quite apologize for the chieftains in Uganda that were selling the blacks to the slave traders, did he? Heh. He didn't talk about what's-his-name, Idi Amin, who killed five hundred thousand people in Uganda. He didn't apologize for that.

You know, he's very quick to apologize for other people's mistakes, and can't apologize for his own, and it comes right down to character."

I winced at the thought that this extraordinary statement had been parsed by Canadians hoping to make some sense of it. Let's see—the American president apologized for America's role in the slave trade, and he expressed regret for having let the genocide in Rwanda go on without much interference. And the congressman finds this offensive.

Uh, I said alertly. Well. The congressman is not expected to go into the diplomatic field anytime in the near future.

"Ah," said the Canadian politely, "I see."

Actually, I don't. I utterly fail to see how apologizing for America's role in the slave trade can be construed as attacking our country. And I cannot think of a single historical lesson that has been more emphasized in the fifty years since the Holocaust than that civilized nations must not let genocide occur without attempting to do something about it.

And by the way, Clinton was never a sixties flower child. By all accounts and records, he was a politically ambitious young man from at least high school on.

"Yours is a curious country," observed a television producer here, in mild Canadian fashion, "more concerned about secondhand smoke than guns." The events in Jonesboro, Arkansas, have of course not gone unremarked by our benevolent neighbors.

Uh. Well. Sure. Guns don't kill—children do.

As for our current obsession, most Canadians are so embarrassed by the whole tawdry mess that they are reluctant even to ask about it. "It couldn't happen here," said a book publisher with a mild Canadian twinkle. "Canadian politicians don't have sex."

Canadians themselves often observe that much of their national sense of identity stems from defining themselves as "not like the States." Some of them describe themselves as the proverbial flea next to the elephant or regret their relative insignificance to the bigger, richer, more go-go States.

But Alan Gregg, a sort of Canadian David Frost, said of this phenomenon: "There's actually a fair amount of moral superiority in our way of contrasting ourselves to the States. The implication is always: We wouldn't have gotten ourselves involved in Vietnam because we are so peaceful; we wouldn't have race troubles because we are so tolerant. We're a bit smug, actually. It's a bad failing." Canadians, unlike DeLay, do not hesitate to examine their national conscience.

The resentments harbored by the World's Best Neighbors are often to be found under that notoriously bland headline, "Canadian Trade Talks

Continue." You may recall that last year, Canadian salmon fishermen finally took action after seven years—seven years!—of trade talks that were supposed to iron out respective fishing rights on the West Coast.

Canada is, of course, enjoying a veritable Renaissance in the arts, with Canadian film and literature flowering in splendid profusion. This is because the Canadians, in their practical Canadian way, set up a commission on the arts in the fifties and decided to invest some money in them, with spectacular results. Unfortunately, many of their films can't even get distribution in Canada because Americans own the distribution system. If you want to see a Canadian in a state that might be described as "somewhat angry," find one in the film business and mention the name Jack Valenti. Canadian Trade Talks Continue in that regard, too.

The long, festering problem of Quebecois separatism has taken a remarkable turn recently. One Jean Charest, head of the Progressive Conservative Party, turns out to be the one Quebecois leader capable of stemming the separatist forces. So, he has just agreed to leave his national post and return to Quebec as leader of the Liberal Party (don't ask me how these things get arranged—Canada is sometimes mysterious), thus saving the country and destroying his own promising career. Although there is a general approbation for M. Charest for having made this sacrifice, there is also a widespread sentiment that as a decent citizen he really had no choice and so too much of a fuss shouldn't be made over him!

Should one have a Clintonian Moment on the foreign soil of Canada and actually utter something vaguely critical about one's own nation (say, referring to Our Nation's Capitol as "stark, raving bonkers"), Canadians immediately rush to console the distressed American by reflecting that they, too, have been known to have peculiar things happen in their political life. Uh. Well, there was this senator quite notorious for spending a lot of time in Mexico and not attending to business at all. Quite Shocking. But after some citizens showed up at the Capitol to lampoon the fellow by wearing sombreros and playing mariachi music, he naturally had the decency to resign.

My question is this: Is there any way we could put Canadianism into pill form so Americans could take it regularly? The pacific, benevolent effects of regular doses of Canadianism cannot be overestimated. We would unquestionably be a better people for it. And now I'm headed back to Texas, where no one ever, ever worries if perhaps we might be slightly dull compared with our neighbors.

# Tom DeLay III

■

W HAT I LIKE ABOUT the new radical, right-wing Republican take-over of this country is how easily they blow past all our defenses against déjà-vu, they-all-do-it cynicism.

There you are—thinking you're way too old and have been around this block too many times to suddenly up and evince moral outrage over a little callousness here or a dollop of favoritism there. Suddenly, you find yourself whomperjawed, outraged, stupefied with disbelief. A Girl Scout again, after all these years. It's enough to make me believe in that nutty fundamentalist theory about "secondary virginity," which claims you can become a virgin again even if you're not a virgin. I swan to goodness, these folks can indeed produce miracles.

My latest walking-on-water moment came while I was reading an *Austin American-Statesman* article about Brother Tom DeLay, now the second-most powerful man in America, right after Dick Cheney. It was a familiar story to those of us who follow DeLay (who is, he has said, hell-bent to "stand up for a biblical worldview in everything I do and everywhere I am").

Brother Tom is given both to preaching holy propriety and running a political machine so shameless it would make Boss Tweed blush. Those who were privileged to see him in action during the last days of the peculiarly hideous process of redistricting the state of Texas know that ruthlessness and Christianity can be combined, no matter what Jesus had to say on the subject.

Among those newly startled by DeLay's tactics last week were, according to the *American-Statesman*, "Four House Judiciary Committee members who protested after an article in the Capitol Hill newspaper *Roll Call* reported that DeLay planned to slip an amendment revising U.S. trade statutes into the annual defense authorization bill."

Now, you may think that revising trade statutes by way of a defense-authorization bill is procedurally unusual—and such was the content of the protest: "The amendment had not been properly vetted by the judiciary panel, which is supposed to oversee trademark law." Still not in a stew over this, eh?

The amendment itself is a little charmer designed to help the Bacardi rum folks (vague memories of many good tropical drinks are stirred) with a trademark problem they have with one of the world's oldest rum labels, Havana Club. Not being an expert on fundamentalist theology, I have no idea whether assisting a rum company fits into a biblical worldview, but I can tell you that Bacardi-Martini Inc. is a Bermuda-based company run by a family of prominent Cuban exiles who happen to be very generous, very large campaign donors. They have been especially generous to Tom DeLay for several years now.

This li'l ol' amendment of DeLay's carries some history. In 1998, then-senator Connie Mack, a Florida Republican, inserted an obscure amendment called Section 211 into a bill that was four thousand pages long. Turns out 211 gave Bacardi a way to win its long-running lawsuit over Havana Club, a label also claimed by Pernod-Ricard, the French company that now sells that brand name in partnership with the Cuban government.

Oops, this touched off a major international stink. France complained to the World Trade Organization, which ruled the United States had violated treaty obligations to protect copyrights. The WTO has given the United States until the end of the year to revise the law.

So what DeLay is trying to do here is fix 211 to bring it into technical compliance with the WTO ruling, while continuing to give Bacardi the edge. According to the *Statesman:* "Critics charge the 'fix' would still violate U.S. treaty obligations going back to the 1930s. Several major corporations have joined in asking Congress to repeal Section 211 altogether to avoid possible retaliation by the Castro government against their own trademarks."

Citizens Against Government Waste, a conservative watchdog group, opposes special treatment for Bacardi. "We think it has an adverse influence on the taxpayers, on consumers, and on the economy," said the group. (Note: In the now-defensive, formerly liberal media—"Oh God forbid anyone should ever call us part of the Liberal Media"—we are pleased to have an actual conservative group protesting along with us here, because if it were just liberals, who would care? A connection between special legislation for Bacardi and huge campaign contributions? What are you, a commie?)

OK, now that you have been fully prepped on this deal, I give you the Outrage Moment. One Jonathan Grella, spokesman for Tom DeLay, when asked about all this, said, "It's wrong and unethical to link legislative activities to campaign contributions."

Let's make sure we all understand what is being said here. Grella asserts that there is no conflict of interest between a public official using his power to change the law in exchange for a hefty campaign contribution—the immorality occurs when the press and/or public interest groups point out this connection. That's when I went slack-jawed.

**October 2003**

# John Ashcroft I

■

**W**ITH ALL DUE respect, of course, and God Bless America too, has anyone considered the possibility that the attorney general is becoming unhinged?

Poor John Ashcroft is under a lot of strain here. Is it possible his mind has started to give under the weight of responsibility, what with having to stop terrorism between innings against doctors trying to help the dying in Oregon and California? Why not take a Valium, sir, and go track down some nice domestic nut with access to anthrax, OK?

Not content with the noxious USA PATRIOT bill (for Uniting and Strengthening America by Providing Appropriate Tools Required to Intercept and Obstruct Terrorism Act—urp), which was bad enough, Ashcroft has steadily moved from bad to worse. Now he wants to bring back FBI surveillance of domestic religious and political groups.

For those who remember COINTELPRO, this is glorious news. Back in the day, Fearless Fibbies, cleverly disguised in their wingtips and burr haircuts, used to infiltrate such dangerous groups as the Southern Christian Leadership Conference and Business Executives Against the War in Vietnam. This had the usual comedic fallout, along with killing a few innocent people, and was so berserk there was a standing rule on the left—anyone who proposed breaking any law was automatically assumed to be an FBI agent.

Let's see, who might the Federal Fosdicks spy upon today? Columnist Tom Friedman of *The New York Times* recently reported from Pakistan that hateful Taliban types are teaching in the religious schools. "The faithful shall enter paradise, and the unbelievers shall be condemned to eternal hellfire." Frightful! Put the Baptists on the list.

Those who agitate against the government, constantly denigrating and opposing it? Add Tom DeLay, Dick Armey, and Rush Limbaugh to the list.

Following the J. Edgar Hoover Rule (anyone who criticized Hoover or the

FBI was automatically targeted as suspect), we need to add the FBI alumni association. According to *The Washington Times:* "A half-dozen former FBI top guns, including once-Director William Webster, have voiced their dismay at Ashcroft's strategy of detention and interview rather than prolonged investigation and surveillance of those suspected of terrorism. They contend the new plan will fail to eliminate terrorist networks and cells, leaving the roots to carry on. The harsh criticism seems calculated to take advantage of growing concerns in Congress about Ashcroft's overall anti-terrorism approach."

Harsh criticism? Put the ex–FBI agents on the list. Come to that, "growing concerns"? Put Congress on the list.

I cannot commend too strongly those hardy, tough-minded citizens ready to sacrifice all our civil rights in the fight against terrorism. It's clear to them anyone speaking up for civil liberties is on the side of the terrorists, and that's the kind of thinking that has earned syllogism the reputation it enjoys today.

Some of us are making lists and checking them twice to see who stood with us on this particular St. Crispin's Day. And when next we see you Federalist Society types at some debate over, say, strict construction, we'll be happy to remind you how much you really care when the chips are down. With the honorable exception of the libertarian right (William Safire, Representative Bob Barr), the entire conservative movement is missing in action, and so are a lot of pious liberals.

And what could be better than the insouciance with which the attorney general himself approaches the Constitution? During his six years in the Senate, he proposed no fewer than seven constitutional amendments. Since we've only managed to amend it seventeen times in the last two hundred years (that's leaving out the Bill of Rights), it's an impressive record. Of course, one of John Ashcroft's proposed amendments was to make it easier to amend. Another was the always helpful flag-burning amendment, which had it been in effect, would have done so much to prevent the terrorist attacks.

Yep, if we had a constitution largely rewritten by John Ashcroft, as opposed to the one we're stuck with by such picayune minds as Madison, Washington, Franklin, Hamilton, etc., we'd be a lot safer today.

Wouldn't we? How? you ask. Well, for example, uh . . . And there's . . . uh. Well at least we could have had a better visa system. So that has nothing to do with the Constitution: picky, picky.

In this fight for our cherished freedoms, those cherished freedoms should definitely be the first thing to go. Sieg heil, y'all.

# John Ashcroft II

B Y GEORGE, we need honest, reasoned debate around here and not fear-mongering, so anyone out there who suspects Attorney General John Ashcroft of being a nincompoop is clearly aiding terrorists and giving ammunition to America's enemies. Ashcroft says so, and if that's not reasoned debate, what is?

Under the high standards of reason set forth by Ashcroft, we are allowed to present CORRECT information (those who present incorrect information, like some people in government, erode our national unity and diminish our resolve) as to what the attorney general is up to. While Operation Enduring Freedom continues in Afghanistan, enduring freedom is not looking so good here at home—and like the A.G., I would be the last to encourage people of goodwill to remain silent in the face of evil.

Here is some CORRECT information about enduring freedom:

* Ashcroft's urpily named PATRIOT Act permits government agents to search a suspect's home without notification. In J. Edgar Hoover's day, this was known as "a blackbag job." As Nat Hentoff reports in *The Progressive:* "A warrant would be required, but very few judges would turn a government investigator down in this time of fear. Ashcroft's 'secret searches' provision can now extend to all criminal cases and can include taking photographs, the contents of your hard drive, and other property. This is now a permanent part of the law, not subject to any 'sunset review' by Congress."

Many of our tough-minded brethren, to whom it is perfectly clear that less freedom equals more security, have dismissed complaints by saying, after all, these measures only apply to non-citizens, and besides, the worst parts of it will sunset in four years. Wrong. This means you, fellow citizens—if you happen to know someone whose brother-in-law rented a garage apartment to a guy who knew someone who might be a terrorist. Benjamin Franklin said, "They that can give up essential liberty to obtain a little temporary safety deserve neither liberty or safety." But I'm pretty sure Franklin didn't mean to aid terrorists, so please don't report him to the A.G.

• The expansion of wiretapping authority to computers simply puts privacy in cyberspace in jeopardy without any concomitant gain to law enforcement. According to James X. Dempsey, deputy director of the Center for Democracy and Technology, neither Congress nor the media have put all this together to see the breadth of the dragnet.

The government can now delve into personal and private records of individuals even if they cannot be directly connected to a terrorist or foreign government. Bank records, e-mails, library records, even the track of discount cards at grocery stores can be obtained on individuals without establishing any connection to a terrorist before a judge. According to the *Los Angeles Times*, al-Qaeda uses sophisticated encryption devices freely available on the Internet that cannot be cracked. So the terrorists are safe from cyber-snooping, but we're not.

• Ashcroft and Co. essentially say, "Trust us, we won't misuse these new laws." But in fact the FBI and the CIA have repeatedly violated such trust to spy on everyone from Martin Luther King Jr. to Jean Seberg. That's why the checks were there to begin with.

• According to an analysis of PATRIOT by the Electronic Freedom Foundation, the government made no showing that the previous powers of law enforcement and intelligence agencies to spy on U.S. citizens were insufficient to allow them to investigate and prosecute acts of terrorism: "Many provisions . . . instead of (being) aimed at terrorism, are aimed at nonviolent, domestic computer crime. In addition, although many of the provisions appear aimed at terrorism, the government made no showing that the reasons they failed to detect the planning of the recent attacks or any other terrorist attacks were the civil liberties compromised by the bill. The government may now spy on websurfing of innocent Americans, including terms entered into search engines, by merely telling a judge anywhere in the U.S. that the spying could lead to information that is 'relevant' to an ongoing criminal investigation."

The person spied on does not have to be the target of the investigation nor is probable cause required.

• The military tribunals idea is so bad the administration has been backing up on it steadily, especially since Spain has already announced it won't turn over its al-Qaeda suspects to a system so violative of international standards. The Spaniards, who have been fighting Basque terrorists for years, are not noticeably "soft on terror-ism."

• Lest you think our only attorney general does not care about rights, I point out that when it comes to the 550 he has "detained" since September, without evidence, without charges, without identi-fication, and without legal counsel, he so fully respects the Second Amendment rights of these noncitizens that he has reversed the Justice Department's previous stand to forbid the FBI to check on their gun-purchase records in order to protect their privacy. Also, Ashcroft fully believes in the rights of the unborn. The born are on their own.

**December 2001**


# John Ashcroft III


SOMETIMES I FORGET how truly simpleminded the Bushies can be. The front page of *The New York Times* reports, "The Bush administration seems to accept and even relish (Attorney General) Ashcroft's role as lightning rod on difficult criminal justice issues."

Since the attorney general has so amply demonstrated his clueless incom-petence, it may seem difficult to plumb why it should be so. But it is precisely, you see, because liberals consider John Ashcroft a dangerous nincompoop that the administration thinks he's doing a good job. They really are that simple.

In the Texas Legislature, the press occasionally gives the If-He-Votes-Yes, I-Vote-No Award for some egregious example of this particular strain of non-thinking. Any halfway smart politician loves to have another pol in this position. That's when you introduce a resolution in favor of Motherhood just to watch the other guy vote against it.

It takes no great detective to see the pattern here. Before September 11, Bush's entire foreign policy consisted of being Not Clinton. If Clinton was for something, Bush was against it, and vice versa. This did not, you may have noticed, lead to an effective foreign policy.

Likewise, most people had difficulty understanding why the administration was so set on drilling in the Arctic National Wildlife Refuge when it didn't make any sense. The U.S. Geological Survey estimates 3.2 billion barrels of economically recoverable oil, which would at most reduce our foreign dependence by a couple of percentage points. We can save twice that with a tiny improvement in fuel mileage, which the Bushies opposed. It's just dumb to drill there, and the enviros were in a snit about it.

Precisely. It was because the enviros were in a total snit that the Bushies felt they were doing the right thing. Unfortunately, this is four-year-old thinking.

Because John Ashcroft has become a bugbear for liberals, the Bushies assume he must be doing something right. Not necessarily.

As David Cole reports in *The Nation*, "To date, despite the thousands of Arab and Muslim immigrants arrested, searched, profiled and questioned, Ashcroft has charged only a single person—Zacarias Moussaoui—with any involvement in the attacks of September 11. And he was arrested before the attacks occurred. Such broad-brush tactics are unlikely to succeed, for they give notice to potential targets, allowing them to evade detection while alienating the very communities we must work with to identify potential threats who may be living among them."

Ashcroft is still "detaining"—such a nice euphemism—hundreds of noncitizens on immigration charges, even though many of those charges have been resolved. Under Ashcroft's orders, they are being tried in secret proceedings closed to all outside observers.

U.S. District Judge Nancy Edmunds has declared the closed proceedings unconstitutional, and Superior Court Judge Arthur D'Italia of New Jersey, calling the secret arrests "odious to a democracy," has ordered the INS to release the names of those detained.

Ashcroft's prosecution of Lynne Stewart, the New York lawyer who has bravely defended some terribly unpopular clients, is a mystery. She is not charged with furthering any illegal or violent activity. Ashcroft has also made prosecution of Moussaoui more difficult by insisting on the death penalty. We knew in advance that meant France would not cooperate by releasing information that could lead to the death penalty. It's all very well to sit around and gritch about the French, but it doesn't get us any forwarder.

Then we have this ludicrous situation at Gitmo, where we now say we may keep these people locked up even if they are acquitted of whatever charges are finally leveled against them. A permanent policy of imprisonment without conviction or even trial—that's worse than stupid, it's horrible.

The administration has already backed down from its original position and will now require public trials, unanimous votes for the death penalty, and some review. But they insist they can put you in a dungeon forever and they never have to say why. It's like the old French lettre de cachet that used to figure as plot device in potboilers like *The Count of Monte Cristo*. One can only conclude the problem is the administration has no idea what to do with these prisoners.

**April 2002**

# Jimmy Carter

■

For those interested in high points in the history of Bad Manners, there was rather a breathtaking moment last week when columnist and television pundit Bob Novak chose to use the occasion of Jimmy Carter's winning the Nobel Peace Prize to trash the man.

"It's one of those inevocable [that's what the transcript says] signs of autumn," said Novak on *Crossfire*. "Year in and year out, we get the inevitable boomlet to give Jimmy Carter the Nobel Peace Prize. The admittedly incompetent president, who is supposed to be a terrific ex-president. Well, this year they slipped up and actually gave him the Peace Prize. So we are giving the peanut man from Georgia something else: our 'Quote of the Day.' "

(They then run a clip of Carter being modest and amusing about getting the call from Sweden that morning. "I thought it was some joker who was calling," he says.)

Novak continues: "You know, James, the Nobel Peace Committee's been making mistakes on that prize, giving it to people like Yasser Arafat and Le Duc Tho. But Jimmy Carter's one of the biggest mistakes. He's the guy that was for the communists in Nicaragua and Fidel Castro in Cuba."

James Carville, rendered speechless for once, finally stammered: "You know . . . I . . . It's stunning that you would sit there—here's a man who's one of the most deeply religious people, goes around building houses for poor people, goes all over the world on his own time, monitors elections, tries to resolve disputes. I mean, what is it about people getting along that so irritates and aggravates you?"

"Ask Bill Clinton," Novak replied. "He couldn't stand him because he was bothering him all the time he was president."

"Maybe he's irritating to some people, but he's a great man," said Carville.

"This guy, he gives his heart. He believes in these things. And I don't understand what's wrong with Jimmy Carter."

Novak: "He screws up everything he touches."

Maybe the exchange was worth it, just to hear Novak cite Bill Clinton as
an authority on anything. Clinton and Carter have had a famously cool relationship ever since President Carter dumped a bunch of Cuban Mariel refugees
on then-governor Clinton, who lost his next election largely because of all the
trouble they caused.

Jimmy Carter needs no defense from me. The man is enough to give
Christianity a good name. Following the Christian doctrine of works as well as
faith, he has done immeasurable good in the world, and no mean-spirited
attack from a petty pundit can diminish him.

The only reason I bother to note Novak's nastiness is because it left such a
bad taste with me. I was traveling on the West Coast that day, and all through
the airports and in cabs and hotels, people were saying to one another with
real pleasure: "Jimmy Carter got the Nobel Peace Prize. Isn't that nice?" A genuine piece of good news in a world with little of it lately. It isn't necessary to
agree with Carter on everything to think he deserves the Peace Prize. Even the
right-wing *Wall Street Journal* managed a negative editorial on what it feels are
the inadequacies of Carter's approach without demeaning the man or his
accomplishments.

The implicit criticism of President Bush in the Nobel Committee's selection (made explicit by the chairman) should not detract from this recognition of how long and how hard Jimmy Carter has worked for peace and
human rights. I think he is an invaluable asset to the nation. Like Nelson
Mandela, he has unique stature, and wherever he goes to help with an election or to try to work out a problem, he is welcomed and listened to. In this
season when the dogs of preemptive war are running loose, it is good to hear
Carter pointing out the obvious: that we would be better off working with
the rest of the world to disarm Saddam Hussein rather than annihilating his
whole country.

Not only do we still not have answers to basic questions about invading
Iraq—why now, how are we going to pay for it, and what do we do when we
win?—but it also seems to me the tragedy in Bali is further evidence that we
need to concentrate on al-Qaeda. We're sure not finished with them, and it's
dangerous to take our eye off that ball.

Now that President Bush has submitted to the formality of getting a resolution through Congress and urged action in the U.N., apparently we are all supposed to forget that he announced initially he didn't need to do either one. It's as though administration officials think they're characters in the *Men in Black* movies: All they have to do is take out one of those little silver jiggers to zap our memory.

**October 2002**

# Dick Cheney

■

VICE PRESIDENT CHENEY'S Christmas card this year not only offers best wishes in this holiday season but also bears the following quotation from Benjamin Franklin at the Constitutional Convention: "And if a sparrow cannot fall to the ground without His notice, is it probable that an empire can rise without His aid?" Food for thought there: a heavy meal, in fact.

Interpreting what the Lord intended by one thing or another has always been a dicey pastime. Ten years ago, we had one of those outbreaks where lots of people do ridiculous things and then claim it was because the Lord told them to. That was the summer a family of twenty people from Floydada, Texas, got naked, piled into a GTO (five kids in the trunk), and drove to Vinton, Louisiana, where they ran into a tree. Surprised hell out of the Vinton cops to see twenty nekkid people get out of one car. The family said the Lord told them to do it. There was so much of that kind of thing going around, I developed a theory about a dangerous Lord impersonator being on the loose.

I'm not saying that either Cheney or Franklin has heard from a Lord impersonator, but just for starters on this empire biz, it was the Roman Empire that crucified Jesus. Then your Turkish Empire, not too tasty. Your Moguls, ditto. Aztec Empire, fairly liberal on human sacrifice. Of the colonial empires—French, Dutch, British, Portuguese—all were contenders for the title of Worst Ever at different times and in different places—but I think the crown probably goes to the Belgian Empire under King Leopold, believed to be responsible for the deaths of ten million Africans when the entire Congo was Leopold's private plantation.

Of course, in the United States, we like to believe in American exceptionalism, to see ourselves as the Shining City on the Hill, a light and beacon unto all the world, and—as it says on that statue given us by our friends, the French—opening our arms to the world's tired, hungry, and poor. We would naturally prefer to forget that the country was founded on genocide and slavery, but we have among us many nags and scolds who keep bringing it up, especially when we're having one of our snits of American triumphalism.

All I am saying is I wouldn't be all too sure about the Lord's intentions regarding empire. Just a cheery Christmas thought brought to you by the vice president and me.

My favorite Christmas card this year says: "We wish you a Merry Christmas" three times on the front. On the inside it says, "AND a Happy New Year . . . or not . . . Depending on what the elves get for Christmas. After all, we wished you a Merry Christmas three times! Only Santa does this for grins."

I have not heard of one good crèche fight this year. We can normally count on a peppy crèche controversy to add to the seasonal joy and festive cheer. This occurs when some citizen or public official suffering from an excess of Goodwill Toward Men puts up a religious symbol, often a crèche, on public property. Then the ACLU or somebody files a lawsuit, and everybody gets mad at everybody else, leading to slightly less Peace on Earth. As Ann Richards once observed of a controversial star on top of the Texas state Capitol: "Oh, I hate to see them take that down. This could be the only chance we'll ever get to find three wise men in that building."

My favorite Christmas visitor (so far) was the chief of the Pojoaque, New Mexico, Volunteer Fire Department. I love to hear true tales from the Pojoaque fire department (the time the food warehouse burned down and all the popcorn popped is a special favorite). The chief observes that they're getting more and more calls from people who don't have a fire, or even a raccoon in the house, but from people who are sick. The fire trucks come with EMTs (emergency medical technicians), who can handle any number of routine medical emergencies (if you can have a routine emergency) like a person in a diabetic coma or in need of a regular shot. The sick person then refuses to let the firefighters call an ambulance because the ambulance and the emergency room cost money, whereas the fire department does not charge. As a consequence, fire departments across the country are now becoming the front line for a medical system in increasing disrepair.

So if some homeless woman by any chance had a child in a stable in Pojoaque last night, most likely neither shepherds nor wise men were summoned, but instead volunteer firefighters. Which makes me very happy because I think volunteer firefighters are, by and large, a perfectly wonderful set of people. Merry Christmas to all.

# Dr. Liz Karlin

■

D R .   L I Z   K A R L I N , that lovely soul, dead of a brain tumor at fifty-four. Happened in a matter of a couple months. "Oh, you know Liz, she hated doctors," said our friend Donna Shalala, who is now Secretary of HHS.

They called from Wisconsin and said, "Didn't you know Liz Karlin, the abortion doctor?"

What a stupid way to remember Liz Karlin, one of the most life-affirming people I've ever run across. I knew her because ten years ago we went on a trek together in the Himalayas in northern India. Liz and I were tent mates, which is an awfully good way to get to know someone well over a short period of time.

We were all allowed one duffel bag on that trip, packed with nothing to spare. Liz brought a tiny bag for her own needs and a very large bag stuffed with medication for the people of the area. We were trekking in places where Westerners were seldom seen. (Who can forget the irremediably blond, blue-eyed Betsy Levin, with three cameras strung around her neck, being mistaken for a Japanese? What else could a person with three cameras be, thought the villagers.)

As we hiked through tiny mountain villages, all the little children would run out to greet us, lined up in rows, saying in their silver-bell-like voices, "Salaam, sa-laam!" I can't even remember how Liz did this, but I think sometimes it was without an interpreter—she would say, "I am a doctor, bring me all the sick babies." Can you say that in Jammu and Kashmir without an interpreter? I think Liz could.

And they would bring all the sick babies. It was an area where people heated with firewood but the chimneys didn't work well, so the babies breathed in too much smoke. Liz would listen with her stethoscope and then diagnose, "pneumonia baby, pneumonia baby," passing them down the line to this ridiculously unlikely crew of nurses she more or less instantly trained: Victor Kovner, the noted libel lawyer; Alice Rivlin, the economist now on the Federal Reserve; Carol Bellamy, a pol from New York; me, a journalist from Texas. And I'm here to tell you that when Liz Karlin told you to help a baby, you helped that baby, whether you'd ever helped a sick person before in your life or not.

I think we mostly gave them antibiotics—Lord knows how she ever got all those meds through customs—but the truly high entertainment was Liz Karlin then proceeding to talk with the mothers on what they should do so their babies wouldn't get sick again. If you think there's such a thing as a language barrier, you never saw Liz Karlin trying to save a baby. And don't get the idea this was some kind of "Me Big White Medicine Chief" routine. Remember how she felt about doctors?

Liz was a doctor; that was her life. Of course she did abortions: When did Liz Karlin ever not do what a patient needed? But something happened after our trek, something I wish I had taken more time to understand. When they started picketing her clinic, hounding her at home, threatening her, making the horrible phone calls late at night—well, as any fool could have predicted, when the going got tough, Liz got tougher. She had to. She started helping more and more women who needed abortions because where else could they go?

Shalala says that just a few weeks before her death, Liz's greatest concern was that "they" would win, the people who had made her life such a hell, people so persuaded of their own moral rectitude they had no idea of the incredible courage and compassion that drove a sunny, funny lady with black curls and extraordinary energy to keep helping the people who needed her.

One finds a tendency (born of tiredness, I think) to excuse those who commit acts of terrorism in the name of "life" on the grounds that they feel so passionately about the issue—as though passion were an excuse. Backing down on abortion rights because those who oppose them are "passionate" is simply rewarding terrorism.

Why should it take as much strength and courage as Liz Karlin possessed to allow women to decide whether they will bear children? The only question is: Who decides? A woman and her doctor, or some set of fanatics with no knowledge of the woman or her circumstances? I know these are old arguments, and that we are all tired of hearing them, but it seems to me we owe it to Liz Karlin to make the arguments again, with all the passion they deserve, with all the passion it cost Liz.

If you believe abortion is wrong, don't have one. No one can force you to have an abortion. By what right do these few fanatics think they can force a woman to have a child? The child is not their responsibility. They bear none of the risks or the consequences. There are always two lives at stake. And by the rules of logic, if you give government the right to force you to have a child you do not want, you also give government the right to force you to abort a child you do want, as has happened in China. Abortion will either be safe and legal or unsafe and illegal. Abortion occurs in any case. The latest numbers from Latin America, where abortion is still illegal, are heartbreaking. The best estimates are that the rate of abortion in the United States is lower today than it was when abortions were dirty, dangerous, and illegal.

I think any fair-minded person will admit there is a terrible strain of misogyny in the anti-abortion movement: One has only to hear the rhetoric about "abortion on demand" or "partial-birth abortions"—as though women used abortion, even in the eighth month, like some casual morning-after pill. As though any woman eight months pregnant ever waddled past an abortion clinic, snapped her fingers, and said, "Oh darn, I knew there was something I'd been meaning to get around to." One aborts a child, and I use the word *child* advisedly, in the eighth month for exactly one reason—because one has to.

Despite the constant misdescription of *Roe v. Wade* as "abortion on demand," it is a carefully calibrated, tripartite system. In the first trimester, abortion is relatively easy to obtain; in the second trimester, more difficult; in the third trimester, it is practically impossible.

Sometimes women who are told they are going to bear a child that is hopelessly deformed or handicapped decide to abort. Sometimes they don't. As God is my judge, I cannot judge them. Sometimes a woman has the physical, emotional, and financial ability to care for such a child. Sometimes she doesn't. Among other factors to be considered in these cases, the divorce rate among couples who have handicapped children is horribly high and the effect on other children in the family is extremely heavy. (I have known families that not only bore the burden superbly, but found having such a child a source of wisdom and joy in their lives: On the other hand, all of them were well-to-do families.)

I know one woman who was divorced and left to fend for herself and her oldest child, and who had to put the younger child, profoundly retarded, into a state home. I sometimes think that has been harder for her than the girl's actual condition.

Another friend, the single mother of five who is a Hispanic housekeeper, has a child with spina bifida. She is a devout Catholic and travels every year forty-eight hours by bus to make a pilgrimage for that child. She has told me, with tears running down her face, that she believes in abortion in such cases. And any fool, from pope to Pentecostalist, who thinks she is wrong is welcome to walk a mile in her moccasins. She was, by the way, recently notified that thanks to the action of our Republican Congress, her handicapped daughter's qualification for Supplemental Security Income would have to be reviewed. You cannot imagine her panic. Have you ever seen a child with spina bifida?

The Republicans said too many people were "abusing" the system. In one totally berserker speech, House Speaker Newt Gingrich actually claimed poor people were "coaching" their children to "act crazy" so they could obtain "crazy money" and then beating the children if they didn't get it. There is no evidence whatever for this insane charge. Try to get a three-year-old to fake cerebral palsy sometime. Gingrich actually implied Congress was justified in cutting SSI as a way of ending child abuse. The sheer hideousness of the insult to the poor families who care so devotedly for their handicapped children is beyond my ability to describe. Gingrich would rather dump them into state hospitals—where their lives are often without any joy, and, incidentally, cost us all a lot more money—than pay their own families a pittance to care for them.

Shalala and others have since at least managed to provide a review procedure for handicapped children who were cut off SSI by this madness. I'm sorry, but if I could find evidence the anti-abortion activists gave half as much of a damn about what happens to the children who are actually born as they do fetuses, I would feel a lot better. I know this is, in some cases, an unfair generalization. I do know fundamentalist Christians who are just as active in helping handicapped children and very poor children as they are in the anti-abortion movement. But not many.

As for people like Gingrich, who promote these nutty anti-abortion amendments on matters as remote as appropriations for the International Monetary Fund and at the same time insist on cutting the very few services that help poor families care for damaged children, O, let me just say that when it comes to anger and a sense of moral rectitude, I think we can match the anti-abortion movement any time.

God bless you, dear Liz.

# Paul Wellstone

■

SAN FRANCISCO — he was the rarest of all rare breeds—a mensch from Minnesota. But this is not a column about Paul Wellstone. No one has to wonder for a minute what he would have wanted. "What would Wellstone do?" The answer all but roars back: "Don't mourn, organize!"

The contrast between Paul's passionate populism and this dreary midterm election is as sad as his death. There's many a contest between political pygmies this year—we're down to seeds and stems again—but even in proud Texas we have to admit that this year's palm for nose-holding voting must go to California. Not to overstate, two of the most titanically unattractive candidates in the history of time—Gray Davis and Bill Simon—are vying for the governorship. A new nadir in modern politics. How we got from the Lincoln-Douglas debates to this—or what we ever did to deserve it—is unclear. The debate between Davis and Simon raised the always-timely question: Is God punishing us?

Naturally, when it comes to voting, we in Texas are accustomed to discerning that fine hairsbreadth worth of difference that makes one hopeless dipstick slightly less awful than the other. But it does raise the question: Why bother?

One sorry excuse for a decent, fighting people's pol or the other; what difference does it make?

Oh, just that your life is at stake.

What stuns me most about contemporary politics is not even that the system has been so badly corrupted by money. It is that so few people get the connection between their lives and what the bozos do in Washington and our state capitols. "I'm just not interested in politics." "They're all crooks." "Nothing I can do about it, I'm just one person. I can't buy influence."

Politics is not a picture on a wall or a television sitcom you can decide you don't much care for. Is the person who prescribes your eyeglasses qualified to do so? How deep will you be buried when you die? What textbooks are your children learning from at school? What will happen if you become seriously ill? Is the meat you're eating tainted? Will you be able to afford to go to college or to send your kids? Would you like a vacation? Expect to retire before you die? Can you find a job? Drive a car? Afford insurance? Is your credit card company or your banker or your broker ripping you off? It's all politics, Bubba. You don't get to opt out for lack of interest.

In this putrid election season, every television ad seems to announce that the other guy sucks eggs, runs on all fours, molests small children, and has the brain of an adolescent pissant. It's tempting to join the "pox on both their houses" crowd. They're close to right, but they're still wrong.

Here's the good news: All of this can actually be fixed. By me, you, us—no kidding, no bull. Nothing you can do about it? Just one person? As an American at this time, you have more political power than 99 percent of all the people who have ever lived on earth. And should you round up four friends who don't usually vote, you'll have four times that much political power. Why throw that away?

And you have other kinds of power as well. Hundreds of thousands of Americans demonstrated against war in Iraq Saturday. I don't know why the mainstream media are so allergic to reporting this, but the turnout was stunning. In San Francisco, middle-aged protesters with gray ponytails mixed with punk kids with orange hair and earrings in their eyebrows and with suburban families toting toddlers. The old coots griped about their feet and about having to listen to speeches through a bad sound system again (digital sound has not yet made it to the peace movement). But the kids were, like, totally awed. They had not, in their young lives, ever seen anything like tens of thousands of Americans peacefully exercising their right to assemble and to petition their government for redress of grievances. The creativity and humor of the signs was fabulous, though often impolite. A grand exercise in citizenship.

And will it make any difference? Does the Bush administration care that 40 percent of Americans are opposed to this war and that almost all of us have doubts about it? Politicians are much more sensitive creatures than is generally assumed. In political science circles, the technical term we use for this is *goosey*. Pols not only listen to public opinion, they usually overreact to it.

The Bush administration has announced this grand imperial plan, the

"National Security Strategy of the United States," under which America is to dominate the world forever, and we'll attack any country that doesn't agree with us. Frankly, it's nutty. But they made a big mistake. They forgot to run it by the people first.

**October 2002**

# Warren Burnett

■

WARREN BURNETT, the legendary Texas trial lawyer—and if ever there was a legitimate use of the word *legendary*, this is it—died on a veranda overlooking a garden in West Texas on a beautiful afternoon in September with a cold beer in his hand. He was seventy-five. He was the least sentimental idealist I ever knew.

Burnett was, simply, the finest trial lawyer in Texas and quite possibly in the nation in his day. Some will argue that Edward Bennett Williams, on the other side of the Ditch, was pretty good too, but I point out that when Burnett visited John Connally's bribery trial as an observer, Williams moved him up to the defense table after the first day. Burnett was so revered by his colleagues that whenever he tried a case, lawyers and law students would show up like groupies to watch him. I once saw former congressman Craig Washington, himself famous for having three times successfully defended an impossible case—a black convict who had killed a white guard—come up to Burnett at a reception, kneel, and kiss his hand.

Burnett was raised poor in the mountains of Virginia, and the only books in the house were the Bible and Shakespeare. He memorized much of both, and as a result his command of language was stunning. I never heard him utter a graceless sentence. He could tell priceless stories, his wit was quick as a cobra; when the occasion called for grand rhetoric, he did grand rhetoric Clarence Darrow would have wept for. But his particular genius, as both a lawyer and a friend, was for telling the mordant truth.

Warren had a habit of marrying badly. At the end of another sad chapter in his love life, he said, in that great, deep, rumbling voice, "Well, I consider this further evidence of a long-held theory of mine, which is that you cannot cure alcoholism with pussy."

He finally got it right on the fourth try, his wife Kay, a woman of such sweetness and devotion that his old friends envied him.

The son of a miner, Burnett had a strong sense of how the legal system in this country grinds down on those without money. As district attorney in Odessa, he didn't enjoy prosecuting people and quit after two terms. His daughter Melissa says he sent a young, homeless man to the electric chair and was ever-after haunted by it. He switched to defense.

Burnett did not practice law just for money—which he never disdained, since he felt he had spent enough of his life being poor—but for justice as well. A dewy-eyed idealist he was not.

Nevertheless, he took cases for the Texas Civil Liberties Union, for the United Farmworkers, for black people and brown people with no money in hopeless circumstances—and won a staggering number of them. But he was just as cutting about the bull on the left as he was about the racists on the right.

At the sort-of famous Wimberly Conference in 1968 between anti-war movement radicals and the handful of Texas lawyers willing to defend them (the anti-war people were then getting busted all over the state and put away for long sentences for exercising their constitutional rights), there promptly developed a grand split, as was the custom of the left in those days. The radicals wanted the lawyers to go into court, call the judges racist pigs, and denounce the system as a fascist fraud. The lawyers, bound by their professional principles, felt that their primary obligation was to keep these damn fools from spending ten years in the Texas pen, as civil-rights lawyer David Richards notes in his memoir, *Once Upon a Time in Texas*.

Burnett, "who had been much in evidence at the open bar," finally rose to announce the consensus. "We are lawyers who are prepared to represent movement causes when the time arises, and to do so in the manner we, as lawyers, feel the cause should best be presented in court; and if this approach is not satisfactory to the young radicals foregathered on this occasion, then, to borrow from the rhetoric of the movement, 'Fuck 'em.' "

Burnett to the bone.

**November 2002**

# John Henry Faulk

■

O N  A  B L A Z I N G  hot summer day last year, the director of the Central
Texas chapter of the American Civil Liberties Union was frantically phoning
members to announce that the First Amendment was in dire peril from the
Austin City Plan Commission. The First Amendment tends to be under steady
fire in the Great State, but the Austin Plan Commission is rarely found on the
side of jackbooted fascism. What happened was, the Reverend Mark Weaver, a
fundamentalist divine with a strong local following, hell-bent on driving all
the dirty bookstores out of town—he had come up with a zoning scheme by
which this was to be accomplished. The Plan Commission held a hearing that
night attended by more than three hundred members of Weaver's group,
Citizens Against Pornography, and by six members of the Civil Liberties
Union. The Libertarians flocked together. Nothing like sitting in the midst of a
sea of Citizens Against Pornography to make you notice that your friends all
look like perverts.

The Reverend Weaver rose to address the Commission. An eloquent
preacher, he took right off into the tale of a woman who lives directly behind
the pornography theater on South Congress Avenue. The very day before, she
had watched a man come out of that theater after the five-o'clock show, go into
the alley behind the theater, right behind her house, and . . . masturbate. Three
hundred Citizens Against and the members of the Plan Commission all sucked
in their breath in horror. Made a very odd sound. "YES," continued the
Reverend Weaver, "that man MASTURBATED right in the alley, right
BEHIND that lady's house. And she has two little girls who might have SEEN
it—if it weren't for the wooden fence around her yard." And with that the
Reverend Weaver jerked the stopper and cussed sin up a storm. It looked bad
for the First Amendment.

When it came their turn, the Libertarians huddled together and decided to send up their oldest living member. He shuffled to the mike, gray hair thin on top, a face marked with age spots and old skin cancers, one eye useless long since. He spoke with a courtly Southern accent. "Members of the Plan Commission, Reverend Weaver, Citizens Against, ladies and gentlemen. My name is John Henry Faulk. I am seventy-four years old. I was born and raised in South Austin, not a quarter of a mile from where that pornography theater stands today. I think y'all know that there was a *lot* of masturbation in South Austin before there was ever a pornography theater there." Even the Citizens Against laughed, and the First was saved for another day.

Thirty years ago John Henry Faulk destroyed the blacklisting system that had terrified the entertainment industry during the McCarthy era. His was one of the most spectacular show trials of that sorry time; he won the largest libel award that had yet been granted in the United States ($3.5 million) and was honored up to his eyebrows by freedom lovers everywhere. Then he went back to Texas—broke, his career still ruined—never saw any of the money, and learned you can't eat honor. This is the story of John Henry Faulk's life since Louis Nizer won out over Roy Cohn in their courtroom battle about whether the man called the Will Rogers of his generation was actually a communist.

BEEN SO long since Texas freedom fighters couldn't count on Johnny Faulk almost no one can remember the time. He is a folklorist and humorist by profession, a storyteller, and a scholar of the Constitution. He's also a good man to have around when guerrilla tactics are called for.

Back in 1975, there was an unholy uproar in the state over another preacher, Brother Lester Roloff of Corpus Christi, since gone to glory. Brother Roloff ran a home for "wayward girls" without a state license; claimed he didn't need permission from the State of Texas to beat the Devil out of those girls and the Lord into them. At one point the state was forced to throw him into the slammer for contempt of court, and this caused his followers to swear vengeance on every godless politician and every godless licensing law in Texas.

Safe in Austin was State Senator Ron Clower of Garland, a cheerful fellow who followed the old legislative precept "Vote conservative, party liberal." Clower had done a substantial amount of beer-drinking, river-running, and good-timin' with a crowd of Austin liberals, of whom Johnny Faulk is one. Vast was the surprise of the senator's friends when an item appeared in the papers saying Clower had introduced a tiny amendment to exempt Brother Roloff from state supervision. It was felt he should have known better.

The day of the hearing on his amendment, Clower's office received a call from a Reverend Billy Joe Bridges of Lovelady, leader of the White Christian Children's Army, a full-immersion, foot-washing fundamentalist sect headed toward Austin to help Brother Clower hold off the forces of Satan. "We're bringin' three busloads of children. Red-white-and-blue buses," crooned Bridges. "We'll take those Christian children right up into the Senate gallery, and they'll float little paper airplanes with the words of Jesus written on them onto the Senate floor. We'll be the Christian Children's Air Force for the day, you see. Heh, heh."

Clower had been hoping to avoid publicity on this misbegotten amendment, but Cactus Pryor, a television newsman at KLBJ in Austin, called to say he'd heard the White Christian Children's Army was coming and the station wanted to have its cameras on the Capitol steps to catch the "charge." Could Senator Clower's office tell him what time the buses were expected? "Oh God, television!" groaned Clower. The liberal *Texas Observer* called: "We've just received a press release from some outfit called the White Christian Children's Army. What the hell is going on?"

"They've put out a press release!" screamed Clower's aide.

Came a call from Belton, the voice low and threatening. "This is Officer Joe Don Billups with the Department of Public Safety. We've just stopped three red-white-and-blue buses for speeding. They said your office could explain."

Clower, no idiot, took only a few more hours to realize it was all a put-on. The culprits never confessed, but a few months later, when Johnny Faulk received a call at 3 A.M. from the Democratic Telethon to verify his pledge of $500,000, Senator Clower was the chief suspect.

IN THE ugly, angry time of "Lyndon's War" against the Communist Vietnamese, which all good Texans felt called upon to support, John Henry Faulk was making a slim living as an after-dinner speaker—and, for that matter, after-lunch—in front of such prestigious and high-paying organizations as the Grimes County Taxpayers Association and the Madisonville Kiwanis. He was never fool enough to come out against the war. But he would recount conversations he'd had with his cousin Ed Snodgrass, an old geezer so retrograde he has a sign over his mantelpiece that says, ROBERT E. LEE MIGHT HAVE GIVE UP, BUT I AIN'T. Cousin Ed would get to fussin' about all the dirty, long-haired peaceniks. "Don't you believe in the right to dissent, Cousin Ed?" Faulk would ask.

"Dissent? Oh hell yes, I believe in dissent. H'it's in the Constitution. What I can't stand is all this criticism. Criticize, criticize, criticize. Why can't they leave ol' Lyndon alone and let him fight his war in peace? Lookit this war. We send our best boys over there, in broad daylight, in million-dollar airplanes, wearin' pressed uniforms, to bomb them Veetnamese, and what do they do? Come out at night. On their bicycles. Wearin' pyjamas. Not even Christian. I tell you what, if we wasn't bombin' 'em, they would not be able to bomb theirselves. If they don't like what we're doing for 'em, they ought to go back where they come from." Johnny Faulk could get laughs out of Republicans with this routine, and no one ever got mad at him. They did, however, go away with the notion that there was something, well, ludicrous about the war.

"I never attack people for what they think," explains Faulk. "That's crucial. If I want to say something I know will stir folks up, I make one of my characters say it. Then I disagree with my character, chide him for being foolish." Which is why the man accused of being a Red is now asked to speak everywhere in Texas.

JOHNNY FAULK got branded a communist when he ran for union office in New York in 1955. At the time, Faulk remembers, "I was choppin' in the tall cotton." He was starring in his own five-day-a-week network radio show on CBS, called *Johnny's Front Porch*, and also appearing twice weekly on television on two panel quiz programs and in a variety of other slots as a guest panelist or guest host. Faulk ran as part of an anti-blacklisting slate for the board of AFTRA, the American Federation of Television and Radio Artists. Other members of the ticket included the CBS News reporter Charles Collingwood and the performers Orson Bean, Faye Emerson, Garry Moore, and Janice Rule. The anti-blacklisters won twenty-seven of the thirty-five seats on the board. A month after the new officers took over, AWARE, Inc.—"An Organization to Combat the Communist Conspiracy in Entertainment-Communications"— issued this bulletin about the group: "The term 'blacklisting' is losing its plain meaning and becoming a Communist jargon-term for hard opposition to the exposure of Communism." The newsletter then presented a number of allegations against Faulk. He once appeared on a program with Paul Robeson. He helped the Henry Wallace campaign in 1948. He sent second-anniversary greetings to a record company that sold "people's folk songs." Item No. 4 said, "A program dated April 25, 1946, named 'John Faulk' as a scheduled entertainer (with identified Communist Earl Robinson and two non-Communists) under the auspices of the Independent Citizens Committee of the Arts, Sciences, and Professions (officially designated a Communist front, and predecessor of the Progressive Citizens of America)."

It turned out that "officially designated a Communist front" meant some witness of indeterminate reliability had once mentioned the group in front of a congressional committee. It also turned out that John Henry Faulk did sure as a by-God have an intimate supper on the night of April 25, 1946, at the Astor Hotel with a known agent of the Soviet Union. And not just any agent—he dined with Andrei Gromyko, the Soviet ambassador to the United Nations. The dinner celebrated the first anniversary of the United Nations, and several hundred other people also showed up. Eleanor Roosevelt and Harold Ickes, the former secretary of the interior, were co-chairmen of the event—presumably the "two non-Communists" mentioned in the AWARE bulletin—and Secretary of State Edward Stettinius was the main speaker. Johnny Faulk, fresh up from Texas, never did get to howdy or shake with the big Red, but his career was destroyed anyway.

CBS fired Faulk a few months after the AWARE bulletin came out. "They didn't want to do it, and felt terrible about it," Faulk says. He was told that his ratings were slipping and that Arthur Godfrey was being given his time slot on radio. His lawyer, Louis Nizer, later proved in the trial that Faulk's ratings were going up at the time he was fired. But AWARE operated by putting pressure on advertisers, invoking the threat of a boycott by the American Legion if companies bought time on programs that employed suspected Reds. The system blacklisted, among others, an eight-year-old actress who was to have played Helen Keller in *The Miracle Worker*. AWARE itself was on retainer from the networks to sniff out subversives, so it had financial incentives to keep doing so.

Faulk filed a suit for libel against AWARE in 1956, but it didn't come to trial for six years, until the spring of 1962. In the meantime, he was out of show business and down to small odd jobs like selling encyclopedias. In his book *The Jury Returns* Louis Nizer wrote of John Faulk's case:

"One lone man had challenged the monstrously powerful forces of vigilantism cloaked in superpatriotism.

"One lone man with virtually no resources had dragged the defendants into the courts, and although outrageously outnumbered, had withstood starvation and disgrace, and summoned enough strength to battle them into submission.

"One lone man was so naïve in his profound patriotism that he did not conceive of himself as fighting a heroic battle, but simply as doing what any

American would do—defy the bully, spit at his pretension, and preserve his faith in his country's Constitution and principles."

This is Nizer at his most magniloquent, a style Faulk adores to imitate. In sorry truth, though, the "lone man" wasn't all that lone. He had the support of family and friends (from Edward R. Murrow to the beloved Texas historian, folklorist, and naturalist J. Frank Dobie), and Nizer was probably the finest trial lawyer in the country. In fact, Johnny Faulk had a wonderful time filing that lawsuit. "It required no courage to fight," he says, "because I never doubted I would win. I never thought of doing anything else."

ONE LEGACY of his seven years on the blacklist is that Faulk almost never publicly criticizes the Soviet Union or communism. He has no use for communists: "I knew a number of 'em on the University of Texas campus back in the thirties, well-intentioned but kind of pitiful people. And off-putting, like all true believers, like anyone who thinks he has The Truth and has no questions, no doubts, just wants to proselytize." But Faulk also believes that Americans hear so much anti-communist propaganda already there's no point in adding another scintilla to it. It galls him that to this good day a person is still expected to profess anti-communism as a way of proving his loyalty. "He must manifest it, say it, swear it, and pledge it," as Nicholas von Hoffman writes in his biography of Roy Cohn, "not once but . . . head covered, hand over heart, in the classroom, the ballpark, at the testimonial dinner."

During preparation for the trial Nizer kept pushing Faulk for proof that he'd done something actively anti-communist. It was fine that he was such a patriot he'd enlisted in the merchant marine at the start of World War II, then managed to get a job overseas with the Red Cross, and finally finagled his way into the army despite being one-eyed. But what had he done *against* communists? After weeks of listening to Nizer press this issue, Faulk launched into a splendid extemporaneous tale of finding his dear old crippled grandmother one day reading the *Daily Worker*. No sooner had he said, "But Granny, that's a COMMUNIST newspaper!" than the oil lamp in her tar-paper shack tumped over, setting the place ablaze. Faulk grabbed her wheelchair and started toward the porch and safety, but "as I wheeled her out, I looked down and saw that *Daily Worker* in her lap, realized she was just a COMMUNIST pawn, and was so filled with loathing I turned her chair and pushed the old lady back into the flames!" Nizer listened to this entire faradiddle without expression and then snapped, "We can't use it." Nizer had so little humor he introduced into evidence Faulk's boyhood award for perfect attendance—seventy-two consecutive Sundays—at the Fred Allen Memorial Methodist Church in South Austin. Faulk is not much of a Methodist, but his mother sure was.

SOUTH AUSTIN was then the city's black neighborhood, and Johnny's father was Judge John Henry Faulk Sr., a man of progressive principles, whose hero was Clarence Darrow. The elder Faulk had served as Eugene V. Debs' state campaign manager in the days when socialists got a sight more votes than Republicans in Texas. As an attorney he had often represented poor black people, so he moved his family to a beautiful old home in South Austin called Green Pastures, now one of the city's best restaurants, run by Johnny Faulk's nephew Ken Kooch. Johnny grew up among blacks, and they were his childhood friends.

John Henry Faulk's great natural gift is an almost freakish aural memory. One day last year, as he walked in South Austin, he began reminiscing about his childhood neighbors. One was an elderly black woman whose only child, a retarded son, had died years earlier. When she got to missing that child too bad she would call to him as though he were still alive, and the neighborhood children made fun of her for it. Suddenly, across a distance of sixty-five years or more, the voice of an old black woman came out of Faulk's throat, a crackled call of love: "Come on, son. Come on, son. Mama's waitin'." The voice hung like a ghost along the dirt lane.

Because the Faulk family had progressive opinions on "colored people" for that time, John Henry did not recognize his own racism until he was at college. He and his mentor, Frank Dobie, so loathed Hitler that they studied his speeches, and it slowly dawned on them that racism could apply to blacks as well as to Jews. Talk about a couple of Texas boys in a quandary—now what to do? They consulted Faulk's childhood chum Alan Lomax, who had not only gone off to prep school and Harvard but was also the son of John A. Lomax, who had started the folklore collection at the Smithsonian Institution. They felt Lomax was wise in the ways of the great world. He advised that among the intelligentsia the word was pronounced "Negro" rather than "Nigra," and that this was the sure sign by which black people could tell you weren't prejudiced against their kind. Johnny Faulk and Frank Dobie sat around solemnly practicing the word—"Kneee-grow, Kneee-grow"—to get it right. Faulk's gift for mimicry made it easy for him, but poor Dobie, a full generation older and with a Texan accent, had to rehearse for ages.

In order to get a master's degree in folklore, Faulk traveled around East Texas in the late thirties with a recorder taping what was then called "colored folklore." In 1941, he was working for his doctorate and teaching at the university when he got a Rosenwald grant to collect more material. "Rural blacks in those days were so isolated. They were too poor to have electricity, so even the radio was unknown to them," Faulk says now. "Many of their cultural traditions have since been so thoroughly wiped out not even many black people know about them." These days Faulk rarely does black characters, but one still in his repertoire is the Reverend Tanner Franklin, who preaches a sermon on David and Goliath in the wondrous, ancient sing-preaching of Afro-Americans that is virtually gone. You can hear it now only on old records and in the voice of Johnny Faulk replicating the Reverend Franklin as he sings:

*"Go down angel, consume the flood.*
*Snuff out the sun, turn de moon to blood.*
*Go down angel, close de door.*
*Time have been, shan't be no more."*

FAULK'S YARNS about Texas frequently have a bizarre flavor. Long before anyone had heard of Lenny Bruce, Johnny Faulk was doing black humor in the form of country stories. Strange deaths, weird funerals, matrons complacently rocking as people go mad around them. It's possible that Faulk's career never would have blossomed on television, because what storytellers need above all else is time. It is an art born of leisure, and a story well told can pause for any number of interesting sidetracks. From 1975 to 1981, Faulk was employed on *Hee Haw*, the corn-pone country version of *Laugh-In*. He was the resident cracker-barrel philosopher, commenting on politics in thirty-second skits. ("Why, the trouble with Jerry Ford is, he played center for so long he looks at the world backward and upside down." HEE-HAW.) Faulk's humor is not suited to one-liners. The show was pretty awful, but it was steady work, and Faulk delighted in it. In addition to his congenital optimism, he has that show-business habit of thinking everything's coming up roses—whatever project he's doing is fabulous, the director is wonderful, he's met the loveliest people.

His *Hee Haw* fame has been useful to him at some odd points. Although he makes a living as an after-dinner speaker, ever since his trial Faulk has considered his real work educating Americans about the First Amendment, and to that end he donates his time and talent without stint. One day, in March 1979, he got a call from a lawyer representing the pornographer Larry Flynt. Flynt was on trial in Atlanta for obscenity, and his goose was pretty well cooked. Georgians have no use for Yankee pornographers, even those who have been shot, crippled, and brought to Jesus by President Carter's sister. The judge had turned down almost every expert Flynt's lawyers had tried to call—scholars from Harvard and Yale. Faulk remembers the attorneys implying they were down to the bottom of the barrel, and if Faulk would come over to Atlanta they'd pay him to testify as an authority on the First Amendment.

Faulk doesn't take money for testifying about the First Amendment, but he agreed to stop by Atlanta on his way to a *Hee Haw* taping in Nashville. Thinking he should know what he was about to defend, he bought his first copy of Flynt's *Hustler* magazine at the Houston airport. Slipped off the plain brown wrapper and like to had a stroke. "H'it was a picture of a nekkid lady with her finger stuck up herself and her tongue out like this . . ." Faulk arrived for a conference of the Flynt defense team that opened with the newly born-again defendant insisting they all form a circle, join hands, and pray. Faulk silently addressed the Lord with a strong sense of grievance over being there at all. The lawyers warned Faulk that security at the courthouse was tight, because of the earlier shooting; the Georgia lawmen hated the Flynt team and daily threw them up against the wall, searched them, emptied their briefcases on the ground, and verbally harassed them.

Next morning the defense team headed into the courthouse and met the first line of the law—Georgia State Troopers. "They wore shiny mirror silver sunglasses, big guns on one hip, big billy clubs on the other," Faulk remembers, "and they were *mean* lookin'." He braced himself for the search, but the troopers parted before him, whispering as they fell back, "H'it's John Henry Faulk, from *Hee Haw*! H'it's John Henry Faulk, from *Hee Haw*!" And the dreaded sheriff's men, said to be even meaner than the troopers, they, too, turned out to be fans, and, instead of throwing Faulk up against the wall, asked for his autograph. Danged if the judge didn't watch *Hee Haw*, and the jurors, who beamed at him. Even the prosecutor told the court he was proud to have Mr. Faulk of *Hee Haw* testify in his case.

Faulk started by talking about growing up in South Austin without indoor plumbing. His family had an outhouse and, being on the poor side, never could afford toilet paper, so his mama used to put the Sears, Roebuck catalog out there for that purpose. But being a good Methodist Sunday-school teacher, she always cut out the pages with the corset ads on them, lest the boys get excited in the outhouse. The judge and the jury were chuckling along at this story, and Faulk had already made points about changing community standards.

The prosecutor, no fool, leaped up, shoved a copy of *Hustler* under Faulk's nose, and roared, "MR. FAULK! Would you have wanted your mother, the Methodist Sunday-school teacher, to have seen THIS?" Sure enough, Faulk reports, there was another nekkid lady with her finger stuck up herself and her tongue hangin' out. "SHUT YOUR MOUTH, BOY!" he replied. "You want lightin' to strike this courthouse? God will call it down at the very IDEA of my sainted mother seeing such a thing!" He continued in a far quieter vein. "Of course I would not have wanted my mother to see such a thing. Nor do I want my wife to see it, nor my son. That's ugly. That's so ugly. But let me tell you about why the Founding Fathers wrote what they did in our Constitution where it says, 'Congress shall make no law ...' " Faulk was eloquent in the cause, but notes, "Didn't do him a damn bit of good. They found his ass good and guilty."

FAULK HAS recently recovered from cancer. Although he admits that having cancer nearly scared him to death, he also loves being the center of attention and reveled in all the concern. Doctors in Houston managed to rid him of a lemon-size tumor in the middle of his head solely by using radiation. His salivary glands were damaged in the process, and that makes his stage work more difficult, but he appears to have regained most of his energy. Right now he's working on a one-man show he already tried successfully in Houston last year. The play, called *Deep in the Heart,* involves a collection of Faulk's characters all placed loosely in some mythical Texas town, and will be in New York this fall under the direction of Albert Marre, who did *Man of La Mancha,* among other productions. It will be the first time Faulk has performed in New York since he was blacklisted. He is so excited he practically dances when he talks about it: He has the capacity for delight of an eight-year-old at Christmas.

No tragedy here, no life destroyed by McCarthyism. He has a close family—three sisters and a brother—and Faulk family gatherings tend to look like county conventions. He had messed up two marriages before he met Elizabeth Peake, a British nurse, in 1964, and struck it lucky. They have one son, Yohann, who is nineteen. Faulk claims he is "the only kid ever born on Medicare." Among Liz Faulk's outstanding qualities is her immense common sense, a commodity for which her husband is not noted—imagine Maggie Thatcher with a heart. She keeps track of his schedule, his money, and his health, while he wanders around blithely being funny about politics and serious about the Constitution. What fun, what joy, thinks he, and wades once more into the battle. It infuriates him to see this country betray its best, basic principles, and he sometimes concludes that most of his fellow citizens are nincompoops. But Faulk is always confident that the genius of the Founders will triumph in the end. He speaks of them with a reverence, love, and depth of knowledge all the flag-waving patriots down to the VFW Hall recognize and respect.

**Summer 1998**

## ABOUT THE AUTHOR

MOLLY IVINS began her career in journalism as the complaint department of the *Houston Chronicle*. In 1970, she became co-editor of *The Texas Observer*, which afforded her frequent fits of hysterical laughter while covering the Texas Legislature.

In 1976, Ivins joined *The New York Times* as a political reporter. The next year she was named Rocky Mountain bureau chief, chiefly because there was no one else in the bureau. In 1982, she returned once more to Texas, which may indicate a masochistic streak, and has had plenty to write about ever since. Her column is syndicated in more than three hundred newspapers, and her freelance work has appeared in *Esquire, The Atlantic Monthly, The New York Times Magazine, The Nation, Harper's,* and other publications. Her first book, *Molly Ivins Can't Say That, Can She?,* spent more than a year on the *New York Times* bestseller list. Her books with Lou Dubose on George W. Bush, *Shrub* and *Bushwhacked,* were national best-sellers.

A three-time Pulitzer Prize finalist, she counts as her two greatest honors that the Minneapolis police force named its mascot pig after her and that she was once banned from the campus of Texas A&M.